Legal Rights for Rivers

In 2017 four rivers in Aotearoa New Zealand, India, and Colombia were given the status of legal persons, and there was a recent attempt to extend these rights to the Colorado River in the USA. Understanding the implications of creating legal rights for rivers is an urgent challenge for both water resource management and environmental law. Giving rivers legal rights means the law can see rivers as legal persons, thus creating new legal rights which can then be enforced. When rivers are legally people, does that encourage *collaboration and partnership* between humans and rivers, or establish rivers as another *competitor* for scarce resources?

To assess what it means to give rivers legal rights and legal personality, this book examines the form and function of environmental water managers (EWMs). These organisations have legal personality, and have been active in water resource management for over two decades. EWMs operate by acquiring water rights from irrigators in rivers where there is insufficient water to maintain ecological health. EWMs can *compete* with farmers for access to water, but they can also strengthen *collaboration* between traditionally divergent users of the aquatic environment, such as environmentalists, recreational fishers, hunters, farmers, and hydropower. This book explores how EWMs use the opportunities created by giving nature legal rights, such as the ability to participate in markets, enter into contracts, hold property, and enforce those rights in court. However, examination of the EWMs unearths a crucial and unexpected paradox: giving legal rights to nature may increase its legal power, but in doing so it can weaken community support for protecting the environment in the first place. The book develops a new conceptual framework to identify the multiple constructions of the environment in law, and how these constructions can interact to generate these unexpected outcomes. It explores EWMs in the USA and Australia as examples, and assesses the implications of creating legal rights for rivers for water governance. Lessons from the EWMs, as well as early lessons from the new 'river persons', show how to use the law to improve river protection and how to begin to mitigate the problems of the paradox.

Erin O'Donnell is a Senior Fellow and sessional lecturer at the University of Melbourne Law School, Australia. She is also an independent consultant on water markets to the World Bank and has worked on water governance in the public and private sectors for more than 15 years.

Earthscan Studies in Water Resource Management

China's International Transboundary Rivers
Politics, Security and Diplomacy of Shared Water Resources
Lei Xie and Jia Shaofeng

Urban Water Sustainability
Constructing Infrastructure for Cities and Nature
Sarah Bell

The Biopolitics of Water
Governance, Scarcity and Populations
Sofie Hellberg

Water, Technology and the Nation-State
Edited by Filippo Menga and Erik Swyngedouw

Revitalizing Urban Waterway Communities
Streams of Environmental Justice
Richard Smardon, Sharon Moran and April Baptiste

Water, Creativity and Meaning
Multidisciplinary Understandings of Human–Water Relationships
Edited by Liz Roberts and Katherine Phillips

Water, Climate Change and the Boomerang Effect
Unintentional Consequences for Resource Insecurity
Edited by Larry Swatuk and Lars Wirkus

Legal Rights for Rivers
Competition, Collaboration and Water Governance
Erin O'Donnell

For more information and to view forthcoming titles in this series, please visit the Routledge website: www.routledge.com/books/series/ECWRM/

Legal Rights for Rivers

Competition, Collaboration and Water Governance

Erin O'Donnell

Routledge
Taylor & Francis Group
LONDON AND NEW YORK

earthscan
from Routledge

First published 2019
by Routledge
2 Park Square, Milton Park, Abingdon, Oxon OX14 4RN

and by Routledge
52 Vanderbilt Avenue, New York, NY 10017, USA

First issued in paperback 2020

Routledge is an imprint of the Taylor & Francis Group, an informa business

British Library Cataloguing-in-Publication Data
A catalogue record for this book is available from the British Library

Library of Congress Cataloging-in-Publication Data
Names: O'Donnell, Erin, 1979- author.
Title: Legal rights for rivers : competition, collaboration and water governance / Erin O'Donnell.
Description: Abingdon, Oxon ; New York, NY : Routledge, 2019. | Series: Earthscan studies in water resource management | Based on author's thesis (doctoral - Melbourne Law School, University of Melbourne, 2017) issued under title: Constructing the aquatic environment as a legal subject : legal rights, market participation, and the power of narrative.
Identifiers: LCCN 2018030343 (print) | LCCN 2018032404 (ebook) | ISBN 9780429469053 (eBook) | ISBN 9781138603257 (hardback)
Subjects: LCSH: RiversLaw and legislation. | Water resources development–Law and legislation. | Locus standi.
Classification: LCC K3496 (ebook) | LCC K3496 .O326 2019 (print) | DDC
346.04/69162–dc23
LC record available at https://lccn.loc.gov/2018030343

ISBN 13: 978-0-367-58416-0 (pbk)
ISBN 13: 978-1-138-60325-7 (hbk)

Typeset in Sabon
by Wearset Ltd, Boldon, Tyne and Wear

To my husband Rob, who celebrated all the tiny victories with me, and made me laugh

Contents

Figures

Tables

Acronyms and abbreviations

CAR	autonomous regional corporation (Colombia)
CEWH	Commonwealth Environmental Water Holder
CWCB	Colorado Water Conservation Board
CWT	Colorado Water Trust
DEWNR	Department of Environment, Water, and Natural Resources, South Australia
DRC	Deschutes River Conservancy
EPBC	Environment Protection and Biodiversity Conservation Act 1999 (Australia)
ESA	Endangered Species Act 1973 (USA)
EWM	environmental water manager
HRA	Healthy Rivers Australia
MDB	Murray-Darling Basin
MDBA	Murray-Darling Basin Authority
NEPA	National Environment Protection Act 1969 (USA)
NFWF	National Fish and Wildlife Foundation (USA)
NGO	non-governmental organisation
NWI	National Water Initiative (Australia)
OEH	Office of Environment and Heritage, New South Wales
RMA	Resource Management Act 1991, Aotearoa New Zealand
SDG	Sustainable Development Goal
UN	United Nations
VEWH	Victorian Environmental Water Holder
WWF	World Wide Fund for Nature

Units of water volume

Acre-foot (AF)	Volume of water required to cover one acre of land to a depth of one foot. One acre-foot is equivalent to 0.001233 GL, so 10 million AF is equivalent to 12,330 GL.
Gigalitre (GL)	1,000 ML or 811 AF.
Megalitre (ML)	1,000,000 litres or 0.811 AF.

1 Introduction

In March 2017 the national government of Aotearoa New Zealand (Aotearoa is the Māori name for the country of New Zealand; the literal translation of Aotearoa is 'land of the long white cloud') passed legislation that established the Whanganui River and its catchment as a legal person. Days later the High Court of the state of Uttarakhand in India ruled that the Ganga (Ganges) and Yamuna Rivers were legal persons, with the status of legal minors. Shortly after that the same court granted legal rights to all the natural objects in the state of Uttarakhand. In May the Constitutional Court of Colombia recognised the 'biocultural' rights of the Río Atrato, conferring legal rights on the river itself. Collectively, these unprecedented developments represent the most significant creation of legal rights for nature since Bolivia's Law of Mother Earth in 2010 and have fundamentally altered the legal status of rivers.

Giving rivers legal rights means the law can see the river itself as a legal person, and the river can take legal action to enforce those rights. Legal personhood confers legal standing (often described as the ability to sue and be sued), which enables rivers to go to court to protect their rights. Legal personhood also includes the right to enter into and enforce contracts, and the ability to hold property. Creating legal rights for nature more broadly has been considered by many environmental advocates and legal scholars as a step forward for environmental protection,[1] although this remains controversial.[2]

The movement to extend legal personhood to natural objects continues to build momentum. In Aotearoa New Zealand a similar form of legal personhood will be extended to Mount Taranaki, and is currently under consideration for the Whangaehu River. In 2018 the Supreme Court in Colombia (Corte Suprema de Justicia, Sala de Casación Civil) ruled that the Colombian Amazon Basin was the subject of legal rights.[3] In Nigeria there is a campaign under way to grant legal personhood to the River Ethiope. Globally, the concept of legal rights for nature is becoming part of mainstream environmental law. There is a growing belief that it offers a powerful new approach to environmental protection and an opportunity to transform radically the relationship between people and the environment.[4]

However, there is a great deal of uncertainty about what these novel legal developments will mean in practice.[5] The rivers have received their legal rights in different ways (via legislation or judicial decision), for different purposes (environmental protection, religious beliefs, and Indigenous values), and by using different legal forms as the basis for legal rights and personhood.[6] Although the implementation of the new legal arrangements is well under way in Colombia and Aotearoa New Zealand, it is still unclear how these new legal rights will affect water governance and river basin management. In fact, there is already evidence that instead of transforming the relationship between people and rivers from one of subjugation to one of fraternal equality and respect,[7] these new legal rights may be encouraging people to consider suing the river for flood damages.[8]

This rapidly changing legal context creates important opportunities, but also presents significant risks for the governance and management of rivers and wetlands around the world. The growing popularity of the legal rights for nature movement means that we cannot simply wait and see how these new legal arrangements work in practice, and whether they represent a real improvement in environmental protection. We urgently need to understand the implications of constructing a river as a legal person, and what it means for water governance.

But where can we find evidence of the practical outcomes of such a powerful and novel idea as legal personhood for rivers? As it turns out, organisations managing environmental water have been using this tool for decades. Around the world, organisations with the status of legal persons have been recovering and managing water rights for the environment since the mid-1990s. Although these organisations (environmental water managers, or EWMs) are not precisely the same as creating legal rights for the river itself, the combination of their legal form, the water rights they hold, and the activities they undertake enables them to construct the aquatic environment as a legal person, albeit in a slightly attenuated way. Examining the EWMs can offer powerful insights into the consequences for water law and governance of giving rivers legal rights.[9]

Constructing the environment in law: a new conceptual framework

When rivers have rights, the rivers themselves are constructed in law as legal persons. However, the natural environment is already constructed in law in multiple ways, including personhood. Understanding how these multiple constructions interact is essential if we wish to identify and manage the outcomes of constructing the environment as a legal person. One of the major contributions of this book is to develop a new conceptual framework to distil the multiple definitions of the environment in law into three main constructions, and show how these different constructions can interact and the potential consequences for environmental law.

What does it mean to 'construct' the environment in law?

For the law to engage with nature, or the 'environment', it must be constructed in a way that makes the environment both *visible* and *comprehensible* (what I term as *legible*) to the law. This process is not straightforward. The 'environment' is a nebulous concept, contingent on both the physical (and ecological) reality and the particular values of human society at a given time. As a result, the environment is particularly difficult for the law to engage with, because it is inherently dynamic (via ecological processes) as well as changing in response to shifting human values.

Legal constructivism emphasises the power of the law to construct its subjects, rather than simply finding existing subjects already in the world.[10] Naffine calls this a 'legalist' perspective, and argues that 'law constructs, rather than finds, its subject and that subject is not intended to reflect, in any direct way, real beings in the real world ... law is always engaged in a process of constructing its subjects for legal purposes'.[11] This approach is particularly apparent when these constructs are explicitly created in statute, as is the case for much of water law and environment law.

Hirokawa argues that a 'legal constructivist view of nature, then, defines nature by implication from particular statements of law'.[12] Historically, environmental law has used a combination of extremely specific definitions of the environment in statute and open-ended, unstated concepts. When the environment is constructed as a legal subject with legal rights, these definitions become crucially important, but there has been little analysis of how these definitions combine or interact.

However, the environment is a physical reality and not a *mere* construction of the law. In his analysis of the power of legal constructivism to embed environmental ethics within the law, Hirokawa identifies both a 'hard' and a 'soft' form of social constructivism:

> Hard constructivism is typically characterized by its existential thesis, which holds that nature is only a social construction. The softer thesis is merely an epistemological one, positing that our concept of nature is socially constructed.[13]

Moreover, a constructivist approach 'acknowledges the historical and contextual contingencies of knowledge and meaning',[14] and makes it possible to observe the multiple ways in which the environment is constructed in law so as to enhance the legibility of the environment to law.

This book applies a 'lightly' constructivist approach, based on Hirokawa's 'softer' form, which enables engagement with the multiple ways that the environment is constructed within law, and supports examination of how and why these constructions have been created without overlooking the physical reality of the environment itself. The lightly constructivist approach makes it possible to discern the connection between the construction of the environment in law and the underpinning cultural narratives about the value of the environment. Making the environment legible to the law means that although the environment as a physical reality has not changed (although it may be altered as a result of the effects of legal interventions), what has changed is the *relationship* of people to the environment.

This lightly constructivist approach is particularly useful for examining the question of legal rights for rivers, and the example of the EWMs, because it offers a method to unpack the multiple ways that the aquatic environment is constructed in water law.

Making sense of multiple constructions: the conceptual framework

In the law there are 'many different "environments", each the focus of social and legal interest'.[15] We can understand the myriad definitions of the environment in law by focusing on the way that the environment is *constructed* in law, which helps to distil the diversity into three main constructs: the socio-ecological concept, the legal object, and the legal subject.

The statutory basis of modern environmental law means it is largely the result of the deliberate creation of law by governments passing legislation,[16] and these '[t]ools never come out of thin air'.[17] Environmental protection statutes reflect, and shape, *cultural narratives* of what the environment means and how it is valued. In Chapter 2 I present a new conceptual framework that connects the multiple constructions of the environment in law to their underpinning cultural narratives. When this conceptual framework is applied to water law, it helps to illuminate the relationships between the different constructions of the aquatic environment in law and shows how the conflicting cultural narratives can interact to influence water law and governance in unexpected ways.

This new conceptual framework highlights a particular vulnerability in the way that the environment is constructed in law: each definition of the 'environment' is context specific, and easily altered by shifts in the way that the community values the environment. New cultural narratives about the environment that enable it to be personified as a legal subject compete with existing narratives about the value of the environment as a legal object, and this competition can fundamentally transform the way that we collectively conceive of, and value, the environment. As the environment is not a fixed constant in law, these transformations and shifts can easily drive further legal reform.

This broader analysis also shows that the construction of the aquatic environment as a legal person has occurred at the intersection of two very different legal trends in environmental law: Earth jurisprudence, and the use of market mechanisms to achieve environmental outcomes.

Earth jurisprudence is a broad legal movement which aims to reshape law around ecological needs. The concept of giving legal rights to nature is only one element of this broader movement, and has recently found real-world application in Aotearoa New Zealand, Ecuador, Bolivia, and some local governments in the USA. Granting legal rights to the environment makes it 'the formal subject of rights and duties',[18] and in effect turns it from legal object to legal subject in the eyes of the law. However, legal rights are only of value to the extent that they can be enforced. While the creation of the capacity for those rights in law may be a relatively rapid process (such as the passing of legislation), the ability to enforce them depends on a particular organisational vehicle to manifest those rights.[19] In 2017, when rivers began to receive legal rights, each granting of rights was accompanied by a process that clearly identified the specific river to which the rights would attach and established a new organisation to be the guardian of the river. The more advanced examples include specific organisations (the EWMs themselves) responsible for acquiring and managing water for the aquatic environment over long periods. The EWMs are an example of how the capacity and competence for legal rights for the environment can come together in the creation and operation of an organisation.

Market environmentalism and the use of market-based regulatory instruments to protect and manage the environment are even more influential when it comes to water governance, given the growing role of water markets. Participation in a market depends on the construction of the environment as being capable of holding transferable 'property' rights[20] and entering contracts, which are attributes of legal personhood. Thus the capacity of the EWMs to participate in water markets depends on their specific legal powers (to hold water rights, to enter contracts, to sue and be sued), and the capacity and freedom to use those legal powers in the particular legal, social, and economic context in which they operate.

This book creates a real dialogue between Earth jurisprudence and market environmentalism, and the findings will be of interest to scholars and practitioners in both fields. In particular, it shifts the debate from *whether* 'nature' could (or should) be constructed as a legal subject to examining the outcomes of what happens when it *is*. As more rivers and other natural objects receive legal rights, the evidence of what happens, and why, will become increasingly important for water law and governance.

Environmental water managers: a useful example of legal personality

Demand for water access, allocation, and services continues to rise, and the OECD (Organisation for Economic Co-operation and Development) predicts that by 2050 almost 4 billion people will live in river basins under severe water stress.[21] Water scarcity is likely to be exacerbated by growing populations, greater pollution of water sources, and increasing frequency and severity of drought resulting from climate change.[22] As the world tries to meet the United Nations (UN) Sustainable Development Goals (SDGs) by 2030, the challenge of sustainably managing rivers will be crucial for the success of SDG 6 (water and sanitation).[23]

Rivers and wetlands are among the most threatened ecological systems in the world.[24] Extraction of water for human use can cut off habitats for fish spawning and bird breeding, and cause the dieback of aquatic vegetation. Too often, the environmental impacts of overextraction are only considered after there is clearly not enough water to go around. This situation is starting to improve as water resource managers begin to include sustainability considerations, but in many parts of the world there is just not enough water for the aquatic environment.[25]

To combat the decline in aquatic ecosystem health, new approaches that deliver more effective protection of the environment and the people who depend on it are urgently needed. Many countries are developing new laws and policies to protect the aquatic environment and ensure that it has the water it needs.[26] Water for the environment, or *environmental flows*, is defined as 'the quantity, timing, and quality of water flows required to sustain freshwater and estuarine ecosystems and the human livelihoods and well being that depend on these ecosystems'.[27] In jurisdictions where access to water resources is managed via the allocation of water rights, providing environmental flows may require the aquatic environment to hold water rights of its own.[28]

One of the mechanisms for managing scarce freshwater resources is the water market.[29] In addition to managing water demands between human users, water markets give an opportunity to increase the volume of water for aquatic ecosystems, provided that the environment can find a way to hold water rights and participate in the market.[30]

EWMs are organisations created to hold and manage water rights on behalf of the aquatic environment (see Chapter 3). They operate in a range of legal frameworks around the world, mostly in Australia and the western USA. The EWM organisations have what Naffine described as the 'particular constellation of rights and duties held by any given legal person',[31] and many EWMs are incorporated entities. They also have specific objectives to improve and maintain the health of the aquatic environment.

However, legal personhood does not begin and end with the creation of an organisational form. In the case of EWMs, their legal personality is strengthened by their operation as decision-makers on the use of environmental water. The EWMs operate at the confluence of three relatively recent water law reforms: modern water rights (transferable and separate from land), water markets (enabling transfers between users), and environmental water rights that have the same legal characteristics as the water rights held by other water users.[32] The EWMs achieve their objectives by increasing the volume and/or improving the efficiency of management of environmental water.[33] EWMs can use their water rights to provide environmental flows, or they can buy and sell these transferable water rights in water markets.

The creation and operation of the EWMs significantly reframe the role of the aquatic environment in water law, changing it from being the mere context in which water resource management occurs to being a holder of water rights, a decision-maker, and a participant in the water market (via the EWMs).[34] These activities depend on the specific legal rights and powers of the EWM as a legal person. In Australia this reframing has been accompanied by a shift in language used to describe the aquatic environment, from a legitimate *need* for water[35] to 'just another *user*' of water.[36] In 2010 the Victorian government created the Victorian Environmental Water Holder (VEWH) to be 'the single voice' for environmental water rights in Victoria.[37]

As a result, the creation and operation of EWMs can be used to tackle an important question: what happens when the aquatic environment is *constructed* in water law, and *participates* in water markets, as a legal subject?

More power, less protection: the paradox of the EWMs

Examining the experience of the EWMs in Australia and the USA over the past two decades shows what can happen as different cultural narratives underpinning the multiple legal constructions of the environment come into conflict (Chapters 4–6). The creation and operation of the EWMs appear to generate a paradox: they are organisations that *increase* the legal rights and powers of the aquatic environment (by constructing it as a legal person), but in doing so they reframe the aquatic environment as 'just another user', a mere participant in a water market, and thus *weaken* the cultural narratives that support environmental protection in the first place. The evidence of the EWMs demonstrates that this loss of support can have significant consequences for water governance, including legal reform that reduces statutory environmental protections.

Although rivers have only had legal rights since March 2017, we can already see evidence of these conflicting cultural narratives emerging and shaping the way that communities and governments are responding to the new legal entities (Chapter 7). For example, in India, when the Ganga and Yamuna Rivers received legal rights, the state government of Uttarakhand was so concerned that the rivers could be sued for flood damages that they appealed the decision to the Supreme Court. Within four months of the rivers receiving legal rights, the Supreme Court had stayed the effect of the original decision (effectively taking away those rights once again), because of the fear that the new construction of the rivers as legal persons had changed the way that Indian people viewed these sacred rivers to such an extent that they would attempt to take the rivers to court.

From competition to collaboration?

The new conceptual framework also shows us how we can begin to mitigate the unexpected paradox of legal rights by finding ways to dampen the competition between the different narratives, enabling them to coexist. The EWMs have struggled to do this, but the ways in which legal rights are being granted to rivers show the possibility of embedding these new legal rights deeply into social values that promote caring for rivers rather than competing with them. Chapter 8 outlines the evidence so far, and identifies new strategies to improve water governance into the future.

Definitions and terminology

One of the recurring themes in environmental protection is that it is often assumed that everyone understands what is meant by the basic terms used to underpin a legal framework. However, this is not always straightforward, as the 'environment' in law reflects both a physical reality and a social value, and specific definitions are often created to reflect the particular objectives of legislation. This definitional problem is even more acute in water law, where environmental protection relies on an understanding of 'aquatic environment', a term that is rarely, if ever, specifically defined in law.

This section gives a short overview of three critical concepts: environmental water, aquatic ecosystems, and water rights.

Environmental flows and environmental water

Healthy rivers and wetlands depend on both water quantity and water quality, but in many catchments high levels of water extraction mean that there is simply not enough water, so water quantity has become the overriding concern. In addition, low water availability drives poor water quality outcomes. While water quantity on its own will not ensure healthy rivers, in highly allocated water systems where there is a risk of overallocation or overuse of water, providing the necessary quantity of water is a crucial first step. Water resource laws in many jurisdictions have recognised the concept of 'environmental flows' to define the water that the environment needs to ensure a healthy, functioning aquatic ecosystem.[38]

Environmental flows are sometimes called instream flows: water provided for environmental purposes within the river which moves through the system and may be available for alternative uses downstream. In Australia, the USA, and Mexico water is also extracted from rivers for environmental purposes, such as wetland watering, but this water is used consumptively at a particular location and is therefore not available for use downstream. In Australia and the US Colorado River Delta water is also released from storage to provide specific flow events (sometimes called 'designer flows' in the USA),[39] a particular form of environmental water management called 'active management'.[40]

Throughout this book the umbrella term 'environmental water' is used to designate both run-of-river flows and water released from storage for environmental purposes, as well as water extracted and used at specific locations, such as wetlands, for environmental purposes.

Environmental water is a mechanism used to maintain ecosystem function at an acceptable level while still supporting human use of water. By definition, environmental water is always part of a trade-off, as it is legally defined and managed in systems where there are competing uses for water.[41] Environmental water is provided to protect ecosystem functions, but also to supply ecosystem services. Different jurisdictions approach this in different ways. In Australia the ecosystem benefits of environmental water are often highlighted, whereas in North America more emphasis is placed on the human benefits of the ecosystem services. Changing social values as well as changing environmental conditions can therefore significantly impact whether environmental water provision is considered to be adequate.

Rivers, floodplains, aquifers, wetlands, estuaries: defining an aquatic ecosystem

Water law is often rather vague when it comes to defining aquatic ecosystems. In Aotearoa New Zealand the Whanganui River is defined as the area 'from the mountains to the sea, incorporating all its physical and metaphysical elements', which is very broad; but rights to the river water itself are explicitly excluded.[42] The objectives for an Australian EWM, the VEWH, are defined using 'water ecosystems', a term which is itself not further defined in the legislation.[43]

At the most basic level, aquatic ecosystems or water ecosystems clearly encompass those ecosystems where water must always be present, such as permanent rivers and lakes. However, aquatic ecosystems can also be ephemeral, such as wetlands. Further, even permanently wet aquatic ecosystems often depend on nutrient inputs from adjacent floodplains, so are these floodplains included? Where groundwater is concerned, the definition gets broader still: any ecosystem with a connection to a groundwater source could be included.[44] As a result, legal definitions of aquatic ecosystems are often left open-ended, which supports the development of context-specific definitions in response to local circumstances. In this book the term 'aquatic ecosystem' is used to identify the wide range of water-dependent ecosystems in which rivers (including floodplains, wetlands, and the wider catchment) may receive legal rights, and in which the EWMs operate.

Water rights

Each water law jurisdiction defines rights to water differently, but some general statements can be made at the outset. First, water rights typically specify the right to use a certain volume of water, in a particular location, in accordance with stated conditions.[45] Second, water rights can be based in common law or created by statute,[46] but there is a trend towards increasing reliance on statutory frameworks for water resource management, even in jurisdictions with a history of common law rights. Third, there is a strong and growing interest in using markets to manage access to water resources.[47] For this reason a water right is often referred to as though it is a form of private property right; but while water rights may be considered property in an economic context, they are not consistently considered property by the law. In this book I use the term 'water right' to refer in a general way to the right to use water as specified in the law of the particular jurisdiction.

Case studies

This book is based on in-depth analysis of two case studies of jurisdictions with EWMs (Australia and the USA), and the jurisdictions that granted legal rights to rivers in 2017 (Aotearoa New Zealand, Colombia, and India).

Environmental water managers

EWMs are organisations with legal personality which act on behalf of aquatic ecosystems (rivers, wetlands, floodplains, and estuaries) to acquire and manage water rights to achieve environmental outcomes. Almost all EWMs in operation today are found in south-eastern Australia and the western states of the USA. As a result, the book focuses on the EWMs of these two regions as case studies.

There are broad similarities between the forms of the EWMs in the case study regions, as well as the water law frameworks in which the EWMs are embedded, but the case studies are also sufficiently different to generate useful comparisons. The two case studies illustrate:

- different water law origins and water rights;
- a range of water market activity levels;
- sophisticated environmental water programmes that have moved beyond protection into recovery and management of environmental water, using a range of different mechanisms and processes;
- diverse EWM organisational forms, including a range of public and private entities;
- a range of EWM origins, including statutory creation and more organic emergence in response to the problem of acquiring water for the environment; and

- persistent activity of the EWMs in acquiring and managing environmental water over time (from the 1990s in the USA and the 2000s in Australia).

The case study methods use a combination of legal analysis of the constructions of the aquatic environment in law (including the EWMs) and long-form, semi-structured interviews with EWM staff.[48] These interviews extend the publicly available information and help to build an understanding of the way that the form and operation of the EWMs reflect the understanding and value of 'specific embodied knowers'.[49] This approach also acknowledges the specific background of the primary researcher: I have worked in environmental water law and policy since 2003, and I have significant personal involvement in the creation and operation of some of the EWMs used in this study. The case studies are presented in Chapters 4 and 5.

Rivers with legal rights

Legal rights for rivers have been explored in many countries, including the USA (the Colorado River), Nigeria (River Ethiope), and Australia (the Yarra and Margaret Rivers), but this book focuses on the examples where legal rights have been explicitly granted to rivers in legislation or as the result of a court decision. Three jurisdictions have actually created legal rights for rivers: Aotearoa New Zealand, India, and Colombia. Each of these jurisdictions has used different legal methods (legislation and court rulings), and implementation of the new legal arrangements has proceeded quite differently. In each jurisdiction legal rights have been granted to the river for different reasons and to achieve different aims. However, there is an important common factor across all three cases: the rivers are highly modified by human activities, but are also of great cultural and social value to the communities (both Indigenous and other local people) who live in the river catchments.

These legal rights for rivers are still very new. The case study analysis focuses on the specific legal creation of the new rights, and the ways in which the new legal arrangements are supported (or not) by new institutional and governance arrangements. The conceptual framework is used to identify early evidence of emerging competition between the rivers and human users, and potential collaboration.

Conclusion

This book explores the implications of giving legal rights to rivers, and constructing the aquatic environment as a legal person, for water law and governance. The next chapter reviews the way in which the law has constructed the environment, using examples from Australia and the USA, and the legal rights for nature movement in South America and Aotearoa New Zealand. Based on this review, Chapter 2 develops a new conceptual framework to identify the multiple constructions of the environment in law and the relationships between them.

This framework is then applied to the EWMs, where it highlights the capacity of legal personhood to strengthen cultural narratives of collaboration, but also competition, between the aquatic environment, water users, and local communities (Chapters 3–6). In Chapter 7 this new conceptual framework and insights from the EWMs are used to examine the new legal rights for rivers.

Ultimately, this book shows how creating legal rights for rivers has the potential both to help and to hinder environmental protection. If this legal tool is to be applied more widely, there are significant hurdles to overcome, and the final chapter explores some options for mitigating some of the negative impacts (Chapter 8).

Notes

1 Christopher D Stone, 'Should Trees Have Standing? Towards Legal Rights for Natural Objects' (1972) 45 *Southern California Law Review* 450.
2 George Dvorsky, 'India and New Zealand Were Wrong to Recognise Rivers as Persons' (25 March 2017) Gizmodo www.gizmodo.com.au/2017/03/india-and-new-zealand-were-wrong-to-recognise-rivers-as-persons/#_ga=2.58512682.1816765965.1526603101–1425698775.1526603101.
3 Everaldo Lamprea and Daniela García, 'Recent Trends in Climate Change Litigation: Colombia's Amazon and *Juliana v US*' (OxHRH Blog, 13 April 2018) http://ohrh.law.ox.ac.uk/recent-trends-in-climate-change-litigation-colombias-amazon-and-juliana-vs-u-s.
4 David R Boyd, *The Rights of Nature: A Legal Revolution That Could Save the World* (ECW Press, 2017).
5 Erin O'Donnell and Julia Talbot-Jones, 'Legal Rights for Rivers: What Does This Actually Mean?' (2017) 32(6) *Australian Environment Review* 159.
6 Erin O'Donnell and Julia Talbot-Jones, 'Creating Legal Rights for Rivers: Lessons from Australia, New Zealand, and India' (2018) 23(1) *Ecology and Society* 7.
7 Laurence H Tribe, 'Ways Not to Think About Plastic Trees: New Foundations for Environmental Law' (1974) 83 *Yale Law Journal* 1315.
8 Erin O'Donnell, 'At the Intersection of the Sacred and the Legal: Rights for Nature in Uttarakhand, India' (2018) 30(1) *Journal of Environmental Law* 135.
9 Erin O'Donnell, 'Competition or Collaboration? Using Legal Persons to Manage Water for the Environment in Australia and the United States' (2017) 34(6) *Environmental and Planning Law Journal* 503.
10 Gerry J Simpson and Hilary Charlesworth, 'Objecting to Objectivity' in Rosemary Hunter, Richard Ingleby, and Richard Johnstone (eds), *Thinking About Law: Perspectives on the History, Philosophy and Sociology of Law* (Allen & Unwin, 1995) 86, 101.
11 Ngaire Naffine, *Law's Meaning of Life: Philosophy, Religion, Darwin and the Legal Person* (Hart Publishing, 2009) 26.
12 Keith H Hirokawa, 'Dealing with Uncommon Ground: The Place of Legal Constructivism in the Social Construction of Nature' (2003) 21(3) *Virginia Environmental Law Journal* 387, 388.
13 Ibid., 391.

14 Ibid., 401; Bruce Ackerman, *Reconstructing American Law* (Harvard University Press, 1984).
15 Jo Goodie, 'The Invention of the Environment as a Subject of Legal Governance' in G Wickham and G Pavlich (eds), *Rethinking Law, Society and Governance: Foucault's Bequest* (Hart Publishing, 2001) 79, 80.
16 Neil Gunningham, 'Environmental Law, Regulation and Governance: Shifting Architectures' (2009) 21(2) *Journal of Environmental Law* 179; Zygmunt J B Plater, 'From the Beginning, a Fundamental Shift of Paradigms: A Theory and Short History of Environmental Law' (1994) 27 *Loyola of Los Angeles Law Revew* 981.
17 Yrjö Haila and Chuck Dyke (eds), *How Nature Speaks: The Dynamics of the Human Ecological Condition* (Duke University Press, 2006) viii.
18 Naffine, above n 11, 1.
19 O'Donnell and Talbot-Jones, above n 6.
20 D E Fisher, 'Markets, Water Rights and Sustainable Development' (2006) 23 *Environmental and Planning Law Journal* 100.
21 OECD, *OECD Environmental Outlook to 2050* (OECD Publishing, 2012).
22 Will Steffen, *Thirsty Country: Climate Change and Drought in Australia* (Climate Council of Australia, 2015); Julie C Padowski and Steven M Gorelick, 'Global Analysis of Urban Surface Water Supply Vulnerability' (2014) 9 *Environmental Research Letters* 104004.
23 Dustin E Garrick et al., 'Valuing Water for Sustainable Development' (2017) 358(6366) *Science* 1003.
24 Millennium Ecosystem Assessment, *Ecosystems and Human Well-Being: Wetlands and Water Synthesis* (World Resources Institute, 2005).
25 Tom Le Quesne, Eloise Kendy, and Derek Weston, *The Implementation Challenge: Taking Stock of Government Policies to Protect and Restore Environmental Flows* (World Wildlife Fund UK, 2010); Rafik Hirji and Richard Davis, *Environmental Flows in Water Resources Policies, Plans, and Projects: Findings and Recommendations* (World Bank, 2009).
26 Andrew Harwood et al., *Listen to the River: Lessons from a Global Review of Environmental Flow Success Stories* (WWF-UK, 2017).
27 Brisbane Declaration, *Environmental Flows are Essential for Freshwater Ecosystem Health and Human Well-Being* (Tenth International River Symposium and International Environmental Flows Conference, 3–6 September 2007, Brisbane, Australia, 2007).
28 Avril C Horne, Erin L O'Donnell, and Rebecca E Tharme, 'Mechanisms for Allocating Environmental Water' in Avril Horne et al. (eds), *Water for the Environment: From Policy and Science to Implementation and Management* (Academic Press, 2017) 361.
29 Terry L Anderson and Gary D Libecap, *Environmental Markets: A Property Rights Approach* (Cambridge University Press, 2014); J Bennett (ed.), *The Evolution of Markets for Water: Theory and Practice in Australia* (Edward Elgar, 2005).
30 D Garrick et al., 'Water Markets and Freshwater Ecosystem Services: Policy Reform and Implementation in the Columbia and Murray-Darling Basins' (2009) 69 *Ecological Economics* 366.
31 Naffine, above n 11, 10.
32 Erin O'Donnell, 'Common Legal and Policy Factors in the Emergence of Environmental Water Managers' in C A Brebbia (ed.), *Water and Society II* (WIT Press, 2013) 321.
33 Dustin Garrick and Erin O'Donnell, 'Exploring Private Roles in Environmental Watering in Australia and the US' in Jeff Bennett (ed.), *Protecting the Environment, Privately* (World Scientific Publishing, 2016) 203.

34 Erin O'Donnell, 'Constructing the Aquatic Environment as a Legal Subject: Legal Rights, Market Participation, and the Power of Narrative' (PhD thesis, University of Melbourne, 2017) http://hdl.handle.net/11343/191749.
35 Department of Natural Resources and Environment (Vic), *Healthy Rivers, Healthy Communities: Victorian River Health Strategy* (State of Victoria, 2002); Department of Sustainability and Environment (Vic), *Victorian Government White Paper: Securing Our Water Future Together* (State of Victoria, 2004).
36 Paul Humphries, 'The Drought We Had to Have?' *Science Alert* (15 August 2008) www.sciencealert.com/opinions/20081508–17809–4.html?utm_source=feedburner&utm_medium=feed&utm_campaign=Feed%25253A+sciencealert-latestnews+%252528ScienceAlert-Latest+Stories%252529.
37 Parliament of Victoria, *Parliamentary Debates*, Legislative Assembly, 26 May 2010, 1920–22 (Tim Holding, Minister for Water).
38 Rafik Hirji and Richard Davis, *Environmental Flows in Water Resources Policies, Plans, and Projects: Case Studies* (World Bank Environment Department, 2009) xiii; Angela H Arthington, *Environmental Flows: Saving Rivers in the Third Millennium* (University of California Press, 2012).
39 Mike Acreman et al., 'Environmental Flows for Natural, Hybrid, and Novel Riverine Ecosystems in a Changing World' (2014) 12 *Frontiers in Ecology and the Environment* 466.
40 Erin L O'Donnell and Dustin E Garrick, 'Environmental Water Organizations and Institutional Settings' in Avril Horne et al. (eds), *Water for the Environment: From Policy and Science to Implementation and Management* (Academic Press, 2017) 421.
41 IUCN, 'Environmental Flows' (29 September 2014) https://cmsdata.iucn.org/downloads/water_briefing_eflows_1.pdf.
42 Te Awa Tupua (Whanganui River Claims Settlement) Act 2017 (NZ), ss 12, 16.
43 Water Act 1989 (Vic) s 33DC.
44 Bureau of Meteorology, 'Frequently Asked Questions' (14 October 2014) Groundwater Dependent Ecosystems Atlas www.bom.gov.au/water/groundwater/gde/faq.shtml.
45 Stephen Hodgson, *Modern Water Rights: Theory and Practice* (Food and Agriculture Organization of the United Nations, 2006).
46 Anthony Scott and Georgina Coustalin, 'Rights Over Flowing Water' in Anthony Scott (ed.), *The Evolution of Resource Property Rights* (Oxford University Press, 2008) 63.
47 R Quentin Grafton et al., 'An Integrated Assessment of Water Markets: A Cross-Country Comparison' (2011) 5(2) *Review of Environmental Economics and Policy* 219; William Easter, Mark W Rosegrant, and Ariel Dinar, 'Formal and Informal Markets for Water: Institutions, Performance, and Constraints' (1999) 14(1) *The World Bank Research Observer* 99.
48 O'Donnell, above n 32.
49 Juliana Mansvelt and Lawrence D Berg, 'Writing Qualitative Geographies, Constructing Geographical Knowledge' in Iain Hay (ed.), *Qualitative Research Methods in Human Geography* (Oxford University Press, 2nd edn, 2005) 252.

2 Constructing the environment in law

Making it count

The specific issue of legal rights for rivers needs to be examined in the broader context of environmental law. As Melinda Harm Benson argues:

> How we think about environmental management challenges is important ... because our characterization of these challenges dictates both how we perceive them and then, correspondingly, how we integrate these perceptions into our legal and institutional frameworks.[1]

This chapter presents a historical overview of the ways in which the environment is *constructed* in law, and uses this to develop a new conceptual framework that identifies the relationship between the multiple constructions of the environment in law. The multiple constructions of the environment in law are:

- recognition and articulation of the environment as a *socio-ecological concept*;
- translation of that concept into a *legal object*; and
- personification of that object into a *legal subject*.

These constructs have emerged in response to a need to increase the *visibility* and *legibility* of the environment to the law, so the power of the law can be harnessed to solve environmental problems.

This conceptual framework offers a unique contribution to our understanding of the effect of extending legal personhood to rivers. There has been a clear chronological trend: narrower, more legible constructs of the environment have emerged from broader, less legible constructs over time. However, the multiple constructions continue to coexist, and can interact with one another. The interactions between these multiple constructions occur via their underpinning cultural narratives about the relationship of humans to nature, which shape the legal and regulatory responses to environmental problems. Thus these cultural narratives also underpin the emerging responses in water governance of competition and collaboration between the environment and other water users.

Legal personhood for the environment has emerged at the intersection of two separate drivers of legal reform: creation of legal rights for the environment as part of the legal rights of nature movement; and, in the case of the EWMs, market environmentalism, which enables (and in some cases, requires) the environment to participate in markets to manage environmental resources. This book lies at the intersection of these two very different but increasingly influential paradigms.

Constructing the environment in 'modern' environmental law

Historically, before the advent of specific environmental protections the law viewed impacts to the environment through the lens of the effect of one person's actions on another, via the torts of trespass, negligence, and nuisance.[2] However, these laws were rather ineffective at protecting the environment, as they were focused on the rights of individuals rather than a collective desire to protect and conserve the environment. Even resource management laws, which attempted to manage the use of natural resources for the overall economic and social benefit of the human community, were often inadequate at protecting the environment *qua* the environment.[3]

It wasn't until the 1960s that the environment was recognised as a legal concept, in response to a new understanding of the impact of human activity on the natural environment and a sense of urgency that this impact must be reduced for the sake of human wellbeing, as well as that of other species.[4] Plater described this process as 'dramatic – a massive upwelling of layer upon layer of substantial public and private law doctrines, almost volcanic in the power and mass of its eruption'.[5] Modern environmental laws established the environment as something legible to, and manageable by, the law.[6]

Defining the natural environment in law is central to the task of protecting, conserving, and managing it. In 1998 Godden argued that 'the essential contingency of any formulation of "nature" means that we need to be clear about what is being regulated', an issue that remains a core challenge for environmental law 20 years later.[7] In a society governed by the rule of law, if environmental claims and interests cannot be expressed in legally meaningful ways, then they are highly vulnerable to marginalisation.[8]

Statutory environmental law has approached this challenge by creating multiple, purpose-specific definitions of the environment to meet the needs of the particular problem at hand. Although scholars such as Klaus Bosselman and Douglas Fisher have identified an emergent norm of ecologically sustainable development,[9] environmental law remains dependent on a varied collection of definitions of 'environment', depending on the jurisdiction and the specific purpose of the legislation. We can begin to make sense of the multiplicity of the way the environment is defined in law by distilling this diversity into three main constructions:

- the socio-ecological concept, the 'natural environment';
- a legal object, to be protected from the actions of others; and
- a legal subject, a legal person with rights of its own.

Recognition in the law as a socio-ecological concept

The *socio-ecological concept* of the environment emerges from the recognition and definition of the environment within modern environmental legislation. Lazarus defines environmental law as being 'concerned, in the first instance, with impacts on the natural environment'.[10] Defining the environment in law brings together the recognition of an ecological reality and the relationship of a particular society to the environment in what Evernden describes as the 'social creation' of nature.[11]

The environment is literally everything that surrounds us, so one of the first challenges faced by environmental law was how to define the 'environment' and thus identify which elements were of interest in a specific context. In response, modern environmental law statutes created many new definitions of the 'environment'. These definitions occur along a spectrum of 'naturalness', exemplifying what Dickens identified as the Western dichotomy 'between "people" ... and "nature"'.[12] At one end is the human-centric definition, where the environment is merely the physical surroundings of humans. For example, in Australia the New South Wales Environment Planning and Assessment Act 1979 defines 'environment' as including 'all aspects of the surroundings of humans, whether affecting any human as an individual or in his or her social groupings'.[13]

At the other end of the spectrum, the environment is defined as 'wildness'; the pristine places where human impact is minimal. Queensland's recently repealed Wild Rivers Act 2005 aimed to 'preserve the natural values of rivers that have all, or almost all, of their natural values intact'.[14] In a deeply controversial move, in this case 'natural' was considered to exclude the impacts and broader cultural values of the Indigenous Australian populations in the wild river catchments.[15]

More recent definitions of the environment include humans as part of the ecosystem, such as Australia's Environment Protection and Biodiversity Conservation Act 1999 (Cth) (EPBC), which defines the environment as 'ecosystems and their constituent parts, including people and communities'.[16] This trend is part of modern environmental law's acknowledgement that moving to the 'holistic, human-species-as-constituent-part-of-nature view is not just an ethical idea, it is fundamentally practical and utilitarian as well',[17] by showing that 'failing to live within the limits that nature imposes not only imperils other species or "nature", it imperils the continued viability of human existence'.[18] Increasing awareness of climate change and the 'Anthropocene' (a new geological epoch that reflects the growing perturbation of the Earth's surface systems by the activities of humans)[19] suggests that this trend is likely to continue.

In addition to specific definitions of the environment, the *socio-ecological concept* of the environment also emerges from the combination of the objectives and purpose of the legislation. Douglas Fisher described these as strategic rules of limitation which indicate 'the direction of decision-making' desired by the legislature.[20] For example, in the USA the National Environmental Policy Act (NEPA)[21] doesn't contain a definition for 'environment', but it's possible to identify common elements of the way the legislation considers the natural environment based on references in the text. First, the preamble refers to the 'environment and the biosphere ... the ecological systems and natural resources' in the context of their importance to the health and welfare of people and the nation. Second, § 4331 part (a) refers to the 'natural environment' and the ways that 'man and nature can exist in productive harmony'. Part (b) is even more specific, referring to 'safe, healthful, productive, and esthetically and culturally pleasing surroundings' for all Americans and the need to 'preserve important historic, cultural, and natural aspects of our national heritage'. So although a clear definition of 'environment' is lacking in NEPA, a picture of the legal vision of the natural environment emerges nonetheless: the natural environment includes ecosystems as well as cultural heritage, and is necessary to support the health and welfare of the people and the nation.

These strategic rules are the basis for identifying the environment as worthy of legal protection, and do so in different ways that reflect the tensions between the different philosophies underpinning environmental law. First, the strategic rules may identify a single clear purpose of environmental protection or conservation, placing the environment at the centre of the legislation. The US Endangered Species Act 1973 (ESA) is one of the most powerful examples of this form of legislation, with the capacity to intervene in a broad range of public and private activities to conserve species and their habitat, but is limited only to those species listed as endangered.[22] Alternatively, and more typically, these strategic rules may include multiple objectives that require balancing against each other,[23] often for the purpose of enabling ecologically sustainable development. Although the primacy of the requirement to pursue ecologically sustainable development does provide environmental protection, the act of balancing environmental impacts and outcomes against economic and social impacts and outcomes frames the environment as merely one of many elements for consideration.

The socio-ecological concept is thus capable of being articulated and defined as needed for the purposes of specific legislation. The ability to tailor the precise shape of the natural environment in law is useful, but it also means that this concept is relatively fluid and consequently vulnerable to changing community attitudes about the environment.

Flexible yet vulnerable to shifting social and ecological values

The law depends on stability to underpin the continued relevance of past precedents and support consistent interpretation of statutory language. However, the natural environment is always changing. Ecologically, very few environments are consistent over long periods of time, as habitats change through abrupt processes such as fire and volcanic eruptions as well as more gradual processes like desertification, glaciations, and continental movements. Human activities can hasten these changes through introduced species, land clearing, mining, and climate change.

When the environment is always changing, how can the law create accountability for environmental protection? Without a clear baseline, and a clear causal nexus for a change, accountability and liability for environmental outcomes are difficult to establish. Environmental water management is a powerful example of this problem, as water availability and ecosystem health are influenced by long-term climate and weather patterns as well as water resource policy.[24]

This ecological dynamism is further compounded by shifting social values. In a democracy, the environment is maintained and protected at the standard required by society.[25] Both Australia and the USA have experienced significant shifts in social values for the environment as each nation has transitioned from a colonial approach to recognition of its own unique environmental values. As the social demand for a healthy environment increased, each country invested significantly in restoring environmental functions degraded by human exploitation. In the USA grey wolves were initially destroyed as a perceived threat to stock before receiving protection under the ESA as a threatened species. Following a successful restoration programme, the wolves are increasingly perceived as threats to farms once again, and attempts are being made to delist the species.[26] In Australia rivers were initially valued for reasons of water supply and transport of goods. As a result many rivers were desnagged, and trees and other debris that had fallen into the river during floods were removed. More recently, as rivers have become valued for fish habitats, the value of these instream habitats was recognised and in some cases rivers have been actively resnagged.[27] In both countries the restoration of environmental flows reflects this shift in social value, as rivers became recognised not only as water resources but as important aquatic environments.[28]

Recognition of the environment in the law as a socio-ecological concept brings a combination of flexibility and vulnerability. The power of this concept of the 'natural environment' in the law is that it is easily adaptable to the concerns of specific legislation. The corollary of this flexibility is that what is meant by 'natural environment' must be constantly and explicitly articulated by the law. The social and ecological dynamism of the environment, in combination with the shifting boundary between what is included and what is excluded, means that it will never be possible to take a 'set and forget' approach to environmental protection and management. Each legal and policy reform remains vulnerable to changing social and ecological states.[29]

While this recognition enabled the law to 'see' the environment, it required an additional step to translate it into a construct with more legal effect.

Translation of the environment into a legal object

The translation of the environment in law was focused on protecting the environment from harm caused by the actions of others, and finding ways to mitigate previously lawful actions and limit the impact of their cumulative effects. Modern environmental law *translated* the socio-ecological concept of the environment into a legal object: a *thing* to be protected from the potential harm posed by the actions of legal subjects.

Translation and incomplete legibility

The vast majority of modern environmental law operates through translation of the environment into a legal object.[30] This translation gave the law the power to directly limit or control specific actions that could cause harm to the environment, but the law could still only 'see' the environment obliquely, through the lens of the actions of legal subjects.

As a legal object, the environment may be used as a resource or protected as an asset under legal rules that empower others to act, or limit their otherwise lawful actions. 'Rules of competence confer powers of management' by establishing the legal right to do something, such as the power of an owner to use a possession, the power of an individual to access the environment, the power to discharge pollution to the environment, or the power of the state to approve or disapprove such actions.[31] These rules of competence confer that power on another legal person, not on the environment itself.

Rules of limitation operate in conjunction with rules of competence to control 'the way in which these powers are exercised'.[32] Regulatory rules of limitation are imposed on other legal subjects, reinforcing the construction of the environment as a legal object and making the environment dependent on the state to enforce these limits to protect it. Under these rules, the environment is the thing that must not be harmed, the medium that must not be polluted, or the native vegetation (for example) that must not be cleared, but it possesses no legal rights of its own.[33]

The real power of these rules is not so much in their limitation of an activity as in the process they prescribe for approving the activity. This process can be more or less effective at protecting the environment, depending on the constraints imposed on the decision-maker.[34]

Remaining blind spots

The translation of the environment into a legal object by the creation of legal rules that control the activities of others (the legal subjects) enhanced the capacity of the law to protect the environment. However, this translation resulted in a form of incomplete legibility, with a number of remaining blind spots.

First, the law is especially good at seeing the special and the iconic, and can easily identify and protect places of iconic wilderness value.[35] The law is similarly able to focus on species that have been identified as endangered, such as those listed under the US ESA.[36] However, protecting the environment requires the law to see and value the entire environment, not merely those few places or species considered as especially valuable.

Second, the law is focused on actions that achieve a measurable shift in environmental quality. Where the law limits actions that reduce air quality or increase noise levels, these are both measured against the existing background (thus limiting the capacity of the law to *improve* the quality of the environment) and focus on single actions or events that cause a *measurable* change in the existing quality. For example, Victoria's Environment Protection Act 1970 states that '[a] person shall not pollute any waters so that the condition of the waters is so *changed* as to make or be reasonably expected to *make* those waters ... *noxious or poisonous*' (emphasis added).[37] Although broader policy and planning regulations can impose unified strategies, the law itself still finds it difficult to consider the effect of cumulative impacts on the environment.

Third, the law can struggle to identify the effects of continuing actions, even where there is a legal capacity to consider the impact of a wide range of activities. For example, the Australian EPBC is limited to consideration of new actions, which means that it has no capacity to be used to assess the impact of ongoing storage and extraction of water under existing water rights.[38] This is in contrast to the USA, where the federal government must relicense existing dams, and this approvals process provides an opportunity to reassess the environmental impacts and alter the operation of a dam to reduce them.[39] Furthermore, the ESA can be applied to ongoing operations, and new information on the requirements of listed species can provide a way to alter existing water uses.[40]

These blind spots are made more problematic by the practicalities of the way in which the law operates. At law, most environmental cases are run by those granted legal standing to seek review of a *decision* to allow an action that has the capacity to affect the environment, so the legal redress is rarely the prohibition of the action but is the requirement for the decision-maker to reconsider the decision. The courts can only provide the 'remedies [that] are available and appropriate to ensure that those possessed of executive and administrative powers exercise them ... in accordance with the laws which govern their exercise'.[41]

In the USA, where the public trust doctrine supports a broader legal approach to the problem of how the state is managing environmental assets, the courts are still limited to an assessment of the human impacts of environmental degradation.[42] In Australia, although the EPBC enables the court or the minister to require remediation of damage to the environment, there are a number of practical limitations on this power, including the capacity of the court to consider the costs of remediation when making the decision to impose the order.[43]

Personification of the environment as a legal subject: legal rights for nature

The third legal construct of the environment is that of a legal person, which 'is to be the subject of rights and duties. To confer legal rights or to impose legal duties, therefore, is to confer legal personality.'[44] A legal person represents the ultimate step in terms of legibility to the law. The legal person is the centre of legal focus, the subject of the law:

> Through its concept of the person, law helps to define who matters … the legal person, in whatever manifestation, corporate or human … represents an act of legal creativity with immense social and political import.[45]

It is also worth noting at the outset that the very idea of framing the environment as a holder of legal rights remains contested.[46]

The idea of constructing the environment as a legal subject is not new. In 1972 Stone argued that legal rights should be extended to 'forests, oceans, rivers and other so-called "natural objects" in the environment – indeed, to the natural environment as a whole', in the same way that legal rights have been extended to other previously 'unthinkable' persons and those who cannot speak for themselves in the adult world (such as children and the mentally ill).[47] Stone's argument directly addressed the question of legibility, and he argued that extending legal rights to the environment would enable the law to see it more clearly, and to respond more appropriately to environmental problems.

Stone identified three legal-operational criteria that 'go toward making a thing *count* jurally': 'that the thing can institute legal actions *at its behest*'; 'that in determining the granting of legal relief, the court must take *injury to it* into account'; and 'that relief must run to the *benefit* of it' (emphasis in original).[48]

Over the past four decades Stone has presented a number of models for personifying the environment in law, centred on the concept of guardianship and legal standing. However, until 2008 there was very little uptake of these concepts in environmental law more broadly. Although some cases have included nature (in the form of a particular species, geographical feature, or location) as a plaintiff, it has generally been a co-plaintiff backed up by a human counterpart, and, as Stone acknowledges, such cases must be 'regarded, at the moment, as curiosities'[49] rather than evidence of a profound legal shift.

The push for legal rights for nature began to enter the mainstream in 2006 as communities began to legislate to protect their environments at the local level, and there are cases where nature exerts its own right to exist and flourish in the courts[50] (although it remains to be seen how these local laws will withstand legal challenges at the state or federal levels).[51] In 2008 Ecuador passed constitutional amendments that created legal rights for nature across the country.[52] In 2010 Bolivia followed suit with new legislation that created legal rights for nature, and committed to establishing a new body to enforce these rights.[53] There is some evidence that these laws are being used by the courts to limit environmentally degrading activities.[54] In 2014 Aotearoa New Zealand adopted the concept of 'legal personhood' when it gave legal rights to a national park, Te Urewera.[55]

In 2017 the concept of legal rights for nature took another leap forward, with four rivers being declared legal persons. The first river to receive legal rights was the Whanganui River in Aotearoa New Zealand.[56] Under the settlement of the Treaty of Waitangi the river itself was recognised as a legal person, in part to sidestep the vexed issue of whether the Māori or the New Zealand government would be considered the 'owner' of the river.[57] New legislation extended legal person status to the river and its catchment, and created Te Pou Tupua to act as the guardian for the river.[58]

One week later the High Court of the state of Uttarakhand in India declared that the Ganga and Yamuna Rivers were legal persons.[59] In doing so, the court blurred the line between a legal person and a human person, and nominated the state government to act as guardians for rivers that extend across the country (well outside the borders of Uttarakhand).[60] In July 2017 the decision was appealed to the Supreme Court of India, which has stayed the original decision (thus leaving the rivers without rights) until the court rules on the appeal.

Finally, the Constitutional Court of Colombia released its judgment from 2016, which extended legal rights to the Río Atrato as part of protecting the culture and livelihoods of various communities who live near the river.[61] The legal rights of the river were articulated by the court as 'biocultural' rights, to emphasise the connection between the river and the people who depend on it.

The concept of legal rights for nature continues to generate widespread interest and application. In Aotearoa New Zealand legal personality has since been granted to Mount Taranaki, and may be granted to the Whangaehu River as part of a recently agreed treaty settlement.[62]

However, what is missing from the scholarship on legal rights for nature is an understanding of exactly what we can expect when nature receives legal rights. How will this relatively new construction of the environment interact with the existing constructions? How can the environment be given both the capacity for legal rights and duties and also the competence to enforce those rights?[63]

Capacity and competence

Ngaire Naffine defines the process of personification within the law as a technical construction *by* the law to make something more visible *to* the law:

> By granting legal rights and duties, law establishes legal relations, and it also personifies: that is, it turns us into legal persons or legal actors, right holders and duty bearers, beings who are therefore capable of acting and relating in law.[64]

Naffine distinguishes this 'legalist' definition from alternatives that focus on the moral nature of personhood or its particular relationship to a 'natural' person.[65] In essence, legal personhood brings three main legal rights: the right to enter and enforce contracts; the ability to own property; and legal standing, or the right to sue and be sued in court.[66]

The most common means by which the law expands the category of legal persons is the corporation, which was recognised in common law as having separate legal personality to its members and owners in 1897.[67] The separate legal personality of the private corporation was originally intended to limit the liability of shareholders and promote investment.[68] Given this history, the corporate form is not a natural fit for the environment, but the emergence of not-for-profit corporations and statutory corporations owned and operated by governments demonstrates its flexibility. Many environmental advocacy and charity organisations are created as not-for-profit corporations, and they have been relatively successful in obtaining legal standing to challenge government decisions that have environmental impacts.[69] However, to date these organisations have not been considered as a legal form personifying the environment itself, but merely a way for concerned citizens to take legal action on issues they care about.[70]

The declaration of rivers as legal persons has been accompanied by the creation of new legal entities that more explicitly represent the environment as a legal person in its own right. In Aotearoa New Zealand the Whanganui River was established as a legal entity with 'all the rights, powers, duties, and liabilities of a legal person', and the river and its catchment will be represented by the guardian, Te Pou Tupua, which will act on behalf of the river.[71]

The EWMs, which are discussed in more detail in the next chapter, are legal persons (usually incorporated entities) that hold water rights for the aquatic environment. The EWMs use their legal personhood to give voice to the needs of the aquatic environment within policy debates, as well as participating in water markets and entering into contractual agreements. In doing so, the EWMs combine the capacity to hold legal powers with the competence to use those powers. The EWMs have emerged in response to the opportunities created by the water markets, and demonstrate that legal rights for nature can also be a response to market environmentalism.

Market environmentalism

Markets have been embraced by governments and regulators around the world to achieve environmental outcomes, as a lower-cost alternative to prescriptive management.[72] Environmental markets generally have two clear aims: first, to address the market failure caused by 'public good' properties of natural resources allocated to the environment (non-rival and non-excludable use) by *increasing* the allocation to the environment; and second, to *manage* that allocation efficiently, so that it generates the maximum possible environmental outcomes.[73] It is thus clear that markets are a form of regulation, not a replacement for it. In particular, environmental markets depend on significant government investment in the creation and enforcement of property rights and the provision of publicly accessible information exchange platforms to facilitate transfers.[74]

Environmentalists have long considered nature as incommensurable with neoliberalisation and markets, private property as an enemy of effective environmental protection, and the coexistence of private property alongside a commons as a recipe for disaster.[75] However, neoclassical economists argue that it is poorly defined property rights and missing markets that cause environmental problems, and enhancing these rights is an integral part of the solution.[76] Part of the resolution to this dilemma lies in the way that the law constructs the environment. Where the environment is still a legal object, private property rights may act to obscure the environment from the law by limiting the capacity of the law to control a property holder's actions that threaten the environment.[77] However, where the environment is constructed as a legal subject, property instead becomes a significant source of legal power for the environment, and a way for the law to see and engage with the environment directly, as a holder of property.

Thompson defined environmental markets as either 'regulatory' or 'public goods' markets.[78] Regulatory markets aim to internalise *negative* externalities, such as point-source pollution, by using a cap-and-trade scheme. A good example is the market for sulphur dioxide pollution in North America, in which the government set the cap on total pollution and created transferable pollution permits, enabling low-cost industries to sell excess permits to high-cost industries.[79] In these markets there is typically one seller (government via auction) and many buyers (the pollution-generating industry), with some on-selling (between industry) but little to no opportunity for organisations representing the environment itself to engage, although occasionally environmental groups have attempted to purchase pollution rights (effectively lowering the cap). This remains rare, because it is unlikely for environmental organisations to be able to afford to acquire the sheer volume of rights necessary to make a real difference, especially in international markets such as carbon emissions trading.

Public goods markets, on the other hand, were introduced to enable efficient investment in increased production of a public good (a non-excludable and/or non-consumable good) or ecosystem service. These markets internalise a *positive* externality (such as a wetland), which provides benefits in ways that are difficult to protect as private property rights. These markets are often structured as the inverse of the regulatory markets: a single buyer (usually government, occasionally an environmental non-governmental organisation (NGO)), with many potential sellers (such as private landowners).[80] However, these markets rarely stimulated further trade of the environmental good, and thus were often simply a one-off mechanism for increasing production without necessarily changing norms or creating private value for ecosystem services, and they have not yet evolved into ongoing multi-buyer, multi-seller markets.

However, there is now a third type of environmental market, which I term the *shared resource* market, which is a means of managing access to scarce natural resources which have value to both the environment and a range of other users. Shared resource markets are multi-buyer, multi-seller markets in which environmental organisations can participate, and they often emerge from existing rights-based regulatory frameworks for managing access to scarce resources. For instance, fishing licences are now traded in many locations, and in one recent example the World Wide Fund for Nature (WWF) purchased a shark fishing licence. Acting on behalf of the environment, the WWF effectively 'acquired' the right to those sharks, which it then retained in the ecosystem.[81]

Anderson and Libecap implicitly engage with the concept of shared resource markets as part of their arguments for government creation of the 'missing markets' that, they argue, underpin many environmental problems.[82] They overlook, however, some of the opportunities of the shared resource market as a unique market form. Shared resource markets are the mechanism that has done most to shift the construction of the environment itself to being a participant in the market, by enabling organisations acting on behalf of the environment to be both buyer and seller. In doing so, they have also reframed the environment as a competitor with other human users.

Water markets as a driver of personhood

Water markets are one of the oldest examples of a shared resource market, and were established to manage access to a scarce resource rather than as a direct mechanism for environmental protection. Water is a resource required by diverse users: people (drinking and hygiene), industry (farms, mines, and other commercial uses), and the aquatic environment. As a result, water markets offer a way of increasing both allocative efficiency (enabling transfers between different uses as demand and supply change) and productive efficiency (enabling transfers to higher-value uses within or between use types).[83]

This type of market creates an opportunity for the aquatic environment to engage and participate. There are multiple buyers and multiple sellers, and the aquatic environment (via the EWMs) can operate as both a seller and a buyer. The EWMs participate in the market, with funds, assets, and the capacity to manage their own ongoing operations (see Chapter 3). The EWMs thus combine the *capacity* for legal rights with the *competence* to use those rights.

For the EWMs, the capacity to hold water rights strengthens their role in water governance. However, despite their similarity to other water market participants, the EWMs continue to face the ongoing challenge of defining how much water is enough for the environment and how to quantify environmental benefits achieved for the cost of the water. This makes the EWMs fundamentally different to private consumptive water users, who can point to the income generated by their use of water as a measure of value. It also places the EWMs in the uncomfortable position of competing with other water users while depending on long-term community support for their operation.

Personification of the environment in law has occurred at the nexus of two global trends: legal rights for nature and explicit use of legal personhood as a vehicle for those rights, and market environmentalism. However, the market has long been recognised as having the capacity to alter social norms: 'the institution of the market, and its ever-expanding proclivities, represents a shift in the normative underpinning to social action which disturbs that which was previously extant'.[84]

Cultural narratives and the construction of the environment in law

There is a complex relationship between the law and the cultural narratives that underpin its form and function, and this relationship is especially close for modern environmental law, which is largely promulgated in the form of legislation passed by governments. Robin Kundis Craig and Melinda Harm Benson have both argued that the way we tell stories about environmental problems shapes the way we think about them, which in turn shapes the legal solutions available to us.[85] Hutchinson goes further, claiming a central role for narrative in shaping the law:

> The life of law is not logic nor experience, but a narrative way of worldmaking ... Like all tales, legal stories gain meaning and significance from the selective emphasis on certain features of our always complex and frequently ambiguous experience.[86]

A narrative can be a useful way of conceptualising a complex problem, using the logic of a story to help frame both problem and solution. Kundis Craig defines cultural narratives as 'deeply embedded social stories that frame and contextualize events within a particular culture to help give them meaning'.[87] In the context of complex, goal-oriented legal frameworks like that of environmental law, cultural narratives 'can also help to instill value systems into members of the community prior to, or instead of, individual experience'.[88] Community members can thus be primed by the dominant narrative to react to new events or information in a particular way.

Narratives are also, by their very nature, specific. They tend to tell a single story, which means that alternative narratives can be excluded or displaced. This is a real challenge for environment law, where there are myriad definitions of environment and multiple narratives underpinning the importance of its protection and sustainable management. The construction of the environment in law as a socio-ecological concept makes the environment particularly vulnerable to narrative shifts. The constructions of the environment as a legal object and a legal subject are each supported by particular narratives about its value to human society.

Public interest and the legal object: weak but worthy of protection

The translation of the environment into a legal object has been largely the result of the intentional creation of new legislation to bring particular actions under legal control. This construct frames the environment as fundamentally *worthy* of protection, but as legally *weak*, depending on the actions of others to protect it. This narrative not only links the two elements of *worthiness* and *weakness*, but makes willingness to protect the environment *dependent* on its construction as legally weak. In addition to framing the way that community members feel about the environment, this narrative embeds a particular regulatory response. A legal object cannot (and in this narrative, *should not*) speak for itself.

As a result, this narrative, which underpins most of modern environmental law, sits under the *public interest* theory of regulation: that the regulators should act to protect vulnerable areas in the interests of broader social good, based on 'a desire to pursue collective goals with the aim of promoting the general welfare of the community'.[89] Morgan and Yeung distinguish between public interest regulation created to fix a market failure (Pigovian welfare economic regulation), to achieve a particular political goal (substantive political regulation), or to establish participatory processes for public engagement in regulatory mechanisms (procedural political regulation). Environmental law can clearly be all three, but the definition of the environment is most closely drawn from 'the public interest goals of the substantive political approach'.[90]

Sunstein argued that the substantive political approach can include the desire to protect vulnerable values (such as endangered species) from irreversible loss. He conceived of the law as a mechanism for people to enforce their political decisions, and that '[as] citizens, people may seek the aid of the law to bring about a social state in some sense higher than what emerges from market ordering'.[91] Regulation in this instance is considered a way to reflect these broader, collective preferences about what *should* be regulated: 'public interest theories place an emphasis on the goals, functions and values that *justify* regulation' (emphasis added).[92]

Modern environmental statutes are a statement about what qualities or features of the environment should be protected. As such, modern environmental law is contingent on both a collective desire to regulate impacts on the environment and a collective belief that such regulation is justified. Modern environmental law relies on the idea that the environment is *worthy* of protection, and constructs the environment as a legal object that others, usually the state, are empowered to protect.

However, such a view is also contingent on the idea that the environment cannot speak for itself. Public interest theories of regulation depend on the idea that regulation must reflect a *collective* belief, which is more than the sum of individual preferences. If the environment has the capacity to voice its own opinions, or the power to seek its own legal remedies, it would be much less reliant on public interest regulation. The idea that the environment is worthy of protection in law is thus indelibly linked to the idea that it cannot protect itself. The environment is presented in modern environmental law as a passive legal object: a locus of deserved protection, but without the power to speak on its own behalf.

Private interest and the legal subject: more power, less protection?

The personification of the environment in law has constructed the environment as a legal subject represented by a specific legal entity. This construct represents the pinnacle of legibility to the law, and establishes the environment with the same basic set of legal powers as any other person in law, including the capacity to speak and act on its own behalf. Again, there is a clear narrative underpinning this construct: the environment has the same legal powers as everyone else, and so it can, *and should*, look after itself. This narrative represents a dramatic shift in community expectations of the environment, and can be linked to the increasing popularity of using market-based instruments to manage environmental assets.[93] Using a Coasian framework,[94] the environment has been shifted from a property right held by others to the holder of property rights and a bargainer in its own right. This narrative also shapes the regulatory response, by depending on private interest theories of regulation (that regulation emerges as a result of competing private interests).[95] The environment is no longer worthy of special treatment, but is expected to compete for regulatory outcomes with other individuals and interest groups.

Traditional debates about legal rights for the environment have emphasised legal standing, but in this book I argue that the capacity to engage in policy debates is at least as significant for the construction of the environment as a legal person. The environment as legal object was able to rely on public interest theories of regulation, where policymakers operated on its behalf to protect it. A person, however, 'is a being who has a sense of self, has a notion of the future and the past, can hold values [and] make choices'.[96] Legal persons, when represented by distinct organisations like the EWMs, have a voice in policy debates and can articulate what they want for themselves. The personification of the environment transitions environmental protection laws out of public interest theories of regulation and into private interest theories, where regulations are the aggregate of different interest group pressures (competition) and the regulators are merely 'conduits and aggregators'.[97]

Creating an entity to represent the environment in law generates real narrative and regulatory tensions. A voice enables participation in policy debates, so environmental needs and values are injected into a policy debate during the formative stages, when they are likely to have the most impact. However, a voice alone is likely to be insufficient. If the legal entity lacks financial support, it will not be able to pursue legal challenges in court.[98] In policy debates, while a voice can give the environment a seat at the table, if the voice does not come with sufficient real-world power it may go unheard. This is the real risk of the creation of a voice for the environment: it suggests that the environment is competing with other interest groups on a level playing field, when that may not be the case at all.

Engaging with both these legal constructs and their underpinning narratives has two important outcomes. First, there is real tension between the narratives that underpin the environment as a legal object and as a legal subject. As a legal object, the environment is positioned as being worthy of protection and humans *should* protect it because it cannot act to protect itself. As a legal subject, this narrative is excluded and the environment is presented as an entity that can, and therefore *should*, act on its own behalf. The simultaneous construction of the environment as both a legal object and a legal subject brings these narratives into competition, and creates tension in how community members conceive of and value their environment.

Second, the construction of the environment as a socio-ecological concept is extremely vulnerable to changes in the way that the environment is articulated in law. This creates a unique vulnerability for the environment that cannot be addressed by merely levelling the playing field or adjusting for historical imbalance. The need to rearticulate continually what the environment is and why it is important means that shifts in these values can have profound effects.

So what does this mean for legal rights for rivers, and particularly the EWMs which embody legal personhood for the aquatic environment? On the one hand, the EWMs appear well placed to represent the environment in policy debates: they hold water rights and they have the same sorts of legal powers as other users of water, including the right to sit on various water user committees. On the other, the EWMs depend on continued support from the relevant community for their environmental objectives, which makes them more vulnerable than other water users.

Constructing the environment in law: a conceptual framework

This chapter brings together the multiple constructions of the environment over time, the processes by which the environment is constructed in law, and the narratives underpinning these constructions in a new conceptual framework (Figure 2.1). This new framework can help make predictions about the consequences for water governance of creating legal rights for rivers, and how to manage these consequences.

At the broadest level, the environment is a socio-ecological concept based on a combination of physical features and social values. This concept is articulated in the purposes, objectives, and definitions of environmental statutes.

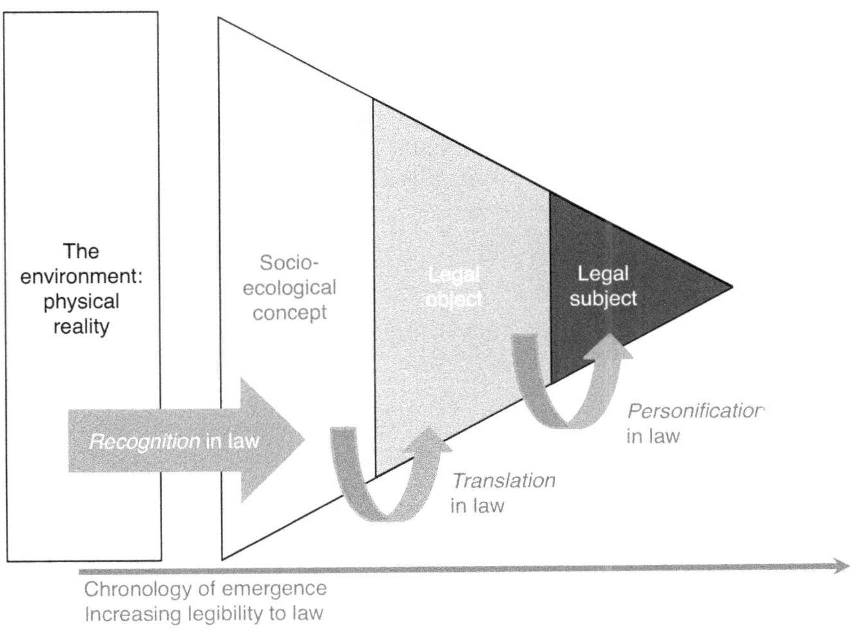

Figure 2.1 Constructing the environment in law.

Next, the natural environment is *translated* into a legal object. This construct enables the creation of procedural protections which place limits on the actions of others that may affect the environment. The environment itself remains passive: it is a thing to be protected. This construct of the environment is contingent on the natural environment being perceived by society as deserving of this protection.

Lastly, the environment can be *personified* as a legal subject, which gives the natural environment legal rights. Where the environment has legal rights but no form, it will be dependent on others to enforce those legal rights (which is the case in Ecuador). Alternatively, an organisation can be created to represent part of the environment (such as the EWMs, or Te Pou Tupua for the Whanganui River). Through the legal powers of this organisation, the environment may take action on its own behalf (at least to a certain extent). The use of markets to achieve environmental outcomes can enhance personification in law, but also reframes the environment as a competitor within the market.

Although there is a distinct pattern of chronology, all three legal constructs of the natural environment currently occur within modern environmental law; they are interrelated by the processes of translation and personification, and underpinned by inconsistent narratives which generate different regulatory responses as the role of the environment shifts between something worthy of protection and something that should be able to protect itself.

By connecting the construction in law to the narrative and the regulatory response, this conceptual framework can be applied to the creation and operation of EWMs to illuminate the legal context of the EWMs and to identify and understand the ways in which the aquatic environment is constructed in water law. The conceptual framework can thus help to help answer the question: what happens when the aquatic environment is constructed as a legal subject, and why?

Notes

1 Melinda Harm Benson, 'Reconceptualizing Environmental Challenge – Is Resilience the New Narrative?' (2015) 21 *Journal of Environmental and Sustainability Law* 99, 99.
2 Lee Godden and Jacqueline Peel, *Environmental Law: Scientific, Policy and Regulatory Dimensions* (Oxford University Press, 2010) 155.
3 Anthony Scott, *The Evolution of Resource Property Rights* (Oxford University Press, 2008); Carol M Rose, 'Energy and Efficiency in the Realignment of Common Law Water Rights' (1990) 19 *Journal of Legal Studies* 261.
4 Rachel Carson, *Silent Spring* (Penguin Books, 1965).
5 Zygmunt J B Plater, 'From the Beginning, a Fundamental Shift of Paradigms: A Theory and Short History of Environmental Law' (1994) 27 *Loyola of Los Angeles Law Revew* 981, 1003.
6 Neil Gunningham, 'Environmental Law, Regulation and Governance: Shifting Architectures' (2009) 21(2) *Journal of Environmental Law* 179, 182.

7 Lee Godden, 'Preserving Natural Heritage: Nature as Other' (1998) 22(3) *Melbourne University Law Review* 719, 722.
8 Mark Stallworthy, *Understanding Environmental Law* (Sweet & Maxwell, 2008) 29.
9 Douglas E Fisher, *Australian Environmental Law: Norms, Principles and Rules* (Thomson Reuters, 2nd edn, 2010) vii and Chapter 6; Klaus Bosselmann, *The Principle of Sustainability: Transforming Law and Governance* (Ashgate Publishing, 2008).
10 Richard J Lazarus, 'Restoring What's Environmental About Environmental Law in the Supreme Court' (2000) 47 *UCLA Law Review* 703, 744.
11 Neil Evernden, *The Social Creation of Nature* (Johns Hopkins University Press, 1992).
12 Peter Dickens, *Society and Nature: Towards a Green Social Theory* (Harvester Wheatsheaf, 1992) 15.
13 Environment Planning and Assessment Act 1979 (NSW) s 4(1), 'environment'.
14 Wild Rivers Act 2005 (Qld) s 5(1) (now repealed).
15 Timothy Neal, 'Overturn, Axe and Bury: The LNP and Queensland's Wild Rivers Act' *The Conversation* (2 August 2012) https://theconversation.com/overturn-axe-and-bury-the-lnp-and-queenslands-wild-rivers-act-8576.
16 Environment Protection and Biodiversity Conservation Act 1999 (Cth) s 528, 'environment'.
17 Plater, above n 5, 1000.
18 David Delaney, *Law and Nature* (Cambridge University Press, 2003) 199.
19 Will Steffen, Paul J Crutzen, and John R McNeill, 'The Anthropocene: Are Humans Now Overwhelming the Great Forces of Nature?' (2007) 36 *Ambio* 614.
20 Fisher, above n 9, 254.
21 National Environmental Policy Act 1969 42 USC § 4321 et seq.
22 Endangered Species Act 1973 16 USC § 1538 et seq.
23 *Parramatta City Council v Hale* (1982) 47 *Local Government and Environmental Reports of Australia* 319.
24 State of Victoria, *Northern Region Sustainable Water Strategy* (Department of Sustainability and Environment, 2009) 150.
25 A Horne, J Freebairn, and E O'Donnell, 'Establishment of Environmental Water in the Murray-Darling Basin – An Analysis of Two Key Policy Initiatives' (2011) 15(1) *Australian Journal of Water Resources* 7, 11–13.
26 *Defenders of Wildlife, et al., Plaintiffs, v. Sally Jewell, et al., Defendants. The Humane Society of the United States, et al., Plaintiffs, v. U.S. Fish and Wildlife Service, et al., Defendants*, F. Supp. 3d, 2014 WL 4714847 (DDC 2014).
27 I Rutherford et al., *Managing Woody Debris in Rivers. Fact Sheet 7* (Land and Water Australia, 2002).
28 Avril C Horne, Erin L O'Donnell, and Rebecca E Tharme, 'Mechanisms for Allocating Environmental Water' in Avril Horne et al. (eds), *Water for the Environment: From Policy and Science to Implementation and Management* (Academic Press, 2017) 361.
29 E O'Donnell et al., 'Cry Me a River: Going Beyond the Crisis Response: Building Trust and Maintaining Legitimacy in Environmental Flows' (Academy of Social Sciences Australia, 2018) www.assa.edu.au/academy-workshop-report-cry-me-a-river/.
30 Gerry Bates, *Environmental Law in Australia* (LexisNexis Butterworths, 2013).
31 Fisher, above n 9, 226–227, 229.
32 Ibid., 255.
33 Ibid., 256.

34 David Grinlinton, 'The "Environmental Era" and the Emergence of "Environmental Law" in Australia – A Survey of Environmental Legislation and Litigation 1967–1987' (1990) 7 *Environmental and Planning Law Journal* 74; Brian Preston, 'Environmental Law 1927–2007: Retrospect and Prospect' (2007) 81 *Australian Law Journal* 616; Richard B Stewart, 'Models for Environmental Regulation: Central Planning versus Market-Based Approaches' (1992) 19(3) *Boston College Environmental Affairs Law Review* 547; Jeb Boyt, 'Struggling to Protect Ecosystems and Biodiversity under NEPA and NFMA: The Ancient Forests of the Pacific Northwest and the Northern Spotted Owl' (1993) 10(2) *Pace Environmental Law Review* 1009.

35 Holly Doremus, 'Biodiversity and the Challenge of Saving the Ordinary' (2002) 38 *Idaho Law Review* 325.

36 Oliver A Houck, 'Reflections on the Endangered Species Act' (1995) 25 *Environmental Law* 689.

37 Environment Protection Act 1970 (Vic) s 39(1)(a).

38 Michael Bennett and Alex Gardner, 'How Do Environmental Conservation Laws Interact With Environmental Aspects of Water Laws?' (2014) 31(3) *Environmental and Planning Law Journal* 3.

39 M Bowman, 'Legal Perspectives on Dam Removal' (2002) 52(8) *BioScience* 739.

40 Holly Doremus and A Dan Tarlock, 'Fish, Farms and the Clash of Cultures in the Klamath Basin' (2003) 30 *Ecology Law Quarterly* 279.

41 *Corporation of the City of Enfield v Development Assessment Commission* (2000) 199 CLR 135; 106 *Local Government and Environmental Reports of Australia* 419 at 437, per Gaudron J.

42 *National Audubon Society v. Superior Court of Alpine County*, 33 Cal.3d 419 (1983); *Lujan v Defenders of Wildlife* 112 SCt 2130 (1992).

43 Environment Protection and Biodiversity Conservation Act 1999 (Cth) ss 480A–480N.

44 Bryant Smith, 'Legal Personality' (1928) 37(3) *Yale Law Journal* 283.

45 Ngaire Naffine, *Law's Meaning of Life: Philosophy, Religion, Darwin and the Legal Person* (Hart Publishing, 2009) 11–12.

46 Holmes Rolston III, 'Rights and Responsibilities on the Home Planet' (1993) 18 *Yale Journal of International Law* 251.

47 Christopher D Stone, 'Should Trees Have Standing? Towards Legal Rights for Natural Objects' (1972) 45 *Southern California Law Review* 450, 456.

48 Ibid., 458.

49 Christopher D Stone, *Should Trees Have Standing? Law, Morality and the Environment* (Oxford University Press, 3rd edn, 2010) 114.

50 Melissa Troutman, 'Pennsylvania Ecosystem Fights Corporation for Rights in Landmark Fracking Lawsuit', *Public Herald* (10 December 2014) www.publicherald.org/archives/19582/invisible_hand/.

51 Peter Burdon, 'The Rights of Nature: Reconsidered' (2010) 49 *Australian Humanities Review* 69, 71–74.

52 Constitution of the Republic of Ecuador 2008, articles 71–74.

53 Ley de Derechos de la Madre Tierra, Law 071 of the Plurinational State of Bolivia.

54 *Wheeler c. Director de la Procuraduria General Del Estado de Loja*, Juicio No. 11121–2011–0010 http:// blogs.law.widener.edu/envirolawblog/2011/07/12/ecuadorian-courtrecognizes-constitutional-right-to-nature/; *República del Ecuador Asamblea Nacional, Comisión de la Biodiversidad y Recursos Naturales*, Acta de Sesión No. 66 (15 June 2011) http://asambleanacional.gov.ec/blogs/comision6/files/2011/07/acta-66.pdf. Spanish translations as per Erin Daly, 'The Ecuadorian Exemplar: The First Ever Vindication of Constitutional

Rights of Nature' (2012) 21(1) *Review of European Community and International Environmental Law* 63.
55 Te Urewera Act 2014 (NZ) s 11.
56 Erin O'Donnell and Julia Talbot-Jones, 'Legal Rights for Rivers: What Does This Actually Mean?' (2017) 32(6) *Australian Environment Review* 159.
57 Julia Talbot-Jones, 'The Institutional Economics of Granting a River Legal Standing' (PhD thesis, Australian National University, 2017).
58 Te Awa Tupua (Whanganui River Claims Settlement) Act 2017 (NZ).
59 *Mohd. Salim v State of Uttarakhand & others*, WPPIL 126/2014 (High Court of Uttarakhand) [19]. This judgment is accessible at http://lobis.nic.in/ddir/uhc/RS/orders/22-03-2017/RS20032017WPPIL1262014.pdf.
60 Erin O'Donnell, 'At the Intersection of the Sacred and the Legal: Rights for Nature in Uttarakhand, India' (2018) 30(1) *Journal of Environmental Law* 135.
61 Centro de Estudios para la Justicia Social 'Tierra Digna' y otros con el Presidente de la Republica y otros: 10 noviembre 2016, Corte Constitucional, Sala Sexta de Revisión (No T-5.016.242) (Colombia).
62 Government of New Zealand, 'Rukutia Te Mana: Deed of Settlement between the Crown and Ngāti Rangi' (2018) www.ngatirangi.com/Data/Sites/5/media/images/201708-aug/7043.pdf.
63 Ngaire Naffine, 'Who Are Law's Persons? From Cheshire Cats to Responsible Subjects' (2003) 66(3) *Modern Law Review* 346, 350.
64 Ngaire Naffine, 'Review Essay: Liberating the Legal Person' (2011) 26(1) *Canadian Journal of Law and Society* 193, 193.
65 Ngaire Naffine, above n 45.
66 Erin O'Donnell and Julia Talbot-Jones, 'Creating Legal Rights for Rivers: Lessons from Australia, New Zealand, and India' (2018) 23(1) *Ecology and Society* 7.
67 *Salomon v Salomon & Co* [1897] AC 22.
68 John Micklethwait and Adrian Wooldridge, *The Company: A Short History of a Revolutionary Idea* (Modern Library, 2003).
69 In Australia, *Booth v Bosworth* (2001) 114 FCR; 117 *Local Government and Environmental Reports of Australia* 168; *Environment East Gippsland Inc. v VicForests* (2010) 30 VR 1. In the USA, *Lujan v Defenders of Wildlife* 112 SCt 2130 (1992); *Friends of the Earth v Laidlaw Environmental Services*, 528 US 167 (2000).
70 Harold Feld, 'Saving the Citizen Suit: The Effect of *Lujan v. Defenders of Wildlife* and the Role of Citizen Suits in Environmental Enforcement' (1994) 19 *Columbia Journal of Environmental Law* 141; Ann E Carlson, 'Standing for the Environment' (1998) 45 *UCLA Law Review* 931.
71 Te Awa Tupua (Whanganui River Claims Settlement) Act 2017 (NZ), s 14.
72 David Driesen, 'Economic Instruments for Sustainable Development' in Benjamin J Richardson and Stepan Wood (eds), *Environmental Law for Sustainability* (Hart Publishing, 2006) 277.
73 Tom Tietenberg and Lynne Lewis, *Environmental and Natural Resource Economics* (Pearson, 7th edn, 2006).
74 Poh-Ling Tan, 'A Property Framework for Water Markets: The Role of Law' in Jeff Bennett (ed.), *The Evolution of Markets for Water: Theory and Practice in Australia* (Edward Elgar, 2005) 56; Terry L Anderson and Gary D Libecap, *Environmental Markets: A Property Rights Approach* (Cambridge University Press, 2014) 86.
75 Nik Heynen et al., 'Conclusion: Unnatural Consequences' in Nik Heynen et al. (eds), *Neoliberal Environments: False Promises and Unnatural Consequences* (Routledge, 2007) 287, 289–290; Eric T Freyfogle, 'Ownership and Ecology' (1993) 43(4) *Case Western Reserve Law Review* 1269.

76 Jonathan H Adler, 'Back to the Future of Conservation: Changing Perceptions of Property Rights and Environmental Protection' (2005) 1 *New York University Journal of Law and Liberty* 987.
77 Joseph L Sax, 'Using Property Rights to Attack Environmental Protection' (1996) 14 *Pace Environmental Law Review* 1.
78 Barton H Thompson Jr, 'Markets for Nature' (2000) 25 *William and Mary Environmental Law and Policy Review* 261.
79 Vivien Foster and Robert Hahn, 'Designing More Efficient Markets: Lessons from Los Angeles Smog Control' (1995) 38 *Journal of Law and Economics* 19.
80 James Salzmann, *Designing Payment for Ecosystem Services* (Property and Environment Research Centre, 2010).
81 Stephanie Small, 'WWF Australia Buys $100,000 Shark Net Licence to Stop It Ending Up in Hands of Fishers' *ABC News* (13 July 2016) www.abc.net.au/news/2016–07–13/shark-fishing-commercial-licence-bought-by-wwf-reef/7625532.
82 Anderson and Libecap, above n 74.
83 A Horne et al., 'Environmental Water Efficiency: Maximizing Benefits and Minimizing Costs of Environmental Water Use and Management' (2018) *Wiley Interdisciplinary Reviews: Water* 5(4) 10.1002/wat2.1285.
84 Mark Peacock, 'Rationality and Social Norms' in John Foster (ed.), *Valuing Nature? Economics, Ethics and Environment* (Routledge, 1997) 67, 73.
85 Harm Benson, above n 1; Robin Kundis Craig, 'Learning to Live with the Trickster: Narrating Climate Change and the Value of Resilience Thinking' (2016) 33(Spring) *Pace Environmental Law Review* 351.
86 Allan C Hutchinson, *Dwelling on the Threshold: Critical Essays on Modern Legal Thought* (Carswell, 1988) 14.
87 Craig, above n 85, 352.
88 Ibid., 355.
89 Bronwen Morgan and Karen Yeung, *An Introduction to Law and Regulation: Text and Materials* (Cambridge University Press, 2007) 17.
90 Ibid., 41.
91 C R Sunstein, *After the Rights Revolution: Reconceiving the Regulatory State* (Harvard University Press, 1990).
92 Morgan and Yeung, above n 89, 75.
93 Anderson and Libecap, above n 74; Jeff Bennett (ed.), *Protecting the Environment, Privately* (World Scientific Publishing, 2016).
94 R H Coase, 'The Problem of Social Cost' (1960) 3 *Journal of Law and Economics* 1.
95 Gary S Becker, *The Economic Approach to Human Behavior* (University of Chicago Press, 1976).
96 Charles Taylor, 'The Concept of a Person' in Charles Taylor (ed.), *Philosophical Papers Volume 1: Human Agency and Language* (Cambridge University Press, 1985) 97.
97 Stephen P Croley, 'Theories of Regulation: Incorporating the Administrative Process' (1998) 98(1) *Columbia Law Review* 1, 58.
98 Chris McGrath, 'Flying Foxes, Dams and Whales: Using Federal Environmental Laws in the Public Interest' (2008) 25(5) *Environmental and Planning Law Journal* 324.

3 Environmental water managers

Examples of indirect legal personhood for rivers

Water is 'fundamental to life'.[1] In 2018 the UN launched the International Decade of Water for Sustainable Development as demand for water access, allocation, and services continues to rise.[2] When more water is extracted and diverted to meet private needs, less remains in our rivers, wetlands, and estuaries, and aquatic environments suffer.[3] The sustainable management of water resources is a critical challenge, and likely to be exacerbated by the effects of climate change on water availability.

To combat the decline in aquatic ecosystem health, many countries are developing new laws and policies to set aside and protect water for the environment, which is then used to provide flows essential for the maintenance of aquatic health.[4] As a result, the aquatic environment is becoming increasingly visible to water law in its own right, rather than simply being the space in which the law regulates access to water resources.[5] One of the ways this has occurred is through the creation of the EWMs: organisations designed to *increase the quantity* of water available to the aquatic environment, as well as *improve the efficacy* of its use, by acquiring and managing water rights using water markets. To do so, they require a specific legal form that gives them the legal powers and capacity to perform their required functions.

The EWMs are legal persons who represent the environment in water resource management, so they are a useful example of the implications for water governance when rivers have legal rights. As discussed in Chapter 1, rivers only received legal rights directly in 2017. Using the EWMs as an example provides an opportunity to observe the consequences of using a legal person to represent the aquatic environment over a much longer timeframe.

This chapter examines the specific functions that the EWMs have been created to perform, and how their legal form and activities combine to give them the rights and powers of legal persons to act on behalf of the aquatic environment. In doing so, this chapter makes the connection between environmental law and the conceptual framework developed in Chapter 2 and water law and governance. Most water law frameworks, if they recognise the environment at all, do so as a form of limitation on other uses of water, so minimum flows may be protected and environmental impacts considered when issuing new rights to water.[6] The EWMs, however, enable the aquatic environment to take on the characteristics of a legal subject: an entity with the power to enter contracts, hold water rights, sue and be sued. The legal context and the activities of the EWMs combine with their legal form to construct the aquatic environment as a legal person (as represented by the EWM organisations), by combining the *capacity* to bear legal rights and duties with the *necessity of using* those powers.

The environment in water law: a transition from object to subject

Historically, water law focused on the management of water resources for human users. Only relatively recently has water law also embraced the holistic, integrated management of aquatic systems.[7] The initial emphasis on water as a resource to be used for consumptive purposes (irrigation, industry, urban supply, domestic supply, and stock) meant that water rights were developed to support this consumptive use of water, and only later adapted to the needs of environmental flows.[8] Even prior to the establishment of a water market, water entitlements used for consumptive purposes had the typical characteristics of what economists refer to as a 'private good': rival use and low costs of exclusion.[9]

Water for the environment, however, has the typical characteristics of a public good: (mostly) non-rival use and non-exclusivity. It is very costly (or impossible) to limit access to the benefits of environmental water to those who pay for it. Indeed, in some cases increased environmental water merely increases the reliability of water availability for a consumptive user downstream, with limited capacity to protect the enhanced flows.[10] Environmental use of water is thus poorly adapted for a system that relies on clear rights to private goods, and the result can be market failure: too small an allocation to the environment and too large an allocation to consumptive use (from the overall perspective of what a particular society values).

In consequence, the environment's need for water is typically only identified in response to the observed problems of environmental degradation caused by overuse of water. From a legal perspective, water law has only been able to 'see' the environment once a problem that affects the rights of other users occurs. For example, the decision to cap total water extraction in the Murray-Darling Basin (MDB), Australia, was in direct response to blue-green algal blooms and salinity – water quality problems that were exacerbated by insufficient river flows. The cap imposed a legal limit on other water users' ability to take and use water, and provided a legal mechanism for water law to engage with the environment to prevent further degradation.[11]

However, limits on the actions of other users, such as the cap, are still an incomplete form of visibility: the environment is only visible to water law obliquely, through the lens of the actions of other water users. Imposing limits on future actions also doesn't address the problem of existing environmental impacts. By recognising the environment's own need for water, water law has finally gone beyond limiting future impacts by creating legal rights to water for the environment. This increases the volume of water (thus redressing the historical imbalance) and transitions the environment towards being visible to water law in its own right (as represented by the organisation holding the water rights).

This inability for the law to 'see' the environment until there is a problem is certainly not unique to water, and, as with other spheres of environmental law, there is often a substantial lag period between the creation of consumptive rights to water and the creation of legal rights to water for the environment. For example, in south-eastern Australia almost 100 years separated the commitment to developing water resources for irrigation and other consumptive purposes and the realisation that a healthy aquatic environment also required water.[12] The transition towards large onstream dams and state-supported irrigation schemes began in the 1880s, but Australia's first commitment to providing environmental flows did not occur until 1967 (a legal allocation to the Macquarie Marshes as part of the Burrendong Dam construction) and the physical water was not provided until 1980.[13]

The effect of this lag period means that environmental water laws have developed along two distinct policy lines.

1 *Protection of existing environmental flows* to prevent further degradation of a highly modified system, or maintain the health of an underused system.
2 *Restoration of environmental flows* to improve aquatic health, particularly in highly modified systems, and the management of those restored flows over time to achieve the maximum benefits.[14]

Protection and maintenance of existing environmental flows

To prevent further deterioration in the ecological health of water systems, environmental flow policies, and the legal frameworks that implement them, take the form of protection and maintenance of existing environmental flows.[15] This approach requires an understanding of the hydrology and ecology of a river basin, and a clear identification of the social values and uses of the water. Connell argues that a minimum definition of environmental sustainability is 'that the region in question should be in an environmentally stable condition system-wide [at a level of health] that is acceptable to the wider community'.[16] This definition demonstrates the interaction between the ecology (the physical processes that enable environmental health) and the social values of the river, which determine the level of health required.

Protection and maintenance policies emphasise setting limits on the extraction of water to protect the existing environmental flows and maintain those flows over time. The legal mechanisms used to protect environmental flows involve placing limits on the way that other users can access water, such as a cap on water extraction, or flow-based limits on the timing of extractions. Maintaining those flows depends on implementing a system of water accounting, and enforcing the limits on water extraction.

Protection policies position the environment as a legal object, only visible to the law through the actions of others (Chapter 2). However, as the focus of environmental flows policies shifted to include restoration of flows, there was a need for a legal mechanism to enable a transfer of water from existing users to the aquatic environment, and a way of constructing legal rights to water for the aquatic environment itself.

Restoration: recovery and management of additional water

Where existing levels of water extraction are causing environmental decline, and where this decline is considered undesirable, the policy shifts to focus on the *restoration* of environmental flows. This policy builds on the hydrological and ecological understandings obtained through the protection and maintenance policies, and focuses on how to increase environmental flows to improve overall aquatic health. This typically requires the acquisition of additional water for the environment, although this is not always the case. For example, dam relicensing in the USA has provided a significant opportunity to change the operation of dams to improve the timing of water delivery to the environment without necessarily increasing the volume of water available.[17] These forms of system optimisation are important, but in many cases there is simply not enough water for the environment at all. For example, in the western USA existing water extraction is so severe that many rivers regularly cease to flow during summer. In these circumstances, additional water must be recovered to improve the ecological health of the rivers (and associated aquatic environments). Although there are occasional examples of alternative methods, water is typically recovered for the environment in two main ways: by generating efficiency savings, or by purchasing water from existing users.

Efficiency savings

Efficiency savings involve changing the way that water is stored and delivered to increase the volume available to the environment.[18] Changing the infrastructure of water delivery can generate savings in water volume, which can be transferred to the environment (although rigorous accounting is required to ensure that this represents 'real' savings).[19] For example, in 2010 Australia's Commonwealth government set aside A$5.8 billion to invest in irrigation infrastructure to generate water savings for the environment as part of the Water for the Future programme.[20] These efficiency savings have been created as new water rights which are then transferred to the Commonwealth Environmental Water Holder (CEWH, a government EWM). In another example, in the western USA the Deschutes River Conservancy (a non-government EWM) worked with irrigator groups to invest in piping or lining irrigation canals to generate water savings, which were then protected as an instream flow right in the Crooked River.[21] In each of these examples the volumetric savings achieved by reducing water losses during delivery were converted to water rights that were then formally transferred to the organisation holding those rights on behalf of the environment.

Water purchase

Water can be acquired directly as a transfer from existing users. In the western states of the USA, EWMs have been using voluntary water transfers to acquire water for the environment since the mid-1990s.[22] Although each state has its own distinct set of water laws, the use of voluntary transactions that involve existing water users being paid to transfer their water rights to the environment (on a temporary or permanent basis) has been widely effective in the states with a prior-appropriation framework. In the western USA these acquisitions are typically the result of one-on-one negotiations with existing water users, and the volume of water recovered through these transactions varies significantly between states.[23] Australia has also made use of water purchase programmes to recover water for the environment. One of the earliest environmental water acquisitions was the state government RiverBank programme in New South Wales, which used tender programmes to purchase water licences from existing users and made that water available to the environment.[24] The largest water purchase programme in Australia is that of the federal government, which committed A$3.2 billion to buying water rights from existing users for the environment in the MDB.[25] By June 2018 this programme had recovered over 1,859 gigalitres (GL) (in long-term average yield) across the basin.[26]

Most water recovered for the environment requires financial investment, either to generate water savings (by investing in more efficient infrastructure) or to pay existing water users to transfer it (via water purchase programmes). This decision to invest funds in water recovery increases the need to demonstrate the efficacy and efficiency of these programmes. A recovery proposal must show sufficient environmental benefit to justify the investment of funds, and the opportunity cost of not using that water for alternative purposes. Further, the water must then be *managed* to generate the maximum environmental benefit.[27] Recovery and management policies therefore embed an efficiency norm in both phases: first in determining how much water the environment should receive, and second in managing that water most effectively to achieve the largest environmental outcome.[28]

The actions required to manage recovered water are dependent on the nature of the water right that has been recovered. For example, in Australia water recovery has focused on water rights in storage, which means that management requires the preparation of plans over multiple timescales to release that water to achieve environmental benefit, either by delivering it to particular locations or by trading the water and investing the income in acquiring additional water or environmental water delivery infrastructure.

In the western USA water recovered for the environment includes both instream flow rights and water in storage. Where instream flow rights are acquired, such as in the Columbia River Basin, management of water over time focuses on two main activities. First, the water acquisition contract must be complied with, and the EWM may need to enforce its instream flow right against other water users, who may seek to take it in contravention of their existing water rights. In some states water accounting proceeds on a complaints basis, so it is up to the organisation that recovers the water to confirm whether its water is actually being delivered.[29] Second, many water acquisitions are temporary, so long-term management requires a decision on whether to proceed with reacquiring water in the same location again in the future.

In all cases, management of acquired water depends on the ongoing availability of water markets to enable these transactions. Decisions to buy and sell will be shaped by the environmental outcomes achieved, as well as the price of water.

Recovery and management policies are dependent on water rights for the environment that receive the same legal protections as other users' rights and can be transferred between users. In turn, enabling the environment to hold, use, and manage these water rights requires the aquatic environment to have the legal rights and powers of a legal person.

Modern water rights for the environment

We have long recognised that the management of water is a matter of public and private interest: 'Water as a commodity has an ultimate private use, either directly or indirectly; private rights are paramount [but] management of those rights is a public matter.'[30]

Under the Dublin Principles of 1992 many countries have adopted what Hodgson calls 'modern water rights': a property rights approach to water access, where some form of property rights in water are held by individuals, separately from the land, and rights to use water are identified under a consistent framework.[31] This *propertisation* of water rights stems from Dublin Principle 4, which called for the capacity to manage water resources as an economic good.[32] Such an approach depends on clear and unambiguous property rights in water that can be transferred between uses and users. These modern water rights are highly context specific, so engaging with the detail of these rights requires understanding the detail of specific jurisdictions. This book focuses on the EWMs of two regions, south-eastern Australia and the western states of the USA, so the water rights of these jurisdictions are discussed here in more detail.

Modern water rights have been created via statute, such as in Australia, or via common law supported by statute where necessary, as in the western USA. Water law in both locations has been shaped by historical context and the need to respond to high levels of variability in water availability, both within and between years.

In Australia water remains vested in the Crown in each state, and water use rights held by individuals are created in state legislation (see Chapter 4). The transition towards transferable water rights was driven by the desire to encourage water transfers between consumptive users as a means to promote efficient water use for high-value outputs.[33] In 1994 the Council of Australian Governments committed to separating water rights from land, capping water entitlements in the MDB, and enabling transfer between water users. This commitment was reinforced in 2004, with the National Water Initiative (NWI) actively embracing water markets as a mechanism for efficient use of water, underpinned by legally secure water rights. The NWI also explicitly committed to ensuring that environmental water had the same degree of statutory recognition and security as the water rights of other users, including the capacity for trade. This reform established the basis for 'modern water rights' and enabled the acquisition of these rights for environmental flows. After 2004 a range of environmental water recovery programmes commenced that explicitly used water markets (either directly or via separate tender programmes) or water donations to acquire water for the environment.[34] The water acquired via transfer from existing users retained its original legal form, and the various EWMs have acquired a significant portfolio of water rights that are legally almost identical to the water rights of other users.

In the western USA water rights confer a 'use' right under a system of prior appropriation, where the first person to divert the water to a beneficial use retains the right to have first call on that water each year.[35] Transition to readily transferable water rights has been patchy. Although prior-appropriation rights have always technically been transferable, the 'use it or lose it' requirement means any transferor must demonstrate that the water has been in use prior to the transfer and any change in location will not detrimentally affect downstream users.[36] The requirement for detailed analysis of water use and assessment of third-party impacts has effectively strangled the activity of water markets in the western USA. The Colorado-Big Thompson water market remains one of the most successful at providing a mix of permanent and temporary transfers in the western USA, with other markets being described as 'more akin to borrowing a cup of sugar from neighbours'.[37]

Unlike Australia, where environmental water acquisition programmes could build on the opportunities created by broader water law reform, in the USA the environmental water organisations are more likely to be driving reform to water law to support their ability to acquire water.[38] In part this reflects the significant legal reform required to recognise instream flows as a beneficial use of water (necessary for the environment to be recognised within the prior-appropriation system). This process began in the 1950s, and now all western states recognise instream flows. However, the late recognition of these flows meant two things: first, that instream flows were typically the most junior rights (and therefore likely to be unavailable to the environment during times of water scarcity), and second, as most rivers were fully appropriated before this recognition, instream flows could only be appropriated in a small number of rivers. As a result, the environmental water recovery organisations had a vested interest in the transferability of water rights to improve instream flows, and have pioneered new processes and legislation to support the evolution towards modern water rights across the western USA.

Although the specifics of water rights in south-eastern Australia and western USA remain significantly different, their application for environmental purposes is strikingly similar. In each jurisdiction the environment has acquired additional water through voluntary transactions (donations, one-on-one negotiated contracts, tenders, or on the water market), and the water rights thus acquired retain their capacity to be traded to another water user as well as being used for environmental flows. The flexibility of these modern water rights acquired for the environment requires an organisation with the capacity to decide actively how best to use its water rights in any given year to achieve the maximum benefit for the aquatic environment. The EWMs are responsible for the recovery and management of the water required to restore the environmental flows, and embody the shift towards restoration (rather than protection) of aquatic health. The capacity to hold environmental water rights that require active management and decision-making is the hallmark of an EWM.

Environmental water managers

EWMs are organisations that hold environmental water rights and make decisions on how to use those rights to achieve the maximum environmental outcome. They focus on restoration of environmental flows to (partially or fully) dewatered systems by acquiring additional water rights on behalf of the environment. EWMs have been in operation since the mid-1990s in the USA and since the mid-2000s in Australia, following the shift in environmental flows policy and legal frameworks from protection to restoration.

EWMs can be government or non-governmental entities, and operate at a range of scales and in diverse hydrological conditions. They may be advocates for developing new environmental flows policies, but they are most usually agents of policy *implementation*. EWMs are currently found in Australia, the western USA, Mexico, and Canada.[39]

EWMs have a number of features in common: they have a clear organisational identity; they acquire and/or manage environmental water rights; and the water rights they hold are transferable and can be traded via the water market. Traditionally, EWMs have been described based on their role in water resource management, but until recently little attention has been paid to their legal forms and powers, or the way they have been constructed as organisations.

In this book, an EWM:

- is an *identifiable* organisation or agency with *legal personhood*;
- has a *specific objective* to improve the health of aquatic ecosystems and maintain these improvements over time; and
- has the *capacity to acquire and/or manage water rights* for the environment to achieve that objective.

Each element of this definition is worth further discussion. First, EWMs have legal personality, which makes them identifiable as organisations. The activities they undertake, the water rights they acquire (and/or continue to hold), and the decisions they make are clearly identifiable and linked to a specific entity. EWMs have what Hart has termed *role-responsibility*, where they are responsible for performing the functions of managing environmental water, and *liability-responsibility*, where they are answerable to the public (or philanthropic donors) for how well they have performed those functions.[40] EWMs are accountable for the performance of their functions in acquiring and managing environmental water, and clarity of identity enables identification of who is making the decisions and why. The identifiability of EWMs also enhances their capacity to represent the aquatic environment. EWMs take legal personhood in a variety of ways (such as a corporation, a statutory corporation, or a trustee), and as legal persons they extend this legal form to the aquatic environment. This enables the EWMs to represent the aquatic environment in court, in water resource planning, and in water policymaking. For example, the CEWH in Australia has a seat in the water services committees in New South Wales, giving it a voice in the broader water planning debates.

Second, while an EWM may have a range of tasks (such as raising awareness and community engagement), there is one dominant objective: to improve the health of aquatic ecosystems by increasing environmental flows. EWMs achieve this by acquiring additional water for the environment and/or managing that water efficiently and effectively. This means that the activities of the EWM are focused on aquatic ecosystems rather than on a more general environmental remit, and helps to distinguish EWMs from other environmental organisations. EWMs also operate over time: they acquire (and/or manage) water in an ongoing way to improve aquatic health. Even where water acquisition programmes are intended eventually to come to an end, the requirement to generate efficient outcomes means that their management of water will continue. This requirement to *maintain* improvement in aquatic health over time, and to do so efficiently, also serves to distinguish EWMs from environmental organisations which contribute to environmental flows as a one-off event. The ongoing relationship between the EWMs and the aquatic environment is an important part of their ability to construct the aquatic environment as a legal person.

Finally, the capacity to acquire water rights legally for the environment is essential for an EWM. This is not a trivial qualification, and in many cases has required legal reform to recognise the environment as a legitimate user of water and create the organisational capacity to hold water on behalf of the environment.[41] In some jurisdictions in the western USA (such as Washington and Colorado), this organisational capacity is limited to a single organisation (a government agency), but other EWMs often initially acquire the water for the purposes of environmental flows. Formal recognition of the water as environmental flows occurs once the acquired water rights are transferred to the relevant body. Both the original acquirer of the water rights and the final recipient (who converts them legally to environmental water rights) can be EWMs, provided that both have an objective to acquire water to improve aquatic ecosystems.

In summary, the EWMs have emerged in response to two important shifts in environmental water law and policy: the transition of environmental flows policies from protection to restoration, and the creation of modern water rights for the environment, transferable to and from other users. EWMs are distinct organisations with legal personhood, which they use to acquire and/or manage environmental water rights in the water market. They use this water to improve aquatic health over time. The EWMs represent a significant step forward in environmental water management, and this is contingent on their legal personality.

Constructing the aquatic environment as a legal subject

The EWM is a novel legal construction of the aquatic environment within water law, and more broadly within environmental law. The EWM makes the aquatic environment visible to law through the twin processes of *creation* of the legal person (the EWM organisation with the capacity to hold and manage water rights for the environment) and *operation* of the EWM in the context of modern water law and water markets (the legal context).

Legal context of the EWMs

EWMs have emerged within a particular legal context, at the confluence of three key water law reforms.

1. *Modern water rights*: property rights in water held by individuals, separately from land, where rights to use water are identified under a consistent framework.
2. *Water markets*: where water rights are capped (by regulation or physical limits) and transfers between users are encouraged by legal processes that refine property rights in water, clarify ownership, and provide full information to potential buyers and sellers.
3. *Legal rights to water for the natural environment*: where the natural environment is legally recognised as a legitimate user of water, and where at least some of that water is held as modern water rights.

To confirm the relationship between the creation of the EWMs and this legal context, a systematic review of water law around the world was conducted in 2013.[42]

Where are the EWMs?

EWMs are found in 19 jurisdictions around the world, most of which are in the USA and Australia (Table 3.1). In all instances where EWMs were located, all three legal elements were present, demonstrating the link

Table 3.1 Jurisdictions where environmental water managers are operating (2013)

Jurisdiction	*Government EWM*	*Private EWM*
Australia (Federal)	X	
Australia: Australian Capital Territory	X	
Australia: New South Wales	X	X
Australia: Queensland	X	
Australia: South Australia	X	X
Australia: Victoria	X	
Canada: Alberta		X
Mexico		X
USA: Arizona		X
USA: California	X	X
USA: Colorado	X	X
USA: Idaho	X	X
USA: Montana	X	X
USA: Nevada	X	X
USA: New Mexico		X
USA: Oregon	X	X
USA: Texas	X	X
USA: Utah	X	X
USA: Washington	X	X

between creation of EWMs and the legal context of modern water rights, water markets, and environmental water rights.

Although the legal context in which the EWMs operate is broadly similar, the variability in the implementation of the legal elements provides further insight into the link between EWMs and the water resource management framework, and how the EWMs have been constructed in law.

First, in Mexico, although water rights can be traded separately to land, intersectoral transfers (i.e. transfers from one 'sector' of users to another) are limited by rules that do not allow water transfers outside the irrigation district boundaries, and within those boundaries specific 'irrigation' licences are required.[43] One of the NGOs operating in the Colorado River Basin, Pronatura Noroeste, has tackled this problem by purchasing land with riparian vegetation, then acquiring irrigation licences for that land and delivering the purchased environmental water to those locations.[44] This situation reflects the incremental nature of change in water law, and the gradual adjustment to full legal recognition of the environment as a legitimate user of water.

Second, according to the reported water transactions available in the literature, two states with active EWMs do not have very active water markets (although leases and sales have been recorded): Washington and Montana.[45] In such situations of less-than-active markets, the focus of the EWM is likely to be on water recovery, with water transfers facilitated through the EWM's outreach programmes and the ability to negotiate changes to on-farm arrangements. However, it is worth noting that there has been a consistent push from the state government of Washington to establish water banks to facilitate trade, and Montana has pioneered a private water-leasing programme to improve instream flows. While an active water market may be necessary to provide flexibility for the long-term management of a water portfolio, the work of EWMs and government departments in these states demonstrates the capacity of EWMs themselves to drive the creation and activity of water markets to access the water they need. What is essential for the EWM is the willingness of other water users to participate in water trades; when water markets are relatively inactive, this willingness to trade directly with an EWM may be a proxy for the presence of an active water market.

Do the EWMs depend on this legal context?

The global review demonstrates a strong correlation between the presence of three elements of the legal context (modern water rights, water markets, and environmental water rights) and the existence of an EWM. All three features are present where EWMs exist today, and EWMs are *not* found where one or more of those elements is absent.

Based on the 2013 review, 42 jurisdictions (countries or states/provinces within them) recognise an agricultural water use right that is transferable and separate from land (modern water rights), but do not have an operating EWM. Three of these jurisdictions (Chile, South Africa, and the Canary Islands) have modern water rights, water markets, and legal protection of environmental flows, but do not yet have an EWM. The primary reason for this absence appears to be the weakness of the allocation of environmental water rights. Chile has focused on a minimum flow provision that remains ad hoc,[46] and South Africa, although it has a strong legal framework, is still grappling with the challenge of implementing environmental flows.[47] The Canary Islands is subject to the EU Water Framework Directive, so it will be interesting to observe whether this begins to encourage more activity in environmental water management in the future.

The remaining 39 jurisdictions that had some form of legally transferable property right to water (although in some cases this is not completely separated from land and use specifications) either did not have an active water market (in some cases it is absent entirely; in others there are very low levels of activity) or do not provide adequate legal protection for environmental flows, or both. None of these jurisdictions had an EWM, which provides the strongest evidence of correlation between the three factors and the operation of EWMs.

How do legal form and legal context combine to create personhood?

Each year EWMs must undertake particular activities: to acquire additional water, to reacquire water (when leases lapse), to transfer water, or to make use of their existing water holdings by delivering water to particular locations (as instream flows or by extracting water for use in wetlands). To do so, however, EWMs require particular legal powers, so their organisational form must include the powers to enter contracts with other persons (to support the acquisition and management of their water) and to own property (especially in jurisdictions where water rights are legally recognised as property), and they must be able to sue in court to protect both their water rights and their contractual rights. In other words, to operate successfully they must be able to make and enforce decisions, which requires the attributes of a legal person.

The law defines a legal person as simply a 'being whom the law regards as capable of rights and duties'.[48] The capacity for EWMs to act in this way does not, therefore, necessarily imply anything more broadly about their status as rights holders beyond their legal context. Using the legalist approach advocated by Naffine, the legal person is 'a relatively autonomous legal fiction and invention',[49] where the sole 'defining characteristic of *law's* construct is the formal capacity to bear rights and duties'.[50] Naffine argues that the law 'constructs, rather than finds, its subject',[51] and the EWMs, in turn, are constructed by various legal sources to enable them to act as legal persons.

Government EWMs are typically established by statute and given the specific rights and duties needed to act as legal persons in this legislation (Table 3.2).[52]

Non-governmental EWMs are generally not-for-profit corporations or trusts established on behalf of a conservation organisation (Table 3.3). The source of legal personhood will vary, depending on the legislation under which the organisation is incorporated (or the trust relationship formalised). The ability of NGO EWMs to represent the aquatic environment thus stems from both the statutory reforms that enable the environment to be a holder of water rights and the contractual relationships the NGO EWMs enter to acquire and manage those water rights for the aquatic environment.

The EWMs, as noted at the outset of this chapter, are created as legal persons, and, as Tables 3.2 and 3.3 demonstrate, they use specific legal forms. They have been created with the specific objective of improving the health of the aquatic environment (within their geographically limited jurisdictions). By acting to acquire and manage environmental water to achieve this objective, within their specific legal context of modern water rights, water markets, and environmental water rights, they act as choice theory's *rational decision-maker*. Harel argues that 'by exercising choice, one manifests one's individuality and personhood',[53] and as Naffine expresses it, 'the very idea of a right … connotes a being with the ability personally to enforce it'.[54] As a combination of their creation and operation within water law, they construct the environment as a legal person.

Prior to the advent of legal rights to water for the environment, and the EWMs, the aquatic environment was merely the terrain in which water resources were located, but was itself largely invisible to the law as it had no legal rights or duties of its own. Even when various limits were imposed on the extraction of water by others, such as caps or the requirement to release minimum flows in dams, these limits did not create legal rights for the environment itself. Only when the aquatic environment had legal rights to water of its own, and had been given legal form through the creation of the EWMs, did water law recognise the legal personality of the environment. Unlike the creation of legal rights for rivers, the EWMs are not a complete personification of the aquatic environment, as legal personhood only extends to the parts of the aquatic environment represented by the EWM, and only to the geographic locations in which environmental water rights are available. However, as Naffine notes, 'If someone or something is a person, it tends to count in its own right. If the being or entity is not a person, its legal protections are dramatically diminished.'[55] An entity with legal personality is the subject of the law, and thus the pinnacle of visibility and *legibility* to the law.

Together, the legal context (modern water rights, water markets, and legal water rights for the environment) and the construction of EWMs as

Table 3.2 Governmental environmental water managers[1]

Organisation type	*Source of legal personhood rights and duties*	*Source of water holding and management capacities*	*Accountability: to whom does this organisation report?*	*Examples*
Statutory corporation	Establishing legislation (creation of the corporate form)	Establishing legislation and/or water statutes in its jurisdiction(s) of operations	Relevant minister(s) and the public through corporate plans and annual reports	Victorian Environmental Water Holder; Murray-Darling Basin Authority; Idaho Water Resource Board
Statutory entity	Establishing legislation (endowed with specific powers in legislation but not a corporate form)	Establishing legislation and/or other water statutes in its jurisdiction(s) of operations	Relevant minister(s) and the public through business plans and annual reports	Commonwealth Environmental Water Holder; Colorado Water Conservation Board
Function within government department (only an EWM when specific and identifiable)	Enabling legislation, policy documents, referral of ministerial powers	Water statutes and regulations in its jurisdiction(s) of operations	Relevant minister(s) through annual plans and reports; parliamentary reports	RiverBank (New South Wales); Washington State Department of Ecology

Note

1 Adapted from Erin O'Donnell, 'Competition or Collaboration? Using Legal Persons to Manage Water for the Environment in Australia and the United States' (2017) 34(6) *Environmental and Planning Law Journal* 503. Reproduced with permission of Thomson Reuters (Professional) Australia Limited, legal.thomsonreuters.com.au.

Table 3.3 Non-governmental environmental water managers[1]

Organisation type	*Source of legal personhood rights and duties*	*Source of water holding and management capacities*	*Accountability: to whom does this organisation report?*	*Examples*
Not-for-profit corporation	Corporation law in the relevant jurisdiction (e.g. Internal Revenue Code (26 USC § 501(c)); Corporations Act 2001 (Cth)); this can include incorporated associations	Water statutes in its jurisdiction(s) of operations, and the objectives of the organisation set out in its constitution	Donors through corporate plans and annual reports, and the public via websites	Healthy Rivers Australia; Murray-Darling Wetlands Working Group Ltd; Freshwater Trust (Oregon); Trout Unlimited Montana; Deschutes River Conservancy
Water trust for environmental purposes	Trust laws in the relevant jurisdictions	Water statutes in its jurisdiction(s) of operations, and the objectives of the trust deed	Donors and the establishing organisation through annual reports, and the public via websites	Environmental water trust of NSW; Conservation Council; Water for Nature SA (a trust established by Nature Foundation SA); Washington Water Trust

Note

1 Adapted from Erin O'Donnell, 'Competition or Collaboration? Using Legal Persons to Manage Water for the Environment in Australia and the United States' (2017) 34(6) *Environmental and Planning Law Journal* 503. Reproduced with permission of Thomson Reuters (Professional) Australia Limited, legal.thomsonreuters.com.au.

legal persons (by their creation in law, and by their own actions as decision-makers in environmental water recovery and management) combine to make the aquatic environment directly visible to the law. The creation of the EWMs, within their legal context, has qualitatively transitioned the aquatic environment over a legibility threshold. The aquatic environment is now visible to the law, and through the medium of the EWM can engage with the law as a legal subject.

Importantly, the EWM is a limited legal vehicle, and 'the artificial yet inventive manner in which law positively constitutes its subject'[56] is highly context specific. Each EWM defines the aquatic environment in a slightly different way, and the legal context for the EWM is specific to the jurisdiction. For this reason, the analysis of the EWMs is conducted using two geographic case studies where most of the EWMs are currently located: south-eastern Australia and western USA.

Two case studies: a brief overview of methodology

In Australia the creation and operation of the EWMs is focused in the south-east (comprising parts of South Australia, Victoria, and New South Wales). In the western USA the activities of the EWMs have been concentrated in two transboundary river systems: the Columbia River Basin and the Colorado River Basin. There are broad similarities between the construction of the EWMs in these locations: modern water rights, water markets, and legal rights to water for the environment. The EWMs have been active in these regions for at least a decade (from the 1990s in the USA and the 2000s in Australia). However, these regions are also sufficiently different to generate useful comparisons, as they each have different water law frameworks and different water market activity levels.

In Chapters 4 and 5 the individual cases are examined in detail to determine:

- how the aquatic environment is constructed in water law;
- how the EWMs are created in law;
- the objectives of the EWMs;
- the activities undertaken by the EWMs; and
- how the activities of the EWMs interact with their legal context.

In Chapter 6 the two geographic cases are then analysed jointly, using the conceptual framework (Chapter 2) to explore the implications of the multiple constructions of the aquatic environment in law, and the power of the different cultural narratives about the value of the environment. This joint analysis considers:

- how the EWMs are formally constructed as legal persons and the precise legal powers are different for each form;

- how the EWMs are choosing to construct themselves by the actions and beliefs of their staff, and which legal powers are considered as 'off limits';
- how the multiple constructions of the aquatic environment in water law affect the activities and operation of the EWMs and the dominant narrative in each geographic location; and
- evidence that other water users fear a legally powerful form of the aquatic environment, and the effects of this fear on the EWMs (the paradox of legal rights).

Investigation of the EWMs in situ required research methods that can engage with both the creation and the operation of the EWMs. Understanding how and why they undertake their activities as legal persons requires a deep engagement with their specific legal context, including the effects of history and location. To do this, two distinct methods have been applied: legal analysis of statutes, case law, and other legal instruments; and an interpretative method drawing on textual analysis of publicly available material and in-depth interviews with EWM staff.[57] The interviews provide nuanced insight into the operation of the EWMs that enables this examination to go beyond the public face of these organisations. This approach shows how the EWMs interact with their legal context, and identifies the different cultural narratives about the aquatic environment that underpin their operation.

Interviews and interviewees

There is often room for interpretation between the formal legal construction of an organisation (including its form and objectives) and the way that organisation operates in the real world. Dingwall and Strong argue that:

> Organizations cannot be sufficiently described solely by reference to their legal form, but there is an enormous difference between saying that such forms are, in principle, indefinitely negotiable and recognizing that they are, in practice, determinate ... How are the legal instruments articulated with members' everyday actions in such a way as to depict them as aspects of the same phenomenon?[58]

The interviews with senior staff of the EWMs bridge the gap between the form and what actually happens in reality. The long-form interviews created an opportunity to lift the veil of the organisation, and go beyond the public face to find out what the staff of the organisation really think and feel.[59]

The interviewees had all been working within the environmental water management sector for some time, and had been in their current role (or a very similar one) for several years. Most interviewees were executive-level staff, and the remainder held senior positions at the operational level within their organisation. As some interviewees preferred not to be referenced by name, they are only referred to by their EWM; where more than one staff member has been interviewed from a single organisation, they are distinguished by a unique number (e.g. staff member 1 from the Victorian Environmental Water Holder is VEWH1). A total of eight interviews were conducted in Australia, and a further 12 in the USA (Table 3.4).

Although the National Fish and Wildlife Foundation is not an EWM, this organisation coordinates much of the environmental water recovery work in the Columbia Basin, so a senior staff member in charge of this programme was also interviewed. As part of scoping the case studies, two interviews were conducted with a senior staff member of the California Department of Water Resources (Cal DWR) and a former senior staff member with American Rivers (AR). These interviews provided helpful insights which, among other things, confirmed the selection of the distinct geographic regions of the case studies.

The interviews give insight into the way that the staff of the EWMs make sense of the form, function, and role of the EWMs within their local contexts. Content analysis based on the interviews helped to provide a richer, deeper, more nuanced interpretation of the findings that emerged from the review of legislation, academic literature, and publicly available reports, plans, and websites. All interviews quoted in the following chapters are drawn from this material.

Conclusion

The EWMs are organisations responsible for acquiring and managing environmental water to improve aquatic environmental health using the water market. They have been created in a response to the need for an active decision-maker for environmental water recovery and management activities. This chapter defined the EWMs as *identifiable legal persons with specific objectives to improve the health of aquatic ecosystems over time, using environmental water rights*.

An EWM is *created* as a legal person (often formalised by using the form of a body corporate, or a trust held by a corporation), so the EWM is a legal subject with rights and duties of its own. The EWMs then *operate* within in a specific legal context, at the confluence of modern water rights, water markets, and environmental water rights. The EWM organisation, combined with the legal reforms of transferable water rights and environmental water rights, can represent at least part of the aquatic environment. The EWMs thus construct the aquatic environment as a legal person, enabling it to engage more fully with the law (via the EWM).

The legal personhood of the EWMs includes the specific legal powers to:

Table 3.4 Environmental water manager staff interviewed in each case study jurisdiction

Country	*Organisation*	*Role*	*Code*
Australia	Victorian Environmental Water Holder	Commissioner	VEWH 1
		Executive Officer	VEWH 2
		Operations Manager	VEWH 3
	Commonwealth Environmental Water Holder	Strategic Policy Manager	CEWO 1
		Operations Manager	CEWO 2
	SA DEWNR	Senior Policy Officer	SA DEWNR
	Healthy Rivers Australia	Chief Executive Officer	HRA
	New South Wales OEH	Regional Operations, South West Regional Manager	NSW OEH
USA	National Fish and Wildlife Foundation	Director, Western Water Program	NFWF
	California Department of Water Resources	Chief Deputy Director	Cal DWR
	American Rivers/Stanford Water in the West	Professor	AR
	Oregon Freshwater Trust	Flow Restoration Director	FWT
		Implementation Officer	
	Washington Water Trust	Executive Director	WWT
	Washington State Department of Ecology	Trust Water Program Director	WDE 1
		Trust Water Program Director	WDE 2
		Manager, Program Development	
		Implementation Officer	
		(Three staff members in a single interview)	
	Trout Unlimited Montana	Director, Montana Water Project	TUM
	Clark Fork Coalition	Legal Director	CFC
	Colorado Water Trust	Executive Director	CWT
	Colorado Water Conservation Board	Chief, Stream and Lake Protection Section	CWCB
	Deschutes River Conservancy	Program Director	DRC

- hold, acquire, and use water rights (although some legal contexts specify that only one EWM can hold water rights on behalf of the environment, other EWMs can acquire these rights with the intent to transfer them to the officially recognised EWM); and
- have legal standing in court (including the ability to sue and be sued), and the power to enter and enforce contracts (most notably for the acquisition and management of water rights).

This establishes the EWM as a useful example for assessing the implications of constructing the aquatic environment as a legal person (such as giving legal rights to rivers). Examination of the EWMs shows how legal personhood creates both opportunities and challenges, especially in the interaction between the multiple constructions of the aquatic environment in water law and the cultural narratives underpinning the social value of the environment. As the majority of the EWMs are located in two regions (the western USA and south-eastern Australia), these regions are used as the two geographic case studies.

Notes

1 Lee Godden and Jacqueline Peel, *Environmental Law: Scientific, Policy and Regulatory Dimensions* (Oxford University Press, 2010) 304.
2 J W Hall et al., 'Coping With the Curse of Freshwater Variability' (2014) 346 *Science* 429.
3 C J Vörösmarty et al., 'Global Threats to Human Water Security and River Biodiversity' (2010) 467 *Nature* 555.
4 Tom Le Quesne, Eloise Kendy, and Derek Weston, *The Implementation Challenge: Taking Stock of Government Policies to Protect and Restore Environmental Flows* (World Wildlife Fund UK, 2010); N LeRoy Poff and John H Matthews, 'Environmental Flows in the Anthropocence: Past Progress and Future Prospects' (2013) 5 *Current Opinion in Environmental Sustainability* 667; Angela H Arthington, *Environmental Flows: Saving Rivers in the Third Millennium* (University of California Press, 2012).
5 Anthony Scott and Georgina Coustalin, 'Rights Over Flowing Water' in Anthony Scott (ed.), *The Evolution of Resource Property Rights* (Oxford University Press, 2008) 63.
6 Stephen Hodgson, *Modern Water Rights: Theory and Practice* (Food and Agriculture Organization of the United Nations, 2006).
7 Patrick Meire et al., 'Towards Integrated Water Management' in Patrick Meire et al. (eds), *Integrated Water Management: Practical Experiences and Case Studies* (Springer, 2008) 1.
8 Daniel Connell, *Water Politics in the Murray-Darling Basin* (Federation Press, 2007); Lawrence J MacDonnell, 'Return to the River: Environmental Flow Policy in the United States and Canada' (2009) 45(5) *Journal of the American Water Resources Association* 1087.
9 Jeffrey M Perloff, *Microeconomics: Theory and Applications with Calculus* (Pearson, Pearson International Edition edn, 2008).
10 K Matthews, *Independent Investigation into NSW Water Management and Compliance: Interim Report* (NSW Government, 2017).

11 Murray-Darling Basin Commission, *Murray-Darling Basin Cap on Diversions Water Year 1997/98: Striking the Balance* (Murray-Darling Basin Commission, 1998).
12 Warren Musgrave, 'Historical Development of Water Resources in Australia: Irrigation Policy in the Murray-Darling Basin' in Lin Crase (ed.), *Water Policy in Australia: The Impact of Change and Uncertainty* (Resources For the Future, 2008) 28, 29.
13 National Water Commission, *Australian Environmental Water Management: 2012 Review* (Commonwealth of Australia, 2012) 13.
14 Erin L O'Donnell and Dustin E Garrick, 'Environmental Water Organizations and Institutional Settings' in Avril Horne et al. (eds), *Water for the Environment: From Policy and Science to Implementation and Management* (Academic Press, 2017) 421.
15 Brian D Richter et al., 'Ecologically Sustainable Water Management: Managing River Flows for Ecological Integrity' (2003) 13(1) *Ecological Applications* 206.
16 Connell, above n 8, 154.
17 M Bowman, 'Legal Perspectives on Dam Removal' (2002) 52(8) *BioScience* 739; Gregory A Thomas, 'Managing Infrastructure to Maintain Natural Functions in Developed Rivers' in A Horne et al. (eds), *Water for the Environment: From Policy and Science to Implementation and Management* (Academic Press, 2017) 483.
18 B Lankford, *Resource Efficiency Complexity and the Commons: The Paracommons and Paradoxes of Natural Resource Losses, Wastes and Wastages* (Routledge, 2013).
19 Charles Batchelor et al., 'Do Water-Saving Technologies Improve Environmental Flows?' (2014) 518 *Journal of Hydrology* 140.
20 Commonwealth of Australia, *Water For the Future: Improving On-Farm Irrigation Efficiency March 2009* (Australian Government Department of the Environment, Water, Heritage and the Arts, 2009).
21 Deschutes River Conservancy, 'Water Conservation Program: Permanent Streamflow Protection' www.deschutesriver.org/what-we-do/streamflow-restoration-programs/water-conservation/.
22 Janet C Neuman, 'The Good, the Bad and the Ugly: The First Ten Years of the Oregon Water Trust' (2004) 83 *Nebraska Law Review* 432.
23 Dustin Garrick and Bruce Aylward, 'Transaction Costs and Institutional Performance in Market-Based Environmental Water Allocation' (2012) 88(3) *Land Economics* 536.
24 NSW Government, *New South Wales RiverBank Business Plan Part A: Program Plan 2006–2011 Buying and Managing Water for the Environment (2010 Update)* (Department of Environment, Climate Change and Water, 2010).
25 Commonweath of Australia, *Water for the Future: Restoring the Balance in the Murray-Darling Basin* (Australian Government Department of the Environment, Water, Heritage and the Arts, 2010).
26 Australian Government Department of the Environment and Energy, 'Environmental Water Holdings' (18 February 2018) www.environment.gov.au/water/cewo/about/water-holdings.
27 A Horne, 'An Approach to Efficiently Managing Environmental Water Allocations' (PhD thesis, University of Melbourne, 2009).
28 A Horne, J Freebairn, and E O'Donnell, 'Establishment of Environmental Water in the Murray-Darling Basin – An Analysis of Two Key Policy Initiatives' (2011) 15(1) *Australian Journal of Water Resources* 7.
29 Dustin Garrick and Erin O'Donnell, 'Exploring Private Roles in Environmental Watering in Australia and the US' in Jeff Bennett (ed.), *Protecting the Environment, Privately* (World Scientific Publishing, 2016) 203, 215.

30 M Carter, 'Legal Providers – Turning Professional Towards 2000' in *Water is Gold, Proceedings of 1998 National Conference and Exhibition* (Irrigation Association of Australia, 1998) 5.
31 Hodgson, above n 6, 60.
32 World Meteorological Organization, 'The Dublin Statement on Water and Sustainable Development' (June 1992) www.wmo.int/pages/prog/hwrp/documents/english/icwedece.html.
33 John Freebairn, 'Principles and Issues for Effective Australian Water Markets' in Jeff Bennett (ed.), *The Evolution of Markets for Water: Theory and Practice in Australia* (Edward Elgar, 2005) 8, 10–12.
34 D Garrick et al., 'Water Markets and Freshwater Ecosystem Services: Policy Reform and Implementation in the Columbia and Murray-Darling Basins' (2009) 69 *Ecological Economics* 366.
35 A Dan Tarlock, 'Prior Appropriation: Rule, Principle or Rhetoric?' (2000) 76 *North Dakota Law Review* 881.
36 Zachary Donohew, 'Property Rights and Western United States Water Markets' (2009) 53 *Australian Journal of Agricultural and Resource Economics* 85.
37 Janis M Carey and David L Sunding, 'Emerging Markets in Water: A Comparative Institutional Analysis of the Central Valley and Colorado-Big Thompson Projects' (2001) 41 *Natural Resources Journal* 283, 283.
38 Steven Malloch, *Liquid Assets: Protecting and Restoring the West's Rivers and Wetlands through Environmental Water Transactions* (Trout Unlimited, 2005).
39 Erin O'Donnell, 'Common Legal and Policy Factors in the Emergence of Environmental Water Managers' in C A Brebbia (ed.), *Water and Society II* (WIT Press, 2013) 321.
40 H L A Hart, *Punishment and Responsibility* (Clarendon Press, 1968) 211–230; Ian Thynne and John Goldring, *Accountability and Control: Government Officials and the Exercise of Power* (Law Book Company, 1987) 1–10.
41 Charlton H Bonham, 'Perspectives From the Field: A Review of Western Instream Flow Issues and Recommendations for a New Water Future' (2006) 36(4) *Environmental Law* 1205.
42 Erin O'Donnell, 'Constructing the Aquatic Environment as a Legal Subject: Legal Rights, Market Participation, and the Power of Narrative' (PhD thesis, University of Melbourne, 2017) http://hdl.handle.net/11343/191749.
43 Jesus R Gastélum, Juan B Valdés, and Steven Stewart, 'An Analysis and Proposal to Improve Water Rights Transfers on the Mexican Conchos Basin' (2009) 11 *Water Policy* 79, 87.
44 Le Quesne, Kendy, and Weston, above n 4, 51.
45 Kristiana Hansen, Richard Howitt, and Jeffrey Williams, 'An Econometric Test of Water Market Structure in the Western United States' (Paper presented at Allied Social Science Association Annual Meeting, Chicago, IL, 2012).
46 E O'Donnell and E MacPherson, 'Challenges and Opportunities for Environmental Water Management in Chile: An Australian Perspective' (2014) 23 *Journal of Water Law* 24.
47 Sharon Pollard and Derick du Toit, 'The Shared River Initiative Phase I: Towards the Sustainability of Freshwater Systems in South Africa: An Exploration of Factors that Enable or Constrain Meeting the Ecological Reserve within the Context of Integrated Water Resources Management in the Catchments of the Lowveld; WRC Report No. TT 477/10' (Water Research Commission, South Africa, 2011).
48 John Salmond, *Jurisprudence* (Sweet & Maxwell, Glanville L Williams (ed.), 10th edn, 1947) 318.
49 Ngaire Naffine, 'Review Essay: Liberating the Legal Person' (2011) 26(1) *Canadian Journal of Law and Society* 193, 194.

50 Ngaire Naffine, *Law's Meaning of Life: Philosophy, Religion, Darwin and the Legal Person* (Hart Publishing, 2009) 21.
51 Ibid., 26.
52 Erin O'Donnell, 'Competition or Collaboration? Using Legal Persons to Manage Water for the Environment in Australia and the United States' (2017) 34(6) *Environmental and Planning Law Journal* 503.
53 Alon Harel, 'Theories of Rights' in William A Edmundson and Martin P Golding (eds), *Blackwell Guide to the Philosophy of Law and Legal Theory* (Blackwell, 2005) 191, 194.
54 Naffine, above n 50, 55.
55 Ibid., 11.
56 Ibid., 9.
57 O'Donnell, above n 42, Chapter 4.
58 Robert Dingwall and Phil M Strong, 'The Interactional Study of Organisations: A Critique and Reformulation' in Gale Miller and Robert Dingwall (eds), *Context and Method in Qualitative Research* (Sage Publications, 1997) 139, 147.
59 Mats Alvesson, *Interpreting Interviews* (Sage Publications, 2011).

4 Just another user

Environmental water managers in Australia

The EWMs of south-eastern Australia are organisations with legal personality which have been created to acquire and manage legal rights to water on behalf of rivers and wetlands (the aquatic environment). Docker described Australia's EWMs in the following way:

> A defining feature of environmental water holders as they presently exist is that for the most part these entities manage entitlements that have the same characteristics as similar entitlements used for irrigated agriculture. This means that ... the environment [is] a legitimate user of the resource with the same rights and obligations as other users.[1]

The activities of the EWMs, and the nature of the water rights they hold, are linked to the way in which the EWM is constructing the environment in law and the legitimacy of the EWM to operate as a water user.

In Australia water availability is highly variable within and between years. The EWMs use their legal personality to hold water rights, to buy and sell rights to water in the Australia's water markets, and to use their water to improve ecosystem health. The EWMs in Australia have been in operation since 2005, and their 12 years of work can shed light on the effect of using a legal person to represent the aquatic environment.

The EWMs of Australia express their legal personality through a combination of their form (a legal person) and function (holding water rights and acting as decision-makers in environmental water management). The EWMs are a legal creation, but their operation is a distinctly human endeavour shaped by the perceptions and beliefs of the EWM employees. To gain insight into the human dimensions, the legal framework of the EWMs is supplemented by detailed interviews with senior staff (see Chapter 3 for more detail).

The EWMs of south-eastern Australia are embedded within water law frameworks that operate at the state and national levels within the federation of Australia.[2] Applying the conceptual framework developed in Chapter 2, we can see how the environment is constructed in Australia's water law. The interaction between the multiple constructions is shaping cultural narratives in Australia about the role of the EWMs. One of the consequences of this is the paradox of legal rights for rivers: as legal power increases, the aquatic environment is being increasingly framed as 'just another user', which is driving legal reform that curtails the powers and activities of the EWMs once more.

South-eastern Australia: the Murray-Darling Basin and southern Victoria

There are two federal-level EWMs (the CEWH and the Murray-Darling Basin Authority, MDBA), which have operated almost exclusively within the MDB (Figure 4.1), although the CEWH has the legal capacity to operate in locations outside the MDB where necessary to give effect to Australia's international agreements.[3] There are also state EWMs in South Australia, Victoria, and New South Wales, and the operations of the VEWH extend across the state of Victoria.

Water law in south-eastern Australia

Australia's water laws have their origins in riparian rights, but over the past century they have transitioned to a statutory regime in response to the need to manage highly variable water supplies.[4] Australia's water resource

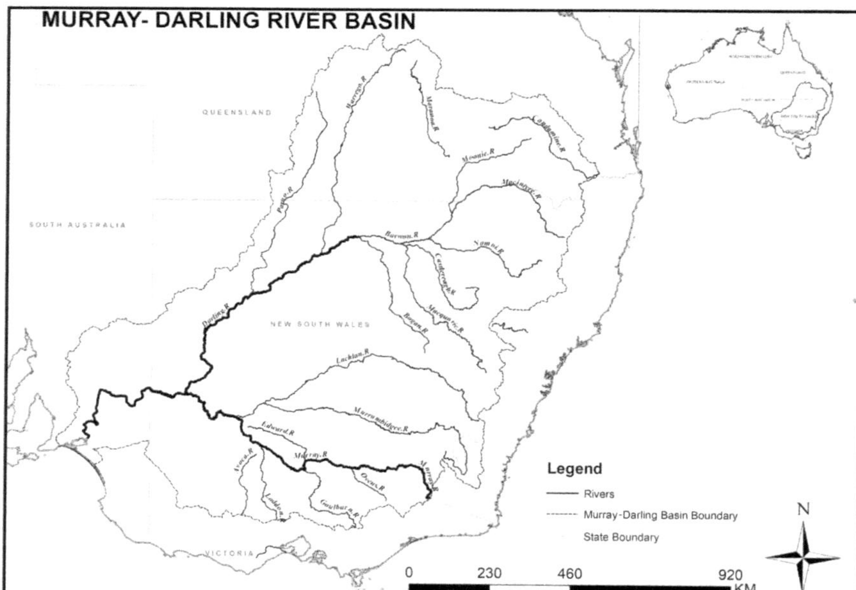

Figure 4.1 Murray-Darling Basin, Australia.

management framework emphasises coordinated, state-based planning schemes that aim to manage water resources sustainably and reliably over time in a highly variable climate. Competition reforms in the 1980s created an additional emphasis on efficiency, by supporting the development of cap-and-trade water markets which are now recognised as some of the most active in the world.[5]

All states and territories have passed their own water legislation that vests the right to control and use water in the Crown.[6] However, the MDB has been jointly managed by state and federal governments since 1915.[7] In 1994, in response to sustained increase in water extractions (and significant environmental decline) in the MDB, the basin states and the federal government entered a new formal agreement.[8] As part of various broad commitments to water reform, this intergovernmental agreement enabled a cap to be imposed on water extractions from the MDB; this cap was set in 1997, at 1994 levels of water extraction. In 2004 a second intergovernmental agreement established the NWI, which included substantial federal government funding incentives for the implementation of water reform. The NWI required the states to develop clearer and more secure legal rights to water that were transferable separate to land, supported the creation and operation of water markets, and created legal rights to water for the environment.[9]

In 2007, in response to an extreme and ongoing drought across south-eastern Australia as well as a 'perceived lack of co-operation between state governments',[10] the basin states agreed to refer some of their powers to the federal government in exchange for substantial federal investment in water infrastructure and water recovery for the environment. The Water Act 2007 gave the federal government a much more substantial role in water resource management, particularly in the MDB. Under this legislation the Murray-Darling Basin Plan was passed in 2012, aiming to streamline water resource management in the MDB, lower the existing cap on water extractions, and allocate more water to the environment.[11] However, the states continue to retain their own legal frameworks, and remain responsible for defining water rights and implementing water resource management plans.[12]

Within this complex multi-jurisdictional water law framework, water rights in Australia are largely segregated by use (e.g. rural or urban) and water source (e.g. surface water or groundwater). Individuals and industries in urban areas have different rights to water than those in irrigation districts; for example, urban rights are typically not transferable at the individual level, whereas individual irrigator water rights are often traded. As a result, the water markets are located in the rural irrigation districts.

Within irrigation districts the legal nature of rights to water differs if water is held in storage (such as dams and weirs) or is accessible as run-of-river flow. Where water is held in storage, water rights have been 'unbundled', a process in which the rights to use water have been separated into different components to stimulate water trade.[13] These water rights have been separated into a 'water access licence', which defines the right to receive water in storage and exists in perpetuity, and a water allocation, which is the physical volume of water available for use (as a share of the water access entitlement), as well as delivery and use licences.[14] Each of these entitlements can be held separately or together. Each state has defined these differently, so for example in Victoria this translates into a water share (the water access licence), a water allocation, and two rights that remain attached to the land: a delivery share (a share of delivery capacity linked to an annual fee to maintain access to delivery infrastructure) and a water use registration (a licence to use water at a particular location).[15] Similar divisions in water rights have occurred in South Australia, New South Wales, and Queensland.[16]

In regions where water is available as run-of-river flow ('unregulated' rivers) or groundwater, unbundling is not yet complete and water rights are held as licences.[17] A licence is highly context specific – it relates to a particular location and has specific conditions attached to it, and thus the collective licences create highly heterogeneous water rights. For this reason, although licences can be transferred separately from land, trades in these licences usually represent personal dealings between landowners, and transferred licences are reattached to a specific land parcel.

In this book, 'water rights' in the Australian context refers to the unbundled water access entitlements and water allocations available in irrigation districts in the MDB and across southern Victoria. These water rights are traded in water markets, which are used to allocate limited and highly variable water supplies between different uses in response to changing water demands.

Water markets in south-eastern Australia

Australia's water markets have emerged in response to water scarcity and variability, and the desire to support continued growth of water-dependent industries within a sustainable limit on water extraction (the cap). The MDB cap was imposed to protect the existing reliability of supply for water users, as well as limiting further decline in the aquatic environment.[18] The cap thus reflected physical scarcity (there was a finite volume of water available each year) and manufactured scarcity (by capping water extractions before reaching that limit, to preserve water for the environment). Trade volumes significantly increased in 2007, in response to the severe water scarcity of the Millennium Drought.[19]

At present Australia has active water markets throughout the MDB.[20] Australia's water markets exemplify Tan's four market fundamentals:[21] many buyers and sellers; mobile resources; reliable and adequate information; and well-defined, largely homogeneous rights. The total value of major water entitlements in the MDB was A$14.5 billion in 2017.[22] Water trading has been an effective way to mitigate drought impacts and support agricultural development in the southern connected MDB.[23] All states have publicly accessible water registers that record ownership, transfers, and mortgages of all water entitlements; in states with highly active water markets, these registers are available online.

The impacts of the creation and operation of water markets on the aquatic environment remain highly contested.[24] Much existing scholarship is focused on attempting to assess quantitatively the effect of the water markets *per se* on the environment, but so far scholars have overlooked the contribution of water markets to the way that the aquatic environment is constructed in law. In Australia, water rights held by other users can be transferred to the environment, and in most cases this transfer is achieved via water trade. The nature of water as a shared resource market helps to highlight the multiple constructions of the aquatic environment within Australian water law (Chapter 2).

Constructing the aquatic environment in Australian water law

In the frequently water-scarce MDB, the construction of the environment in water law is underpinned by the legal concept of 'environmental water'. At the most basic level, Australian water law recognises two types of use: *consumptive use*, when water is usually, but not always, extracted from the river; and *environmental use*, when the water remains in rivers, lakes, wetlands, and estuaries to maintain the health of the aquatic environment.[25] Environmental water was defined by the National Water Commission as 'the water regime provided to achieve environmental objectives', including maintaining ecosystem function, biodiversity, water quality, and river health targets.[26]

In Australian water law environmental water is created in three ways.

1 By legislation, as water set aside for environmental purposes through a range of mechanisms, but with no mention of the volumes or locations of this water.[27]
2 By specific rules for river operators or obligations on consumptive water users, often referred to as *planned environmental water*.[28]
3 By individual water entitlements, including those that have been acquired from consumptive users as well as those specifically created for environmental use,[29] now referred to as *held environmental water*.[30]

The concept of environmental water, however, is relatively new. In the 1980s and 1990s the aquatic environment was recognised in water law as an important part of sustainable resource management[31] and, more rarely, as a specific iconic location considered worthy of protection.[32] Next the aquatic environment was translated into a legal object, to be protected by limiting others' access to water by, for example, setting a cap on water extractions.[33] Only since 2005 has the aquatic environment been a legal subject, and represented by EWMs able to acquire and hold water rights for the environment.[34]

Recognition of the aquatic environment as a socio-ecological concept

In south-eastern Australia the oldest water statute still in operation (although repeatedly amended) is Victoria's Water Act 1989, which constructs the aquatic environment as something that supports a range of social and ecological uses. The purposes of this legislation include the provision of 'formal means for the protection and enhancement of the environmental qualities of waterways and their in-stream uses', which include cultural, recreational, commercial, and environmental values.[35]

Water legislation in Queensland, South Australia, and New South Wales is more recent, and includes explicit support for the principles of ecological sustainable development.[36] In Queensland the statute also includes specific objectives that protect 'the biological diversity and health of natural ecosystems'.[37] New South Wales, on the other hand, appears to limit the aquatic environment to ecosystems associated with water sources, and also explicitly recognises that benefits to the environment are part of the 'the significant social and economic benefits to the State that result from the sustainable and efficient use of water'.[38] The New South Wales statute contains a set of water management principles to guide the administration of the Act, including that:

a water sources, floodplains and dependent ecosystems (including groundwater and wetlands) should be protected and restored and, where possible, land should not be degraded, and
b habitats, animals and plants that benefit from water or are potentially affected by managed activities should be protected and (in the case of habitats) restored, and
c the water quality of all water sources should be protected and, wherever possible, enhanced, and
d the cumulative impacts of water management licences and approvals and other activities on water sources and their dependent ecosystems, should be considered and minimized.[39]

The most recent water statute in Australia is the Commonwealth Water Act 2007. This legislation was cobbled together based on agreement from the states and the limited constitutional remit of the Commonwealth of Australia to legislate on water resource management.[40] The statute aims to return water extraction to 'environmentally sustainable levels' and 'protect, restore and provide for the ecological values and ecosystem services of the

Murray-Darling Basin'.[41] It is explicitly concerned with water-dependent ecosystems,[42] and defines the environmentally sustainable level of water extraction as:

> the level at which water can be taken from that water resource which, if exceeded, would compromise: (a) key environmental assets of the water resource; or (b) key ecosystem functions of the water resource; or (c) the productive base of the water resource; or (d) key environmental outcomes for the water resource.[43]

Like all water laws, the federal legislation defines environmental outcomes to include ecosystem function and biodiversity, as well as the socio-economic values of water resource health and water quality,[44] and the aquatic environment is constructed as one factor among several to be optimised in the management of the MDB water resources.[45] The construction of the environment in this statute exhibits some of the tensions discussed in Chapter 2: the aquatic environment is both special (with the legislation's focus on the biodiversity of the iconic Murray-Darling River system) and commonplace (as it includes the necessary water quality and quantity to support commercial use).

Translating the aquatic environment into a legal object

The environment has been *translated* from this broad, socio-ecological concept into a legal object in two ways. First, the environment is protected by placing limits on the actions of others, primarily by broadly limiting the water available for consumptive use.[46] Second, under the Commonwealth Water Act 2007, as well as water laws in Victoria and New South Wales, planned environmental water itself is explicitly identified and protected.[47] Although 'held' environmental water is created by transferring rights to water to the environment (and forms part of personification, discussed below), 'planned' water is merely the water left behind after there have been further limits placed on the extraction activities of other users. The most common mechanisms for the legal establishment of planned environmental water are:

- a cap on total water extractions, for example the sustainable diversion limit set under the Commonwealth Water Act 2007;[48]
- a requirement to release a minimum environmental flow from a storage; and
- conditions on water licences that require water users to cease pumping from a river when flows fall below a certain level.[49]

Although such water is clearly intended to be part of the water available to the environment, and is often the vast majority of available environmental water,[50] it is not a legal right in itself. The aquatic environment is only obliquely visible to water law, through the lens of the legal rights of others.

The situation is slightly different in Victoria, where the environmental water reserve is an attempt to bring together all the various forms of environmental water under one legal umbrella.[51] However, the environmental water reserve does not create any additional legal rights to water, and has simply expanded the construction of the aquatic environment as a legal object.[52]

Australian water law is also peculiarly isolated from the broader protections of environmental law.[53] Although the water statutes refer to environmental impact assessments and planning laws when new developments are proposed (such as the constructions of new storages or pipelines), the use of water available under existing water rights is generally not an action that triggers further assessment or review outside the water law framework.[54] The aquatic environment is almost solely constructed, and interpreted by water lawyers and resource managers, within the paradigm of water resource management, which has focused on managing the extraction and use of water from various sources for consumptive purposes.

This construction of the aquatic environment as a legal object is legally weak, and dependent on the continued support of communities and governments to take action to protect it, including enforcing compliance with conditions on water licences that protect flows in rivers. In 2017 this reliance on the action of others became a significant problem in the northern MDB, where poor levels of compliance in New South Wales resulted in environmental water being diverted for use by irrigators.[55]

Personifying the aquatic environment as a legal subject

Since the 1990s inadequate levels of environmental water have caused blue-green algal blooms, rising salinity, and loss of wetland ecosystems throughout south-eastern Australia. To combat these problems, Australian governments have invested in recovery of additional water. The need to afford environmental water the same level of legal protection as other users' rights meant that the water law frameworks had to include legal rights to water for the environment itself. Once such rights were established, an organisation with the attributes of legal personality was required to hold these rights on behalf of the aquatic environment.

Although some environmental water entitlements were created in the late 1980s and early 1990s, large-scale environmental water recovery in the MDB began with The Living Murray First Step in 2002, which recovered 500 GL for six 'icon sites'.[56] In 2004 this was followed by the NWI, which committed to legal recognition of environmental water and additional investment in water recovery.[57] In 2007 the federal government committed to a massive increase in water recovery as part of the Murray-Darling Basin

Plan,[58] which was adopted by the Australian parliament in November 2012. The Murray-Darling Basin Plan committed to increase water for the environment to 2,750 GL by 2019 and a further 450 GL by 2024. This is an unprecedented volume of environmental water in Australia (although a formal review process currently under way may see these targets reduced). The largest investor in water recovery for the environment has been the federal government, with A$5.8 billion to water efficiency projects and A$3.1 billion to purchase water rights for the environment,[59] but state governments and NGOs have also invested substantially.[60] Outside the MDB, actions by state governments have recovered additional water for the environment.[61]

As the water recovery process nears completion, the focus of environmental water provision has shifted from *recovery* to *management*.[62] The volumes of environmental water available are large and represent a substantial public investment, which creates an imperative to manage the water effectively and maximise the potential environmental outcomes. For example, by 2017 in the southern MDB the CEWH had obtained almost 1,000 GL of entitlement, or just over 13 per cent of the entitlement on issue.[63] In addition, as environmental water recovery has progressed, water markets within the MDB have increased in activity, and the value of entitlements almost doubled between 2013–2014 and 2016–2017.[64]

Legally, this environmental water includes both environment-specific entitlements and water rights previously held by consumptive users. For example, the Commonwealth Water Act 2007 defines held environmental water as 'water available under: (a) a water access right; or (b) a water delivery right; or (c) an irrigation right'.[65] New South Wales and Victoria both create water entitlements for the environment in legislation,[66] as well as enabling the transfer of water rights from other users. In Queensland and South Australia the legislation does not distinguish between water rights held by the environment and by other users. In both cases water rights that have been previously held by irrigators can be transferred to the environment.[67]

The EWMs emerged in response to the need for organisations with the capacity to operate within the water markets to acquire water and the ability to make decisions on how to use that water most effectively. Government EWMs with responsibility for holding and managing environmental water were explicitly created in water legislation, and over the same period NGOs were established with the intent of providing an alternative method of recovery of, and management arrangements for, environmental water (Table 4.1). The NGO EWMs operate within water law frameworks by virtue of their legal personhood, which enables them to hold water rights.

The EWMs, as a result of the combination of their legal personality, their organisational objectives, and their legal rights to water for the environment, operate to create legal personhood for parts of the aquatic environment within the water law of south-eastern Australia. This combination of legal form with water rights in the context of a water market creates a particularly powerful combination of legal capacity and competence (Chapters 2 and 3). However, the Australian EWMs still face the challenge of how to use their power without undermining the cultural narrative that the environment is worthy of protection (Chapter 6).

The environmental water managers of south-eastern Australia

The EWMs are identifiable organisations that are accorded legal personality, with specific objectives to improve the health of aquatic ecosystems over time using environmental water rights.[68] The existence and operation of the EWMs in Australia are beginning to lead to changes that affect water law, which in turn affects the operation of the EWMs. In Australia this interaction is particularly clear in environmental water recovery, but is also becoming apparent in response to the environmental water management activities.

Legal form: how the EWMs are given legal personality in water law

There are eight EWM organisations operating (or recently operating) in Australia. Each EWM in south-eastern Australia is a specific type of organisation with a specific geographical focus and particular accountability arrangements (Table 4.1).

Healthy Rivers Australia (HRA), one of the earliest NGO EWMs with ongoing environmental watering activities, has ceased operations but is included in Table 4.1 for the sake of historical completeness. Several other environmental NGOs have operated in the environmental water space for a short time (such as the 'Just Add Water' campaign by the Australian Conservation Foundation, which represented a one-off investment in environmental water recovery), but do not meet the definition of an EWM (Chapter 3).

Government EWMs

The EWM with the widest geographical range of operations is the CEWH. The CEWH was established in 2007, in response to severe drought across south-eastern Australia, with responsibility for managing the environmental water holdings of the federal government.[69] This water must be used accordance with the Murray-Darling Basin Plan requirements, and may be traded (in limited circumstances) or carried forward for use in future years. The CEWH is a legal person, and its statutory functions are performed by an employee of the Australian public service and the

Table 4.1 Legal form of the environmental water managers of south-eastern Australia

EWM	*Geographical extent of activities*	*Organisation type*	*Source of legal personhood rights and duties*	*Source of water holding and management capacities*	*Accountability: to whom does this organisation report?*
Commonwealth Environmental Water Holder	Australia, but primarily the Murray-Darling Basin	Statutory entity: a person appointed to hold the water and make decisions, supported by the Commonwealth Environmental Water Office	Water Act 2007 (Cth) s 105	Water Act 2007 (Cth) ss 105, 108 The specifics of the water rights held are defined by the legislation of the state in which those water rights originated	Minister for Environment (Commonwealth), although the Minister for Water oversees the administration of the Water Act 2007 (Cth)
Murray-Darling Basin Authority	Murray-Darling Basin	Statutory corporation: chief executive, chair, and four other members appointed by Governor-General, plus staff	Water Act 2007 (Cth) ss 173, 176	Water Act 2007 (Cth) ss 173, 239C–E The specifics of the water rights held are defined by the legislation of the state in which those water rights originated	Minister for Water (Commonwealth) and Murray-Darling Basin Ministerial Committee (including ministerial representatives from all MDB states)
RiverBank (now New South Wales Office of Environment and Heritage)	New South Wales	Function within department; funded by the Environmental Trust	Unclear personhood of the EWM itself Licences held by Minister for Environment on behalf of NSW and funds managed by the Environment Trust	Water Management Act 2000 (NSW)	Minister for Environment (NSW)

continued

Table 4.1 Continued

EWM	*Geographical extent of activities*	*Organisation type*	*Source of legal personhood rights and duties*	*Source of water holding and management capacities*	*Accountability: to whom does this organisation report?*
Victorian Environmental Water Holder	Victoria	Statutory corporation	Water Act 1989 (Vic) s 33DB	Water Act 1989 (Vic) ss 33DD–DE, 48B; as a person, the VEWH can also hold water shares and water allocations	Victorian Minister for Environment
South Australian Department of Natural Resources and Environment	South Australia (but water licences only in the River Murray)	Government department	The department operates as a delegate of the Minister for Water	Natural Resources Management Act 2004, ss 124–125, 146; see also Draft River Murray Water Allocation Plan	Minister for Water
Environmental Water Trust	Murray-Darling Basin	Trust and tax-deductible gift recipient public fund owned by Murray-Darling Wetlands Working Group (a public company limited by guarantee)	The trustee is a registered company under Corporations Act 2001 (Cth) ss 117–119, 124	State-based water resources legislation in area of operation; the purposes of the trust include the holding of water access licences	Murray-Darling Wetlands Working Group; members and donors in annual reports

Healthy Rivers Australia (now inactive)	South Australia, Victoria, and New South Wales	Incorporated association registered as a tax-deductible gift recipient and charitable organisation	Associations Incorporations Act 1985 (SA) s 25	State-based water resources legislation in area of operation	Office of Consumer and Business Affairs, South Australia; members and donors in annual reports
Water for Nature	River Murray, South Australia	Trust established by Nature Foundation SA, an incorporated association registered as a tax-deductible gift recipient and charitable organisation	Associations Incorporations Act 1985 (SA) s 25	Natural Resources Management Act 2004 (SA)	Nature Foundation SA; Office of Consumer and Business Affairs, South Australia; contract partners (e.g. CEWH), members and donors in annual reports

necessary staff to support that person (now known as the Commonwealth Environmental Water Office).[70] The CEWH is responsible to the Commonwealth Minister for Environment, who can issue directions on how the water should be used, and the Commonwealth Minister for Water, who retains the overall responsibility for administering the Water Act 2007 (Cth). The CEWH reports publicly on the water it holds and how that water has been used.

At basin scale, the MDBA is responsible for managing the portfolio of water entitlements obtained through The Living Murray programme. The MDBA is a statutory corporation created in federal legislation and underpinned by intergovernmental agreement between the states and the Commonwealth of Australia.[71] Each year annual environmental watering plans are prepared by the Environmental Watering Group, which comprises representatives of the state governments and the MDBA. Since 2007 the MDBA has had a much broader planning and enforcement role in water resources management across the MDB, and this potentially conflicts with its responsibilities as an EWM.[72]

At the state level, the VEWH, the New South Wales RiverBank/Office of Environment and Heritage (OEH), and the South Australian Department of Environment, Water, and Natural Resources (DEWNR) all have the capacity to use, trade, and carry over environmental water, although these capacities are limited in each state in different ways.

The New South Wales and South Australian examples demonstrate the importance of an EWM organisation being identifiable and specific for it to extend legal personality to the environment. Although both departments hold environmental water and can decide to use or trade it, they do not do so *as a distinct legal person speaking for the environment*. Their decisions may only be scrutinised as an exercise of the administrative powers that otherwise reside with a minister. Such ministerial decisions are almost always a question of balance, and the environment is only one factor to be considered. Without a clear legal identity, and specific limited focus on the aquatic environment, these government departments do not operate to enhance the legibility of the environment to the law, which continues to see their activities obliquely through the lens of administrative law. The aquatic environment itself remains obscured.

In New South Wales, RiverBank was initially created as a legally distinct mechanism for water recovery and managed separately to the broader activities of the department (OEH).[73] For this reason it is included in Table 4.1, although RiverBank has since been reabsorbed into the department. OEH still transparently holds and manages water rights on behalf of the aquatic environment, but the lack of a clear identity separate to the government limits its ability to extend legal personality to the environment.

South Australia's DEWNR previously had an early form of an EWM in the River Murray Environmental Manager, which has since been merged back into the overall department. According to the interview data, South

Australia is still considering the creation of an EWM, but is limited by budget considerations:

> We don't have an environmental water holder in the sense of the VEWH or the CEWH, but we are investigating setting one up ... The issue we come up against: we are a small state, and we don't have the resources to set up this massive entity; if we did set one up it would be a smaller scale than the VEWH or the CEWH. The previous River Murray Environmental Manager got brought back into the agency as part of the merger of the NRM [natural resource management] and water management agencies; this was a largely budget-driven process.[74]

The VEWH, on the other hand, has both legal personality and organisational separation. It is a statutory corporation with four commissioners and a small staff.[75] As a body corporate, the VEWH has an independent legal personality. While the VEWH must report to the Victorian environment minister, the minister is prohibited from issuing directions on how the VEWH will use its water,[76] thus insulating the VEWH from the politics of the government of the day (to at least some extent). It was a deliberate decision to create the VEWH as a distinct legal person, providing a voice for environmental water that was separate from the minister and the government.[77] However, any permanent sale of an environmental entitlement (unlike the temporary sale of water allocation available under such an entitlement) requires approval from both the Minister for Water and the Minister for Environment prior to the sale.[78] Each year the VEWH prepares annual watering statements that specify the environmental watering priorities for the year ahead, and reports on the watering activities that it has undertaken.[79] These statements and reports are made publicly available on the VEWH website.

Non-governmental EWMs

The severe drought across south-eastern Australia from 2006 to 2010 crystallised the need for additional water for the environment, and most of the non-government EWMs were established during this period.

One of the NGOs, HRA, was established as a not-for-profit incorporated association.[80] HRA was in operation from 2007 to 2014; it was originally established to obtain donations of environmental water available at the end of the irrigation season (as earlier South Australian law prevented irrigators carrying this water over for use in future years), and was registered as a tax-deductible gift recipient with the Australian Charities and Not-for-Profits Commission.[81] HRA was the first organisation to obtain a tax concession on the basis of a donated water allocation, and combined its water donations with corporate and individual charity donations to acquire additional environmental water on the temporary water market. HRA reported publicly on the donations it received and how it used those donations to improve environmental flows in wetlands in South Australia.[82]

The remaining NGOs include several water trusts operated by a parent organisation, such as the Environmental Water Trust,[83] Water For Nature,[84] and the Murray-Darling Foundation (an initiative of the Murray-Darling Association), which has been operating a water bank for environmental purposes since 2007.[85] The Murray-Darling Foundation is not considered to be an EWM (and excluded from Table 4.1), as holding and managing environmental water is not a primary objective of the foundation, which limits its ability to extend legal personality to the environment.[86] Although the Murray-Darling Foundation operated as a water bank for community environmental water holdings, it relied on other organisations (namely the Murray-Darling Wetlands Working Group) to make decisions on how that water would be used for the environment.

In general, the NGOs have relatively small environmental water holdings, and have focused on acquiring water for temporary use rather than permanent water entitlements. They rely on philanthropic donations (of both money and water). In 2012 the CEWH entered into an unprecedented agreement with Water For Nature to manage some of its environmental water in South Australia. Typically, the CEWH works with state government agencies to deliver its water, and this agreement with a NGO remains unique. The CEWH and Water For Nature have a five-year agreement in which the CEWH will make up to 10 GL of water available each year for Water For Nature to deliver.

The activities of NGOs are limited by their own objectives and their capacities under the water resource management statutes of the jurisdictions in which they operate, which can lead to very different outcomes. For example, in Victoria NGOs may purchase water rights, but environmental entitlements can only be allocated to the VEWH.[87] In New South Wales, on the other hand, the Murray Wetlands Working Group (the predecessor of the Murray-Darling Wetlands Working Group Ltd) was given responsibility for managing two adaptive environmental water licences, effectively as an arm of the government. In South Australia the environmental water access licences were previously allocated for a specific purpose, so the government department held a large water access licence to cover the evaporative losses associated with wetlands in South Australia, and licences purchased for environmental purposes could still be classed as irrigation entitlements. The draft River Murray Water Allocation Plan now removes this need for a purpose, but the environmental licences are still part of different consumptive pools. As a result, the Water For Nature trust may manage water available under water access licences in consumptive pool E (as part of its agreement with the CEWH), but not the Wetland Consumptive Pool.[88]

The next section shows how the EWMs of south-eastern Australia leverage their legal personality to support their activities in water recovery and water management for the aquatic environment.

Operation of the EWMs: recovery and management

The operation of the EWMs in south-eastern Australia is a consequence of the particular emphasis of Australia's water laws, which are intended to manage the *use* of water *resources*. In the regulated river systems of south-eastern Australia, water law requires that water access licences be held by a legal person; and similarly that a legal person is required when deciding how to deal with the water allocation (either calling it out from storage or transferring it to or from another user). The capacity to recover and manage legal rights to water for the environment in Australia is therefore contingent on the legal personality of the EWM.

Table 4.2 summarises the objectives of each of the currently operating EWMs in south-eastern Australia. The objectives of the EWMs focus on the use of environmental water to improve and maintain the health of the aquatic environment, but may also include references to the broader community and the need to support continued use of the environment by people.

Table 4.2 establishes the specifically environmental focus of the EWMs. However, the EWMs do not exist in a vacuum. The *raison d'être* of each EWM is dependent on the continued desire of the public (and governments) to improve the quality of the aquatic environment; and the EWMs' actions are affected by the tensions between the different constructs of the environment and vulnerable to changing community perceptions of why the environment is worth protecting (see Chapters 2 and 6).

Australia's EWMs focus on both *recovering* sufficient water for the environment and *managing* this water to achieve the maximum environmental outcomes (such as fish spawning, bird breeding, or maintaining native vegetation).

Recovery of environmental water: right to hold and acquire water rights

Recovery of water for the environment involves a number of steps, and this subsection focuses on the specific work involved in three phases.

1 Planning and prioritisation – how much water and where is it needed?
2 Process of recovery – how can the water be obtained at the lowest cost?
3 Formal legal transfer to the environment – who is legally capable of holding environmental water?

Table 4.2 Objectives of south-eastern Australian environmental water managers

EWM	*Objectives*
Commonwealth Environmental Water Holder	'(1) The functions of the Commonwealth Environmental Water Holder are, on behalf of the Commonwealth: (a) to manage the Commonwealth environmental water holdings; and (b) to administer the Environmental Water Holdings Special Account ... (3) The functions of the Commonwealth Environmental Water Holder are to be performed for the purpose of protecting or restoring the environmental assets of: (a) the Murray-Darling Basin; and (b) other areas outside the Murray-Darling Basin where the Commonwealth holds water; so as to give effect to relevant international agreements.' *Objectives of the environmental watering plan:* '(d) protect and restore the wetlands and other environmental assets of the Murray-Darling Basin; and (e) protect biodiversity dependent on the Basin water resources and achieve other environmental outcomes for the Murray-Darling Basin.' Source: Water Act 2007 (Cth) ss 28, 105.
Murray-Darling Basin Authority (The Living Murray entitlements)	*The Living Murray Initiative* Commits to recovering water over five years to 'maximise environmental outcomes' at 'six Icon Sites ... Barmah-Millewa Forest; Gunbower and Koondrook-Perricoota Forests; Hattah Lakes; Chowilla Floodplain (including Lindsay-Wallpolla); the Murray Mouth, Coorong and Lower Lakes; and the River Murray Channel', where the water is managed in accordance with the Living Murray Environmental Watering Plan (LM EWP). The LM EWP 'will aim to apply available water in a way that enhances ecological outcomes across the six Icon Sites, protects existing high value areas or areas in good condition and realises the greatest environmental benefit from the water'. Source: Murray-Darling Basin Commission, *The Living Murray Business Plan: 25 May 2007* (Murray-Darling Basin Commission, 2007).
Victorian Environmental Water Holder	'[T]o to manage the Water Holdings for the purposes of – (a) maintaining the environmental water reserve in accordance with the environmental water reserve objective; and (b) improving the environmental values and health of water ecosystems, including their biodiversity, ecological functioning and water quality, and other uses that depend on environmental condition.' Source: Water Act 1989 (Vic) s 33DC.

Table 4.2 Continued

EWM	*Objectives*
Environmental Water Trust	Seven objectives, including: '(a) to protect and enhance the natural water resources of Australia which includes protecting, enhancing and restoring water sources, their associated ecosystems, ecological processes and biological diversity throughout Australia;... (c) to apply for, acquire, manage, hold or dispose of Water Access Licences (WAL) as the Trustee determines for these purposes'. Source: Environmental Water Trust, 'Home' (13 March 2013) http://environmentalwatertrust.org.au/.
Water For Nature	'Work with SA River Murray communities to source water and deliver community-driven projects that benefit wetlands and floodplains and the species they support.' Source: Nature Foundation SA, 'Water For Nature: Our Work' (14 March 2016) http://naturefoundation.org.au/what-we-do/water-for-nature/our-work.

In south-east Australia the planning and prioritisation phase establishes the demand for environmental water, and is generally undertaken by government agencies. The Murray-Darling Basin Plan, prepared by the MDBA, establishes the sustainable diversion limit on water extraction from the MDB, as well as the limits on water extraction for each catchment. At the state level, long-term water resource plans such as Victoria's sustainable water strategies also set targets for environmental water recovery in local catchments, based on specific environmental flow requirements. These plans identify how much environmental water is needed to achieve a stated level of environmental health, and are used to target environmental water recovery. Even when water recovery is undertaken by NGOs, where the water is intended for public land the planning process is based on government programmes that identify endangered species and appropriate wetting and drying periods for wetlands. A South Australian NGO EWM staff member commented that:

> The general setting has been the government policy framework set up around needing to provide water and recover it ... In this jurisdiction, it's mostly driven by state government policy ... In South Australia, you're not permitted to put water in a [public] wetland unless you have approval from the state government ... all the sites we looked at required approval from the state environmental manager.[89]

In Australia the second phase, the process of recovering the water, has been the joint work of government and non-government agencies. The earliest large-scale water recovery programme, the Living Murray Initiative, involved A$500 million of government investment and established three mechanisms for water recovery that are still in use today. One of the cheapest in terms of financial outlay was Victoria's regularisation of water entitlements in northern Victoria. As part of meeting the NWI requirement to create permanent, secure, tradable rights to water, Victoria converted a poorly defined right to low-reliability water (called 'sales' water) to a permanent water share, retaining the historical reliability of the right. In return for formalising irrigators' rights to this water in an ongoing way, Victoria converted 20 per cent of this water (equivalent to 120 GL in long-term average yield) into environmental entitlements for the Snowy and Murray Rivers. This water recovery had an extremely low financial cost, and remains an excellent example of finding a win-win for irrigators and the environment when changing water policy.

However, the water recovered in Victoria was low reliability, and unlikely to be available in dry years. In Victoria, water access entitlements are classified as 'high reliability' or 'low reliability'. High-reliability water access entitlements must receive 100 per cent of their allocation before any water is allocated to low-reliability water access entitlements. To acquire high-reliability water access entitlements, other methods of water recovery were needed.

Investing in water efficiency savings is often the most politically popular option, and remains the mechanism of choice for government water recovery in south-eastern Australia.[90] The Living Murray Initiative depended heavily on investment in infrastructure to create water savings, and water recovery under the Murray-Darling Basin Plan has also focused the largest part of government investment in this option, with A$5.8 billion going towards water efficiency savings. However, large-scale water efficiency investments take a long time to generate water savings, and typically cost much more than the market price of water.[91]

Lastly, water can be acquired from existing users; here again, the largest water recovery programmes have been run by governments. In 2005 the Living Murray Initiative ran a small pilot programme, demonstrating how water could be obtained using the market. Also in 2005, New South Wales's RiverBank set aside almost A$150 million to acquire and manage water access licences for the environment. This was followed by substantial investments made by Water For Rivers, a joint venture of the federal, New South Wales, and Victoria governments in recovering water for the Snowy and Murray Rivers.[92] Finally, in 2010, the federal government committed A$3.2 billion to buying permanent water access entitlements from existing irrigators. This water was ultimately transferred to the CEWH, and the process of acquiring the water was conducted by the Commonwealth Department of Environment in a series of tenders. The involvement of the department was an attempt to separate the management (by the CEWH) from the purchase, but is likely to have been in vain: the sellers knew that the CEWH was the person ending up with the water, and that they were offering their water only to the CEWH as part of the tender.

Non-government EWMs have also successfully established processes for water recovery via transfer of water rights. One of the best-known examples in south-eastern Australia is the work of HRA (formerly the Waterfind Environment Fund), which pioneered the legal capacity to donate water access entitlements and water allocations to the environment as a tax-deductible donation.

The legal form and legal personality of the EWM are critically important during the third phase of water recovery, where the water is formally transferred to the EWM. Australia's water laws enable legal persons to hold water access entitlements and water allocations, and the EWMs depend on their legal personhood to hold water rights for the aquatic environment.

The operation of the EWMs (and government agencies) in recovering water for the environment had two significant effects on water law frameworks. First, the smaller water recovery programmes (such as RiverBank, the Living Murray, and the donation-driven activities of the NGOs) demonstrated the capacity to use the market to recover water for the environment, and that significantly more investment would be required to acquire enough water to achieve the desired environmental outcomes. This led to the new Commonwealth Water Act 2007 and the massive federal government water recovery programme across the MDB, which in turn caused many of the smaller water recovery programmes to cease operation to avoid competing with the federal government water purchase programme. As a South Australian NGO staff member stated, 'we're generally of the view that the role of water trusts is no longer to acquire water'.[93]

Second, the early water recovery programmes included different types of environmental water. Some of this was planned environmental water (without a clear legal right attached to it), and even when this water was held environmental water, it was sometimes of a different reliability to the water rights held by irrigators. During the Millennium Drought (2006–2010), water scarcity was so severe across south-eastern Australia that water for the environment was sometimes reallocated to other uses, to meet critical human needs or support industry. Much of this occurred prior to the establishment of the government EWMs, but it was quickly learned that water rights with the same legal attributes as the rights of irrigators were much less vulnerable to reallocation, as a rule, than water rights that were distinctly different to the rights of irrigators. In response, water recovery activities began to focus on held environmental water, with rights that were identical to those of irrigators, largely by acquiring them from irrigators. The CEWH often referred to itself as 'the largest irrigator in the Murray-Darling system'.[94] As a staff member from the Commonwealth

Environmental Water Office remarked, the CEWH is now 'someone who pays the same fees and charges as anyone else ... just another user'.[95]

The VEWH was created in direct response to the political challenges of holding environmental water during droughts, and a staff member commented: 'Having [the] VEWH established as water holder with same rights and same obligations has given [the] environment a legitimacy that will be very useful in the next drought.'[96]

While the overall position of the EWM organisations seems to be one of aligning themselves with the irrigators as just another user, not everyone is convinced of the wisdom of this approach. Both Commonwealth Environmental Water Office staff interviewed expressed this ambivalence:

> I do wonder: do we really want to be just another user? Do we really want to be like everyone else? What's happened to date has been really positive, but is there a limit to this?[97]

> We say we want to be treated as any other irrigator, the irrigators say the same thing, but we also want to evolve the rules to a more flexible environment to suit us, and this flexibility should also be available to irrigators ... But they certainly have views about what we should and shouldn't be doing. On some things they want us to be the same, on others (e.g. carry over) they want us to be different.[98]

When it comes to water recovery, the EWMs of south-eastern Australia are trying to maintain a delicate balance between being treated just the same as an irrigator (with the opportunities that creates for security of water rights and participation in water planning discussions), and maintaining the 'special' nature of the environment. Navigating the tension between these two concepts becomes even more challenging for the management of environmental water.

Management of environmental water: the EWM as decision-maker

> The question of water acquisition is no longer a question – it's really been solved. The Feds have more than they know what to do with... Now the question is: who holds it? Who delivers it? Who monitors it?[99]

In south-eastern Australia the EWMs are the decision-makers for how water is used in a given year. This decision occurs within a broader cycle of policy and planning, implementation, monitoring, and evaluation. The EWMs are often engaged in these activities, but the work is generally undertaken by government departments or other agencies, such as catchment management authorities.

The EWMs of south-eastern Australia typically hold water access entitlements, and receive a water allocation under these entitlements. This water allocation is the physical volume of water available, which may be released for use at a particular location, held back for use at a future time, or transferred to another water user (traded). The non-government EWMs generally hold lower volumes of water access entitlements than government EWMs, but more frequently acquire a water allocation from another water user or another EWM. In some cases EWMs also hold water access entitlements to unregulated flow, which does not require release from a dam but may be shepherded carefully downstream to deliver maximum environmental benefits along the way.[100]

The unique, and essential, role of the EWMs of south-eastern Australia in managing environmental water is therefore to act as the decision-maker for environmental water use. As a staff member from the VEWH remarked, 'Holding and managing – means making decisions about use, trade or carry over.'[101] Each year, the EWMs must decide:

- whether and when to use the water, and where it will be used; and/or
- whether, when, and how much water to trade to (or from) another user as part of meeting their objectives, by improving their environmental water portfolio or investing in an alternative mechanism for enhancing the benefits of environmental water; and/or
- whether and how much water to leave in storage, to be available for use in the following year.

The EWM is the key decision-maker, and while they may rely on the actions of others to gather information and implement decisions once made, they are responsible for making the decisions.[102]

The role of the EWM as decision-maker reflects the desire for environmental water management to be transparent, which depends on the capacity to identify and hold the decision-maker to account for the use of environmental water. Staff from the VEWH and CEWH repeatedly emphasised the importance of transparency and accountability in decisions on how to use environmental water:

> [The VEWH was] set up to provide more independent, accountable, and transparent decision-making ... everyone wanted to know it was being managed in an accountable and robust way that was independent from politics.[103]

> Three things: independence, transparency, and accountability ... There is a big onus on us for transparency, to publish decisions and rationale for decisions ... we're focused on ... getting the best we can from the water we've got ... Transparency and accountability are flipsides of the same thing ... it is very much about real-time decision-making.[104]

> The need to make transparent independent decisions outside of government … The need to show the rigour and transparency of achieving environmental objectives based on criteria that are about maximising environmental outcomes.[105]

> To get the best environmental outcome for the whole basin, it's that decision-making role the CEWH was set up to achieve. It was also established to have more independent governance around the holdings themselves.[106]

The legal personality of the EWMs creates the capacity to hold and deal with the water access entitlements and water allocations, but, more fundamentally, also enables them to act as decision-makers. Their decisions can be identified, and they can be held to account: 'if things go wrong, the responsibility for things that go wrong won't lie with others, [it] will lie with us'.[107]

In making decisions on how to use the environmental water available to it each year, each EWM is also seeking to maximise the environmental outcomes it can achieve (Table 4.2). Maximising the environmental outcomes for the volume of water available can sometimes mean selling water on the market to generate funds that can be used to improve the water portfolio by buying water in alternative locations (or of differing reliability). Both the CEWH and the VEWH have sold water that they have determined as being in excess of their requirements, and early EWMs such as RiverBank were founded with the explicit intent to sell water to help cover the costs of managing environmental water.

The capacity of the EWM to trade its water creates a direct link between the water recovery and management activities.[108] Even where the EWM was not established with the intent to recover significant volumes of environmental water (which is the case with the VEWH), the combination of selling water to fund purchases of other water entitlements into the future means that all EWMs act in both water recovery and water management capacities. The capacity to use the market to manage water 'puts the environment in a whole new field to be an active participant in a water market. It must communicate to the public what its objectives and outcomes are, and account for public money.'[109]

In addition to being active participants in the water market, the operation of EWMs as managers of water has embedded them within the water resource management framework as water users. As part of a national workshop in 2013, two environmental water experts identified the resulting shift in the relationship between EWMs, irrigators, and water corporations (including storage operators):

> Environmental water holders within the Murray-Darling Basin have become the largest single owners of water entitlements. That means they are also the biggest customers of (state) water service providers,

> an important shift in the relationship dynamics in the water sector ... No longer is the environment an interested observer through environmental groups and others providing comment from the sidelines. Through environmental water holders, the environment is now sitting around the table, inside the room as a partner in water delivery.[110]

> A frequent call amongst water users is for environmental water deliveries, based on held environmental entitlements, to be treated exactly the same as all other deliveries utilising water entitlements ... the desire on all sides is for the environment to be seen as just another customer. The reality is that the environment is a very large customer with special needs, so the relationship with water corporations will need to be different to address these needs in comparison to a 'standard' consumptive user.[111]

This is evidence of the tensions between the different ways in which the aquatic environment is constructed in law. The aquatic environment is now simultaneously both insider and outsider. As an EWM, the environment is now *inside* the business of water management, and can participate in policy debates and build relationships with other water users and water corporations. Even the framing of the aquatic environment as a 'large customer with special needs' reduces and constrains the aquatic environment within the water resource management framework and is at odds with the broader legal constructions of the aquatic environment, which remain *outside*: an object which is affected by the acts of others, and a socio-ecological concept vulnerable to changing community values.

These tensions are already affecting the operation of the EWMs in environmental water management. For example, the narrow, identifiable construction of the EWM ensures that it can make decisions for which it can then be held to account. But in 2011 a review of the CEWH considered that the nature of the single-person decision-maker isolated the CEWH from the interests of the broader community.[112] In response, the CEWH was formally embedded within a newly created Commonwealth Environmental Water Office. In 2018 these tensions came to the fore when a letter from the Commonwealth Environmental Water Office was leaked to the media, in which the CEWH expressed concern that:

> the Authority was withholding detailed information from [the CEWH] on the ground that he was an irrigator, like commercial irrigators, a practice [the CEWH] said was 'simply unacceptable, particularly in the interests of public accountability and transparency'.[113]

Despite their eager adoption of the narrative that the CEWH operates just like another irrigator, the CEWH now realises the severe limitations imposed by that narrative.

The VEWH has been likewise affected by these tensions, albeit in a different manner. The early years of the VEWH were focused on using environmental water for ecological benefits, but this narrow focus was not necessarily aligned with the socio-ecological concept of the environment in the communities of Victoria. During the period 2011–2013, locals from the Stawell area in western Victoria believed that the aquatic environment should include recreational values, and argued that environmental water should be used to maintain the lake levels to enable boating and other recreational activities. The community (via the newly formed Lake Lonsdale Action Group) met with the Victorian Ministers for Water and Environment in an attempt to convince the ministers to change the legislation and direct the VEWH on how to use its water. While this was ultimately unsuccessful, and a short-term victory in demonstrating the robustness of the newly created institution of the VEWH, it revealed a long-term problem by showing how the inconsistent constructions of the aquatic environment interact to generate conflict, and the vulnerability of all EWMs to changing community values.

Conclusion

This chapter shows how water law constructs the aquatic environment in south-eastern Australia. At the broadest level, the aquatic environment is *recognised as a socio-ecological concept*, which supports a range of socio-ecological and economic uses. The aquatic environment has been *translated into a legal object*, making it visible to the law through the lens of managing the use of water by legal persons. Lastly, the aquatic environment was *personified as a legal subject*, which occurred in two phases. First, and indirectly, the environmental water rights were created, but merely held by a government minister. Although the minister was indeed a legal person, the decisions on water use were often obscured from the law as part of a broader policy position. Second, in response to the political challenges of ministerial management of environmental water, the EWMs were established within water law (or under other legislation), as legal persons with responsibility to hold and manage water for the environment.

Australia's EWMs include a range of public and private organisations that have been accorded legal personality. Their operations include both recovery and management of environmental water, and they are obliged to meet specific objectives for improving aquatic environmental health and function. In undertaking these activities, the EWMs are altering their legal and social context, by changing public perceptions and (indirectly) by altering legislation. This interaction demonstrates the tensions between the different constructions of the aquatic environment in water law, and the challenges of constructing the aquatic environment as a legal person. The EWMs are trying to maintain a delicate balance between retaining their special nature as environmental organisations and framing themselves as just another user of water and participant in the water markets.

Australia's EWMs use their capacity for legal rights and duties primarily as a means to hold and manage water, giving them an entrée to both the water market and policy debates on how to manage water resources (operationally and strategically). In Australia the EWMs have embraced a narrative of being 'just another user' of water, which enables them to participate in water markets and act as a water customer. However, the EWMs of the second case study, in western USA, are much more likely to focus on collaboration with water users. They similarly rely on their legal personality to assist in the acquisition and management of environmental water rights, but continue to emphasise the coexistence of environmental flows and consumptive water use. Chapter 5 explores the EWMs of western USA to see what happens when the aquatic environment is constructed as a legal subject in the context of prior-appropriation water laws.

Notes

1 Benjamin Docker, 'Discussion Paper Topic 1: Structural Issues and the "Big Picture": What Institutional Mechanisms and Legal Status Can and Should We Provide for Environmental Water as a "Partner" in Water Use?' (Paper presented at Mainstreaming Environmental Water Law and Policy Workshop, Melbourne Law School, Centre for Energy, Resources and Environment Law, 2013) http://law.unimelb.edu.au/centres/creel/research/workshops 2.
2 Alex Gardner, Richard Bartlett, and Janice Gray, *Water Resources Law* (LexisNexis Butterworths, 2009).
3 Water Act 2007 (Cth) s 105(3).
4 Jennifer McKay, 'The Legal Frameworks of Australian Water: Progression from Common Law Rights to Sustainable Shares' in Lin Crase (ed.), *Water Policy in Australia: The Impact of Change and Uncertainty* (Resources For the Future, 2008) 44.
5 R. Quentin Grafton et al., 'An Integrated Assessment of Water Markets: A Cross-Country Comparison' (2011) 5(2) *Review of Environmental Economics and Policy* 219.
6 Water Act 1989 (Vic), Water Management Act 2000 (NSW), Water Act 2000 (Qld), Natural Resources Management Act 2004 (SA), Rights in Water and Irrigation Act 1914 (WA), Water Act (NT), and Water Management Act 1999 (Tas).
7 Daniel Connell, *Water Politics in the Murray-Darling Basin* (Federation Press, 2007).
8 COAG, *Communiqué – Water Reform Framework* (Council of Australian Governments, 1994).
9 COAG, *Intergovernmental Agreement on a National Water Initiative* (Council of Australian Governments, 2004).
10 Maureen Papas, 'The Proposed Governance Framework for the Murray-Darling Basin' (2007) 4(2) *Macquarie Journal of International and Comparative Environmental Law* 77, 77.
11 Murray-Darling Basin Authority, *Murray-Darling Basin Plan* (Commonwealth of Australia, 2012).
12 COAG, 'Communiqué 3 July 2008 Intergovernmental Agreement on Murray-Darling Basin Reform' (20 July 2011) www.coag.gov.au/coag_meeting_outcomes/2008-07-03/index.cfm#water.

13 National Water Commission, *Australian Water Markets Report 2011–12* (NWC, 2013).
14 Gardner, Bartlett, and Gray, above n 2.
15 Water Act 1989 (Vic) ss 33E, 33F, 33U, 33AC, 33AL, 64J, 223.
16 Water Management Act 2000 (NSW) s 56; Water Act 2000 (Qld) ss 121, 122, 128, 128A–B; Natural Resources Management Act 2004 (SA) ss 146–158, 164A.
17 Water Act 1989 (Vic) s 51.
18 Murray-Darling Basin Commission, *An Audit of Water Use in the Murray-Darling Basin: June 1995* (Murray-Darling Basin Commission, 1995); Murray-Darling Basin Commission, *Murray-Darling Basin Cap on Diversions Water Year 1997/98: Striking the Balance* (Murray-Darling Basin Commission, 1998).
19 National Water Commission, *Australian Water Markets: Trends and Drivers 2007–08 to 2012–13* (National Water Commission, 2014).
20 ABARES, *Australian Water Markets Report 2015–16* (Department of Agriculture and Water Resources ABARES, 2016).
21 Poh-Ling Tan, 'A Property Framework for Water Markets: The Role of Law' in Jeff Bennett (ed.), *The Evolution of Markets for Water: Theory and Practice in Australia* (Edward Elgar, 2005) 56.
22 Aither, *Water Markets Report: 2016–17 Review and 2017–18 Outlook* (Aither, 2017).
23 Frontier Economics, *The Economic and Social Impacts of Water Trading: Case Studies in the Victorian Murray Valley* (Rural Industries Research and Development Corporation, 2007); National Water Commission, *The Impacts of Water Trading in the Southern Murray-Darling Basin: An Economic, Social and Environmental Assessment* (National Water Commission, 2010).
24 Janice Gray, 'The Legal Framework for Water Trading in the Murray-Darling Basin: An Overwhelming Success?' (2012) 29 *Environmental and Planning Law Journal* 328.
25 A Horne, J Freebairn, and E O'Donnell, 'Establishment of Environmental Water in the Murray-Darling Basin – An Analysis of Two Key Policy Initiatives' (2011) 15(1) *Australian Journal of Water Resources* 7, 9–10.
26 National Water Commission, *Australian Environmental Water Management Report 2010* (National Water Commission, 2010) 8–12.
27 Water Act 1989 (Vic) ss 4A, 4B; Water Management Act 2000 (NSW) s 8; Water Act 2007 (Cth) ss 4, 6.
28 Water Management Act 2000 (NSW) s 8; Water Act 2007 (Cth) s 6.
29 Water Act 1989 (Vic) ss 48A–48PA, 'environmental entitlement'.
30 Water Act 2007 (Cth) s 4, 'held environmental water'.
31 See Water Act 1989 (Vic) s 1, (b), (d), (j), (k); Water Act 2007 (Cth) s 3(c).
32 Heritage Rivers Act 1992 (Vic).
33 Water Act 2007 (Cth) ss 22 (item 6), 23.
34 Erin O'Donnell, 'Australia's Environmental Water Holders: Who Is Managing Our Environmental Water?' (2013) 28(3) *Australian Environment Review* 508.
35 Water Act 1989 (Vic) s 1.
36 Water Act 2000 (Qld) s 11; Natural Resources Management Act 2004 (SA) s 7; Water Management Act 2000 (NSW) s 3.
37 Water Act 2000 (Qld) s 10(2).
38 Water Management Act 2000 (NSW) s 3.
39 Water Management Act 2000 (NSW) s 5.
40 John M Williams and Adam Webster, 'Section 100 and State Water Rights' (2010) 21(284) *Public Law Review* 267.
41 Water Act 2007 (Cth) s 3.
42 Water Act 2007 (Cth) s 4.

43 Water Act 2007 (Cth) s 4.
44 Water Act 2007 (Cth) s 4.
45 Water Act 2007 (Cth) s 3.
46 Water Act 1989 (Vic) ss 22C, 22J, 33J, 40; Water Management Act 2000 (NSW) ss 20, 21, 23; Water Act 2000 (Qld) s 47; Natural Resource Management Act 2004 (SA) s 76.
47 Water Act 1989 (Vic) ss 4A, 4B; Water Management Act 2000 (NSW) s 8; Water Act 2007 (Cth) ss 4, 6.
48 Water Act 2007 (Cth) ss 20, 22, 23.
49 Avril Horne, Erin O'Donnell, and Rebecca Tharme, 'Chapter 17: Mechanisms for Allocating Environmental Water' in Avril Horne et al. (eds), *Water For the Environment: From Policy and Science to Implementation and Management* (Academic Press, 2017) 361–398.
50 Department of Sustainability and Environment (Vic), *Northern Region Sustainable Water Strategy* (State of Victoria, 2009).
51 Water Act 1989 (Vic) ss 4A, 4B.
52 Anita Foerster, 'Victoria's New Environmental Water Reserve: What's in a Name?' (2007) 11(2) *Australasian Journal of Natural Resources Law and Policy* 145.
53 Michael Bennett and Alex Gardner, 'How Do Environmental Conservation Laws Interact With Environmental Aspects of Water Laws?' (2014) 31(3) *Environmental and Planning Law Journal* 3.
54 Environment Protection and Biodiversity Conservation Act 1999 (Cth) ss 43A, 43B, 345(2).
55 Ken Matthews, *Independent Investigation into NSW Water Management and Compliance: Interim Report* (NSW Government, 2017).
56 Murray-Darling Basin Authority, *The Living Murray Story: One of Australia's Largest River Restoration Projects* (Murray-Darling Basin Authority, 2011) 6–11.
57 COAG, *Intergovernmental Agreement on a National Water Initiative* (Council of Australian Governments, 2004) par 35, 43.
58 Murray-Darling Basin Authority, above n 11.
59 Commonwealth of Australia, *Securing Our Water Future* (Australian Government Department of the Environment, Water, Heritage and the Arts, 2010).
60 Department of Sustainability and Environment (Vic), *Victorian Government White Paper: Securing Our Water Future Together* (State of Victoria, 2004) 43; Department of Sustainability and Environment (Vic), *Our Water Our Future: The Next Stage of the Government's Water Plan* (State of Victoria, 2007) 4; NSW Government, *New South Wales RiverBank Business Plan Part A: Program Plan 2006–2011 Buying and Managing Water for the environment (2010 Update)* (Department of Environment, Climate Change and Water, 2010); M A Siebentritt (ed.), *Water Trusts: What Role Can They Play in the Future of Environmental Water Management in Australia? Proceedings of a Workshop Held on 1 December 2011* (Water Trust Alliance and Australian River Restoration Centre, 2012).
61 Victorian Environmental Water Holder, 'Water Holdings' (11 March 2016) www.vewh.vic.gov.au/managing-the-water-holdings.
62 Mike Young, 'Managing Environmental Water' in Jeff Bennett et al. (eds), *Making Decisions About Environmental Water Allocations* (Australian Farm Institute, 2010) 51.
63 Aither, above n 22.
64 Ibid.
65 Water Act 2007 (Cth) s 4.
66 Water Act 1989 (Vic) ss 48A–48PA, 'environmental entitlement'.

67 National Water Commission, *Australian Environmental Water Management: 2012 Review* (Commonwealth of Australia, 2012).
68 Erin O'Donnell, 'Constructing the Aquatic Environment as a Legal Subject: Legal Rights, Market Participation, and the Power of Narrative' (PhD thesis, University of Melbourne, 2017) http://hdl.handle.net/11343/191749.
69 Water Act 2007 (Cth) ss 104–105.
70 Water Act 2007 (Cth) ss 115–116.
71 Water Act 2007 (Cth) ss 18E, 171–176.
72 A Horne and E O'Donnell, 'Decision-Making Roles and Responsibility for Environmental Water in the Murray-Darling Basin' (2014) 18(2) *Australian Journal of Water Resources* 118.
73 State of NSW, *Environmental Water Use in New South Wales: Outcomes 2014–15* (Office of Environment and Heritage NSW, 2015).
74 Interview DEWNR.
75 Water Act 1989 (Vic) ss 33DF, 33DM.
76 Water Act 1989 (Vic) s 33DS.
77 Erin O'Donnell, 'Institutional Reform in Environmental Water Management: The New Victorian Environmental Water Holder' (2012) 22 *Journal of Water Law* 73.
78 Water Act 1989 (Vic) s 48OB.
79 Water Act 1989 (Vic) ss 33DT–DY.
80 Healthy Rivers Australia, 'About Us' (11 March 2013) www.healthyrivers.org.au/about-us.
81 Siebentritt, above n 60, 7.
82 Waterfind Environment Fund, *Annual Report 2007–2008* (Waterfind Environment Fund, 2008).
83 Environmental Water Trust, 'Home' (13 March 2013) http://environmentalwatertrust.org.au/.
84 Water For Nature, 'Welcome to Water For Nature' (13 March 2013) www.waterfornature.org.au/.
85 Murray-Darling Foundation, *Murray-Darling Foundation Annual Report 2011–2012* (Murray-Darling Association, 2012) 5.
86 Murray-Darling Association, *Constitution* (Murray-Darling Association, 2006).
87 Water Act 1989 (Vic) s 48B.
88 South Australia Murray-Darling Basin Natural Resources Management Board, *Draft Water Allocation Plan for the River Murray Prescribed Watercourse* (Government of South Australia, 2014) 17.
89 Interview HRA.
90 Department of Environment (Cth), *Water Recovery Strategy for the Murray-Darling Basin* (Commonwealth of Australia, 2014).
91 Productivity Commission, *Market Mechanisms for Recovering Water in the Murray-Darling Basin (Final Report, March)* (Productivity Commission, 2010).
92 Water For Rivers, 'About Water For Rivers' (12 April 2011) www.waterforrivers.org.au/.
93 Interview HRA.
94 Warwick Long, 'Coalition Split as Commonwealth Environmental Water Holder Stays With Environment Department' *ABC Rural* (23 September 2015) www.abc.net.au/news/2015–09–23/anger-over-environmental-water-holder-split-from-water-departmen/6797094.
95 Interview CEWO 1.
96 Interview VEWH 2.
97 Interview CEWO 1.

98 Interview CEWO 2.
99 Interview HRA.
100 Commonwealth Environmental Water Office, *Framework for Determining Commonwealth Environmental Water Use* (Commonwealth of Australia, 2013) 20–21.
101 Interview VEWH 2.
102 O'Donnell, above n 34.
103 Interview VEWH 2.
104 Interview VEWH 1.
105 Interview VEWH 3.
106 Interview CEWO 1.
107 Interview CEWO 2.
108 A Horne et al., 'Environmental Water Efficiency: Maximizing Benefits and Minimizing Costs of Environmental Water Use and Management' (2018) *Wiley Interdisciplinary Reviews: Water* 5(4) 10.1002/wat2.1285.
109 Interview OEH.
110 Docker, above n 1, 5.
111 Garry Smith, 'Discussion Paper Topic 2: How Can, and How Should, the Environment Fit Within "Mainstream" Water Law and Policy Mechanisms?' (Paper presented at Mainstreaming Environmental Water Law and Policy Workshop, Melbourne Law School, Centre for Energy, Resources and Environment Law, 2013) http://law.unimelb.edu.au/centres/creel/research/workshops 1, 6.
112 House of Representatives Standing Committee on Regional Australia, *Of Drought and Flooding Rains: Inquiry into the Impact of the Guide to the Murray-Darling Basin Plan* (Parliament of the Commonwealth of Australia, 2011).
113 Peter Martin, 'If It's a Crisis for the Environmental Water Holder It's a Crisis for Us', *Sydney Morning Herald* (13 February 2018) www.smh.com.au/politics/federal/if-it-s-a-crisis-for-the-environmental-water-holder-it-s-a-crisis-for-us-20180212-p4z014.html.

5 Partnership as success

The environmental water managers of the western USA

The EWMs of the western USA are part of a larger set of legal reforms to recognise and protect legal rights to water for the environment, and enable the transfer of existing rights to water to instream (environmental) uses. This chapter presents the findings of the second case study, examining how the aquatic environment is constructed in water law and investigating the creation and operation of these EWMs.

The EWMs of the western USA aim to improve the health of aquatic ecosystems by increasing the volume of environmental water. Achieving this aim required not only the construction of the EWM as a legal person, but specific and targeted legal reform to recognise the aquatic environment as a beneficial use of water under prior-appropriation water law frameworks.[1] Under the doctrine of prior appropriation, water must be used for a beneficial purpose (which did not originally include environmental flows) and all available water can be extracted,[2] so some rivers in the western states of the USA had completely dried out: 'After a century and a half of water policy and practice designed to promote water use by cities, farms and mines, most water has been claimed, leaving inadequate water for the West's fish and wildlife.'[3]

As a result, the processes of translation and personification of the aquatic environment within the US water laws are much more closely linked than they are in Australia. The environment was first *translated* as a beneficial use of water, either in its own right or as a proxy for various human uses that depend on environmental function (such as recreational fishing). However, for water to be used for environmental purposes, it had to be appropriated *by someone* to protect the aquatic environment. Recognising the environment as a beneficial use and creating state capacity to appropriate (effectively create) new water rights for the aquatic environment were part of the same set of legal reforms, and in most cases occurred as part of the broader development of environmental law during the 1970s and 1980s.[4]

However, in places where the existing water use had already dried up the stream, these legal reforms were of no help in restoring flows to the environment. Further legal reform was required to enable water rights to be transferred from existing users to *restore* instream flows, and these reforms finally established the aquatic environment as being able to hold water rights of the same value and type as those of any other user.[5] Most of the western states now recognise the aquatic environment as a beneficial use of water, enable water to be appropriated to create new water rights for the aquatic environment, and enable existing senior water rights to be transferred to aquatic environmental organisations to restore instream flows.[6]

The model of using an EWM to acquire environmental water rights from existing users to improve instream flows in the western USA has been in existence since 1994, and there are many EWMs operating at different spatial scales. It is not possible to include all of them in this detailed examination, so this book focuses on the EWMs that are operating under the National Fish and Wildlife Foundation (NFWF) Western Water Program, which includes investment in the Columbia, Colorado, and Rio Grande River Basins and the terminal Desert Lakes.[7] NFWF is an NGO that leverages funding from the federal government by finding private donors to match the federal funds used for environmental water recovery and management. The Columbia and Colorado River Basins have been the focus of significant investment in EWM establishment and water recovery operations for over two decades, while water recovery in the Rio Grande and the terminal Desert Lakes is more ad hoc and often linked to land purchases.[8] As a result, the analysis in this chapter focuses on the EWMs of two major transboundary river basins in the western USA: the Columbia River Basin (Figure 5.1), and the Colorado River Basin (Figure 5.2).

The Columbia River stretches from western Canada down through the states of Washington, Oregon, Idaho, and Montana (with small areas crossing over into Wyoming, Utah, and Nevada). The Columbia Basin has been extensively affected by the construction of multiple dams for flood control and hydropower, as well as extraction for irrigation in the more arid regions.[9] In 2002, as part of a strategy to mitigate the effects of hydropower production on the health of aquatic ecosystems throughout the Columbia Basin, the Bonneville Power Administration partnered with the NFWF to restore environmental flows in the Columbia River Basin.[10] The Columbia Basin Water Transactions Program is the longest running of the NFWF programmes, and provides insight into how the US EWMs operate to improve instream flows using a range of different state water laws. This book makes an original contribution to the existing scholarship on the EWMs of the Columbia Basin, which have been extensively examined as a mechanism for environmental water recovery.[11]

The Colorado River is one of the best-known transboundary river systems in the world, and has been much studied as an example of multi-jurisdictional water management.[12] The river basin extends across Wyoming, Colorado, Utah, Nevada, Arizona, California, and New Mexico

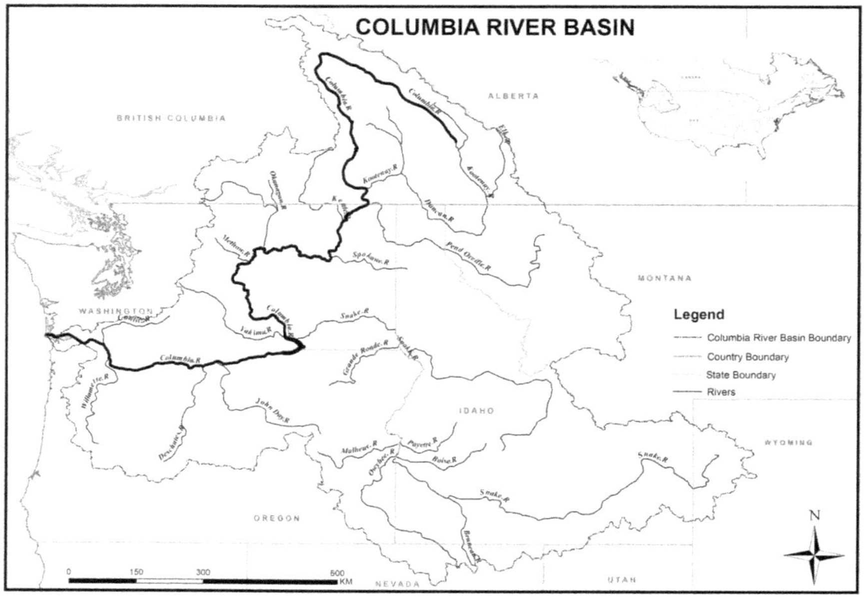

Figure 5.1 Columbia River Basin, USA.

before crossing into Mexico. Several environmental water programmes operate in each of these states. In 2014 a multi-government effort enabled water savings in the northern basin to be used to generate a significant environmental flow event in the Colorado River Delta in Mexico.[13] However, including the entire basin requires discussion of the complex Colorado River Compact (governing water sharing between the US states and Mexico),[14] which is not possible due to space limitations, so this book focuses explicitly on the role of the EWMs.

Including the state of Colorado provides a valuable point of comparison in hydrology, water laws, and environmental water management to the Columbia Basin. Colorado was one of the earliest adopters of a comprehensive instream flows appropriation programme, with the establishment of the Colorado Water Conservation Board in 1973, and continues to provide an interesting example of a judicial rather than permit-based water law administrative system. Colorado is also a jurisdiction in which the government and NGO EWMs have been aligned from the outset to work in partnership.[15] For these reasons, this book focuses on the EWMs of the Colorado River that operate within the state of Colorado.

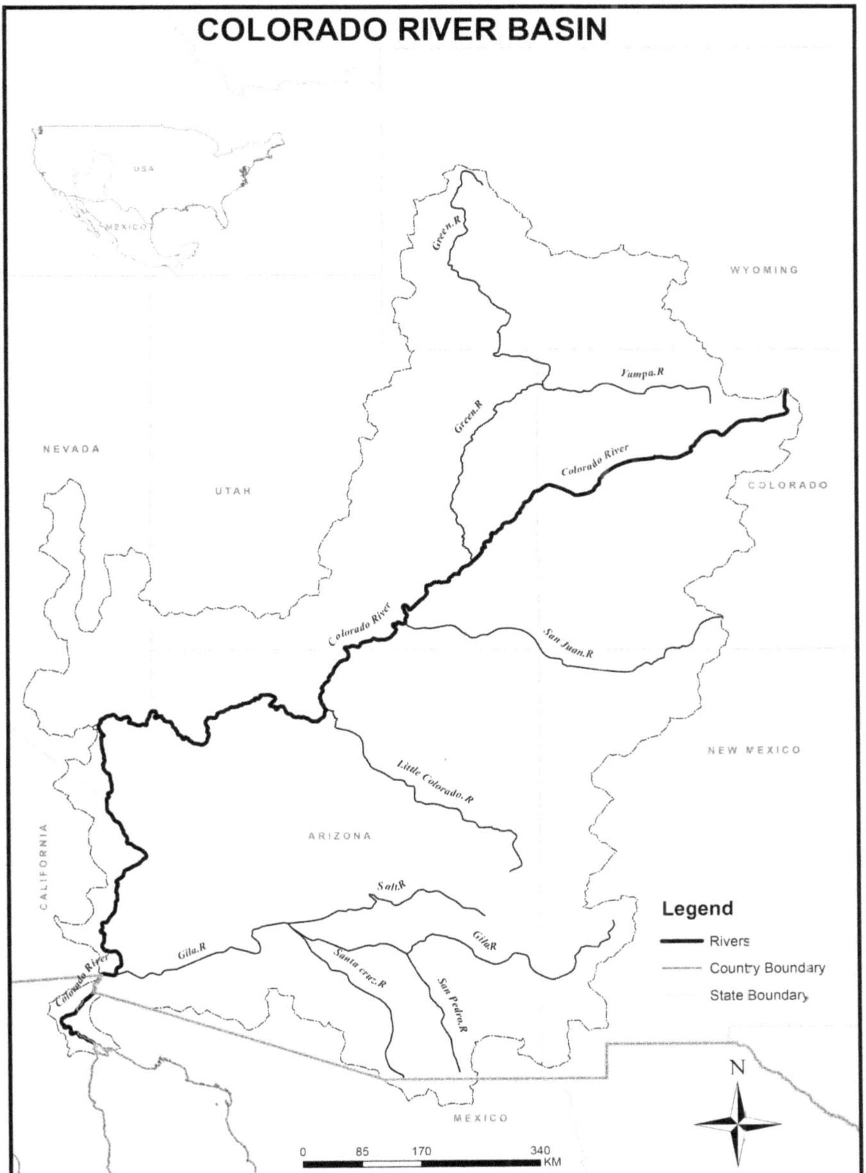

Figure 5.2 Colorado River Basin, USA.

Water law in the western USA

In the western USA each state has its own body of water laws created by a combination of statutory amendments to a common law prior-appropriation framework, and these water laws are all slightly different.[16] The overlay of federal environmental law is also important, as the federal Endangered Species Act (ESA) 1973, for example, has stimulated significant investment in water recovery for the environment and been a catalyst for the creation and operation of some of the EWMs.[17] This section provides an overview of the water law frameworks of the western USA, and examines the way that the aquatic environment is constructed at the intersection of state water law and federal environment law.

Water law in the Columbia River and Colorado

Unlike Australia, where water rights have a strong statutory basis going back over 100 years, water rights in the western USA are based on individual legal rights to water based on initial claims by individuals under the prior-appropriations framework.[18] In addition, water rights in the western USA are legally based on the water that is actually used (i.e. the quantity extracted from the source, less any water returned to the source as drainage); this is significantly different to Australian water rights, which only account for the quantity of water extracted from the source.

In the western USA the water rights are use based and the state retains ownership of the water itself,[19] although the role of the state in regulating the water rights largely consists of administering existing rights.[20] Groundwater rights in the western USA are still poorly defined and monitored, and although there has been recent investment in creating groundwater markets,[21] this has yet to drive major water use reform (or environmental water recovery), so this book focuses on surface water rights.

The Columbia and Colorado River Basins deal with the issue of a cap on water extraction quite differently, reflecting their different hydrology and water law frameworks. In the Columbia River Basin a 'cap' on water use was usually the result of reaching the physical limit of water availability in a particular stream (which means streams run dry in summer).[22] In Washington and Oregon state departments have attempted to cap some basins by placing a moratorium on new appropriations of water,[23] but state legislatures have demonstrated a willingness to overrule these 'caps' to ease development pressures.[24]

In the Colorado River limits on water extraction are set at state and national levels as part of the 1922 Interstate Compact and the 1944 Mexico–United States water treaty.[25] Each state has its own limits on use, and headwater states such as Colorado must pass a certain volume of water downstream. This difference affects the way environmental water is treated in each state, too. As discussed below, when water is recovered for the environment in the western USA, it is typically left in stream and measured as a flow at a particular location. In the Columbia Basin, once these instream flows pass downstream they may be accessed by other users (including the environment) until the Columbia enters the Pacific Ocean. In Colorado, however, increasing instream flows all the way to the state border may result in a net increase of water leaving the state of Colorado. The state of Colorado is unwilling to lose a potentially productive resource, so environmental water recovery in Colorado often results in an improved flow at a specific location, followed by the trade of the aquired water right to another user further downstream. A Colorado Water Trust staff member stated:

> If we acquire water permanently and change it into instream flow, we will as a policy look to see if we can reuse water as a consumptive flow after it meets the instream needs. For example, there might be a seven-mile stretch that is totally dry and we want the water back in it, but at the bottom of this reach, return flows or another tributary comes in and the river is in great shape below this point. If this happens, we may seek to remarket the historical consumptive use to a downstream user ... We try to do a holistic project, with the most uses wrung out of a single drop of water.[26]

Although the precise legal nature of water rights varies from state to state, surface water rights in the states of the Columbia and Colorado Basins have four legal features in common. First, the states apply the prior-appropriation rule: the first person to divert the water has the highest claim to it.[27] This means that the earliest user has the first right to extract their share of the available water, before the next most senior right can take their share, 'no matter what their need'.[28] This is very different to the Australian statutory water law frameworks, where water access licences are grouped into two or three classes of reliability in each basin (Chapter 4). Second, prior appropriation hinges on a diversion for the purposes of a *beneficial use*, which requires that the water is actually used on land and does not reenter the stream (via drainage or groundwater). This, in combination with the variation in stream-flow volumes available in any given year, is often referred to as the difference between 'paper' water (water that has been claimed under prior appropriation) and 'wet' water (water that is physically available and where the legal ownership rights have been established). Typically, the more senior the water right, the more likely it is to be 'wet' water, although in all cases this requires a demonstration that all the water claimed has in fact been used.[29] Third, although prior-appropriation water rights are theoretically tradable, all states require any transfer to comply with the no-injury rule, which means that changes in the location or use of the water must not impact other water users, and must be assessed (by a state administrator or a court) to confirm this.[30]

The confirmation assesses the volume of water that has actually been put to beneficial use, to ensure that any transfer does not remove water that would have made its way to other users. Finally, as part of the beneficial use requirement, many states also enforce a 'use it or lose it' clause: if water is left unused in the river for a certain period, it can be considered as relinquished by the original holder of the right. For example, the state of Washington imposes a five-year relinquishment clause, while Colorado has a ten-year forfeiture period.

In each state water rights are typically grouped into particular time periods, reflecting the evolution of water law from the free-for-all of the original diversions to the better-documented rights granted under the early statutory procedures (typically the late 1800s to the early 1900s) and the most modern (and junior) water rights, often belonging to the environment, and the result of statutory amendments to recognise various instream uses.[31] The evolution of water law in each state means that some water rights are well defined and others reflect a historical usage that may not be clearly stated. The situation has been complicated in many states by two other factors: the federal land reserves, and the recognition that Indian tribes have been using water since before colonisation.[32] In response to a number of high-profile and controversial cases that firmly established the priority of senior rights (and gave short shrift to more recent users),[33] in the 1970s and 1980s most of the western states began formal processes of adjudicating the rights to water based on historical use. These adjudication processes did not overturn the prior-appropriation rule, but created a process to determine formally the legal nature of all water rights in a given basin, including the volume and priority of each right.[34] These adjudication processes are extremely long and costly, and many are still ongoing. Without a complete adjudication, to comply with the no-injury rule a water right holder must be prepared to establish the date of earliest usage and ongoing usage volumes. This becomes critical when seeking to enforce a right to water (for example, if a water right holder believes that another user is taking water to which they have no right) or selling a water right to another user.

Water markets in the western USA

One of the ways that an EWM can obtain senior water rights is to purchase them from another user. Unlike Australia, where water markets are highly active and relatively straightforward for the environment to access, water markets in the western USA are more fragmented, with fewer buyers and sellers, and individual transactions can take a long time, all of which increase transaction costs.[35]

Water trade rules vary from state to state and region to region. At one end of the spectrum the Colorado-Big Thompson water market is considered highly active, handling over 70 per cent of trades in the western

USA from 1987 to 2007.[36] Institutionally, water rights in this location are relatively well defined, trades are facilitated by water brokers, and there are publicly available water prices.[37] Many of the other markets throughout the western USA are relatively thin, with only small numbers of sales and leases in any given year. Brewer et al.'s analysis of the *Water Strategist* data from 1987 to 2005 shows that the total number of transactions (sales, short-term leases, and long-term leases) for Colorado was only 1,707, with only 3,232 transactions in total across the 12 most active state water markets.[38] As a comparison, in 2007–2008 alone Australia recorded over 22,000 trades of water allocation.[39] Although water markets appear to be growing across the western USA, they are still relatively inactive when compared to Australia.

Water markets in the Columbia and Colorado Basins struggle to meet Tan's four market fundamentals: many buyers and sellers; mobile resources; reliable and adequate information; and well-defined, largely homogeneous water rights.[40] Water rights in both basins generally suffer from poor definition, both legally and practically. As discussed above, all water rights must be defined based on actual consumption, not merely water diverted, and in the absence of a completed adjudication process any proposed transfer requires an assessment to determine the volume that has been actually consumed. This assessment can be expensive and time-consuming, adding cost and delay to water transfers. To overcome this, some states employ a streamlined approvals process for short-term (one year or less) transfers by ensuring that at the end of the lease period the water right reverts to its original owner. However, longer-term transfers are still frustrated by this process.

The requirement to undertake an assessment of historical use also exposes potential traders to the possibility of forfeiture: the assessment may well determine that they have not in fact used their full water entitlement during the forfeiture period. Even commencing a potential trade can come with substantial risk, particularly in locations where water rights have not been through the complete adjudication of historical use. This cost, delay, and risk of forfeiture combine to reduce the potential sellers in the market, and mean that water rights are difficult to transfer between locations and uses.

Under prior appropriation each water right is defined at a point in time, and further by the relative seniority in a particular location: the right to water is defined by the dates of other users, so even knowing the specific date of a water right is not enough on its own to know whether it is a senior right or not. Water rights in the Columbia Basin are particularly heterogeneous, defined by a range of dates and locations of use, making it difficult to identify a market price for water. In the Colorado the situation is better in some reaches (especially the Colorado-Big Thompson, where water rights are much more homogeneous),[41] but still challenging in the upper reaches of the Colorado River and its tributaries.

Finally, there is often difficulty in finding information on water prices and potential buyers and sellers, and there is no single location where details of trades are routinely updated.[42] This difficulty reduces the number of potential buyers by creating uncertainty in the market price of water. In response, individual states such as Washington have created water banks and water marketplaces to help facilitate water markets, and this situation is continuing to improve slowly.

Constructing the aquatic environment in western USA water law

In the western USA the environment's need for water has, in general, been poorly articulated in law until relatively recently.[43] The capacity to allocate water to the aquatic environment has been limited by a historical refusal to acknowledge the aquatic environment as a 'beneficial use' of water, and the prior-appropriation doctrine, which gives priority to the earliest users of water. The combined effect of these two legal rules effectively excluded the environment from the water law framework, and overcoming this hurdle required substantial legal reform.

In both the Columbia and the Colorado Basins environmental water is referred to as 'instream flows', reflecting the nature of the beneficial use *in stream* (rather than being extracted for use on land). Various statutes distinguish between minimum flows, instream flows, and lake levels as mechanisms for setting aside water for environmental purposes, and may treat instream flows as slightly different legal rights to water rights held for consumptive purposes.

Recognising the aquatic environment as a beneficial use

Prior-appropriation water laws in the western USA reflect a frontier mentality and support the extraction and use of water to generate economic return, so the first to claim and use water had the best right to it.[44] Leaving water in the river was historically viewed as a waste of a valuable resource, and it wasn't until rivers began running dry and fish populations began to collapse that there was any real change in attitudes.[45]

In changing the state laws to enable instream flows, the states had to *recognise* the environment as a 'beneficial use' of water (without requiring extraction from the river), which required legislation. The states could then create rights for the environment within the prior-appropriation framework. Oregon was the first state to establish an instream flows protection programme in 1955, followed by Washington in 1967. As the environmental movement grew during the 1970s and 1980s, most of the remaining western states enacted instream flows legislation.

Each state defines instream flows slightly differently, and the recognised purposes for appropriating an instream flow are also highly variable. This affects how much water can be allocated to the environment, as the water appropriated for environmental uses must be reasonable under the purpose(s) identified in the legislation. Common purposes for instream flow protection include maintaining water quality and protection of fish and other aquatic species, often to support recreational uses such as angling (see Table 5.1).

State laws also distinguish between using instream flows to *maintain* or *improve* environmental condition (Table 5.1). A maintenance goal effectively limits the appropriation of instream flows to that required to maintain the current state of the aquatic ecosystem. In highly degraded rivers, limiting water recovery in this way prevents the rivers from recovering health and function.

Although water law remains the responsibility of the states, the federal ESA creates an obligation to protect habitats of threatened species, which has been interpreted as creating an additional purpose for instream flows. For example, threatened species affected by the operations of the Bonneville Power Authority helped give rise to the Columbia Basin Water Transactions Program, which aimed to recover sufficient environmental water to protect the habitat of the listed species.

In the states of both the Columbia and the Colorado Basins, the aquatic environment is now recognised in statute as a beneficial use of water. This recognition focuses on the need for healthy aquatic environments to support a range of human uses, and constructs the aquatic environment in water law as a socio-ecological concept. Although this recognition required specific legal reform, the reform merely framed the environment as a legally acceptable *use* within the water law framework. The essential nature of the water law framework as a mechanism for managing use of a resource remained unchanged.

Translating the aquatic environment: a legal object/subject hybrid

Once instream flows for the environment were legally recognised, each state undertook a process of appropriating water to provide these instream flows. This process effectively translated the environment into a legal object, which placed limits on other water users.

The translation of the environment into a legal object in US water law has occurred in two distinct ways. First, the operation of the ESA created an obligation to protect the habitat of threatened species. Although state water laws do not specifically engage directly with the ESA, it is used by the courts to compel water resource managers to change the way in which they use water.[46] As a result, the ESA can significantly limit existing users' water rights.[47]

Second, this translation has occurred as a practical outcome of the operation of western US water law. Early instream flow protections were created as rules that limited existing users' access to water. However, the water law frameworks of the western states emphasise private *rights* to water, so early rules-based forms of instream flows were later converted ('appropriated') to private water rights for the environment. Appropriation of an instream flow is the creation of a new water right. In a formal sense, the appropriated instream flows, even when they are the most junior (and thus most vulnerable) rights on the system, are still explicit legal rights. These water rights are *formally* identical to those of other water users, with a specific seniority, purpose, and location of 'use'. However, the states generally place limits on the ways in which the instream rights can be appropriated, held, and dealt with that are not placed on consumptive water rights (Table 5.1). For example, there are often limits on who can hold the instream flow right, as well as the purpose for which it can be used.

In addition, due to the delay in recognising the environment, instream flow rights are usually the most junior rights on the system. This means that instream flow appropriations often operate more as a *limit* on further water appropriation, as any water rights appropriated after that point in time can only be met once the instream flow has been provided.

Finally, appropriation of instream flows is often limited to maintenance of aquatic health, a protective function that attempts to place limits on water resource development. As a result, although the appropriated water rights for instream flows are as legible and directly 'visible' to water law as the rights of any other user, in practice the combination of the specific legal limits on their creation and management and their junior nature means that they are intended to operate more like limits on other water users' rights, rendering them more akin to a legal object.

When the distinction between the legal object and legal subject is blurred by the appropriation of legal rights to water for the environment, it is the intent of the legislature and the government agencies responsible for the appropriation that is especially important. In the Columbia Basin and Colorado, the instream flow rights have been appropriated as part of broad government programmes to constrain development of water resources within the bounds of sustainability. The use of the legal water rights themselves reflects the real challenge of trying to protect the environment from within a system of law so focused on regulating the *use* of water resources. The attempt to limit the use of water, and protect the environment, by creating these limited legal rights to water for the environment results in a legal object/subject hybrid.

Recognising the environment as a beneficial use and appropriating instream flow rights were a significant step. However, in overappropriated rivers there may be no water left to appropriate for instream flows, and even when instream flows have been appropriated they are often the most junior water rights, so in dry years rivers may still run dry. To actually *improve* aquatic environmental health, a further legal construction is necessary.

Table 5.1 Constructing the environment in western US water law: recognition, translation, and personification

State	*Recognition: instream flow purpose*	*Translation: appropriation and closing of basins to future appropriation (capping)*	*Personification: acquisition and water banking*
Federal	Federal law does not cover instream flows	Clean Water Act (which creates an obligation to maintain water quality) and Endangered Species Act (which creates an obligation to protect habitat of threatened species) by altering existing water management where necessary	Federal law does not cover instream flows
Montana	Beneficial use includes fish, wildlife, and recreational uses. However, water quality can only be protected through reservation of instream flows, and any acquired instream flows must be for the benefit of the fisheries resource (Mont Code Ann § 85-2)	Instream flows can be created through reserves, and these reserves can be applied for by a range of state agencies, including Fish, Wildlife, and Parks (Mont Code Ann § 85-2)	Any individual or corporation, or the Montana Department of Fish Wildlife and Parks, can temporarily change an appropriation right to 'maintain or enhance instream flow to benefit the fishery resource' (Mont Code Ann § 85-2)
Oregon	Protected uses include 'fish life, wildlife, fish and wildlife habitat', 'water quality standards', and 'recreation and scenic attraction' (Or Rev Stat § 537)	Department of Fish and Wildlife, Department of Environmental Quality, and State Parks and Recreation Department can apply for new instream water rights, which are then are held in trust by Water Resources Department (Or Rev Stat § 537)	'Any person may purchase or lease all or a portion of an existing water right or accept a gift of all or a portion of an existing water right for conversion to an in-stream water right' (Or Rev Stat § 537); once acquired for the purpose of instream flows, these water rights are held in trust by Water Resources Department

continued

Table 5.1 Continued

State	*Recognition: instream flow purpose*	*Translation: appropriation and closing of basins to future appropriation (capping)*	*Personification: acquisition and water banking*
Washington	'The department of ecology may establish minimum water flows or levels … for the purposes of protecting fish, game, birds or other wildlife resources, or recreational or aesthetic values of said public waters … [or] necessary to preserve water quality' (Wash Rev Code § 90.22)	Washington State Department of Ecology can appropriate instream flows via administrative procedures to establish base flows in all perennial streams, which can include closing catchments to future appropriations and imposing minimum flow limits on other users (Wash Rev Code § 90.54)	Individuals can transfer (permanently or temporarily) water rights to the state via the Trust Water Program, which protects the water rights against relinquishment
Idaho	Instream flow is a beneficial use to maintain 'minimum stream flows required for the protection of fish and wildlife habitat, aquatic life, recreation, aesthetic beauty, transportation and navigation values, and water quality' (Idaho Code Ann § 42-1501)	Anyone can petition the Idaho Water Resources Board to file application for an instream flow water right, but only the Idaho Water Resources Board can hold that right (Idaho Code Ann § 42-1504)	Acquisition of existing water rights remains unclear, except in the Lehmi River, where a water bank was created to enable an instream flow appropriation in a fully appropriated river
Colorado	'[R]ecognizing the need to correlate the activities of mankind with some reasonable preservation of the natural environment … [beneficial use includes] minimum stream flows or for natural surface water levels or volumes for natural lakes to preserve the natural environment to a reasonable degree' (Colo Rev Stat § 37-92-102) Instream flows have been appropriated for fisheries, riparian habitat, and other aquatic organisms	Colorado Water Conservation Board may appropriate such waters as needed to meet the minimum instream flow needs to maintain the aquatic environment No other person may appropriate instream flows (Colo Rev Stat § 37-92-102)	Colorado Water Conservation Board may receive acquisitions for the purpose of conversion to instream flows to improve the aquatic environment; no other person may convert existing rights to instream flows

Personification of the aquatic environment: acquisition of water rights

To improve environmental condition and keep rivers flowing, the aquatic environment needed access to the senior water rights in the river. There are two ways this could happen: by reducing existing appropriations of water to recognise a new 'senior' instream water right (a controversial and deeply unpopular option),[48] or by purchasing such water rights from existing users. In the Columbia and Colorado Basins the environment needed a water market, and in many cases providing environmental water was a key driver in the creation of such markets.[49]

Senior water rights acquired from existing users retain their legal features (most importantly, their original prior-appropriation date), and are both formally and practically identical to other users' rights to water. These senior water rights mean instream flows can have the same set of legal rights as any other water user. However, obtaining senior water rights requires the further construction of an entity with the legal power to acquire existing water rights.

State water laws explicitly enable the acquisition of instream flows under particular conditions, which include limits on who can hold such rights once they have been formally converted to an instream flow (Table 5.1).[50] For example, in Colorado only the Colorado Water Conservation Board (CWCB) may legally hold the instream flow rights. To acquire the water rights the CWCB works in partnership with a private organisation, the Colorado Water Trust (CWT). The CWT identifies potential water rights that may be available for sale and completes the commercial transaction before donating the water rights to the CWCB for official conversion to instream flows. In Montana, on the other hand, the rules of ownership are more relaxed: the state agency or private organisations may hold the instream flow rights, but these rights are only available for a limited-term lease (up to 20 years). In Washington the state government has provided another alternative: individual users' water rights may be 'banked' with the state agency (Department of Ecology), which protects them from relinquishment and can also enable them to be used as instream flows. The Department of Ecology works closely with the Washington Water Trust, which may acquire a right from an existing user before banking that right with the department. In all cases throughout the Columbia and Colorado Basins, state agencies work closely with private organisations and individuals to obtain senior water rights through voluntary transactions (sale or donation) for the purposes of instream flows. This process is not easy, and shepherding potential sellers through the transaction process while maintaining goodwill towards environmental water recovery forms a large part of the work of the EWMs in these basins.

In summary, the states have *recognised* the aquatic environment as a beneficial use (a socio-ecological concept), and *translated* the environment into a legal object via setting limits on others' use, including the appropriation of new junior water rights that act as a cap on future water allocations (although this formally creates a legal object/subject hybrid). The aquatic environment is personified by establishing the EWMs to acquire existing senior water rights through purchase, donation, or water savings (Table 5.1).

The environmental water managers of the western USA

The EWMs are identifiable organisations with legal personality, and have the objective to improve the health of aquatic ecosystems by increasing instream flow rights (Chapter 3).

Legal form: how are the EWMs constructed in law?

There are two organisational forms of EWMs in the USA (see Table 5.2). First, in the Columbia and Colorado Basins each state government has an organisation legally recognised as responsible for holding instream flows. Second, NGOs work in partnership with the state agencies to acquire (and occasionally hold) instream flows. Both the state agencies and the NGOs often have a range of objectives beyond just water recovery for the environment, and their capacity to be sufficiently identifiable as an EWM is not always straightforward.

Government EWMs have statutory responsibility for appropriating instream flows, and they have specific legal personhood powers to enable them to hold the water rights (Table 5.2). Government EWMs are typically large organisations with multiple policy objectives and responsibilities. However, these EWMs retain sufficient identifiability by virtue of their explicit statutory responsibilities for holding the instream flow rights and the nature of instream flow rights as legal rights to water. Each government EWM can be identified within the government department, and websites typically provide contact details for the person responsible for the programme. As a result, they can be held accountable by the public for both the quantity of instream flow rights in a particular river system (within the limits prescribed by the legislation) and the enforcement of those instream flow rights. However, the government EWMs often have a range of water resource management responsibilities, which can cloud the issue when it comes to both acquisition and enforcement of water rights more broadly.[51]

For example, Washington's Department of Ecology includes the Trust Water Program, a public trust to hold the water for beneficial use, ensuring that the water can remain instream without being relinquished for non-use.[52] In Colorado and Idaho the instream flow rights are held by water boards, which have clear organisational identities but a multitude of objectives (see Table 5.3).

Table 5.2 Environmental water managers of the Columbia Basin and the state of Colorado

EWM	*Geographical extent of activities*	*Organisation type*	*Source of legal personhood rights and duties*	*Source of water holding and management capacities*	*Accountability: to whom does this organisation report?*
Clark Fork Coalition	Clark Fork River, Montana	Internal Revenue Code 501(c)(3) non-profit corporation with 15-person board	Mont Code Ann § 35-2 (non-profit corporation)	Articles of incorporation; Montana Water Use Act, Mont Code Ann § 85-2 (1973)	Members Donors Partners US Internal Revenue Service Montana secretary of state
Trout Unlimited MT Water Project	Montana	Internal Revenue Code 501(c)(3) non-profit corporation established under national organisation Trout Unlimited	Mont Code Ann § 35-2 (non-profit corporation)	Articles of incorporation; Montana Water Use Act, Mont Code Ann § 85-2 (1973)	Local chapters and members Donors Trout Unlimited (national) Partners US Internal Revenue Service Montana Secretary of State

continued

Table 5.2 Continued

EWM	*Geographical extent of activities*	*Organisation type*	*Source of legal personhood rights and duties*	*Source of water holding and management capacities*	*Accountability: to whom does this organisation report?*
Montana Fish, Wildlife, and Parks Department (FWP)	Montana	State government department	Personhood under Montana Water Use Act limited to capacity to acquire water rights for instream flows	Montana Water Use Act, Mont Code Ann § 85-2 (1973); FWP is explicitly identified as a recipient of instream flows	Department of Natural Resources and Conservation Montana citizens Fish and Wildlife Commission Governor of Montana
Deschutes River Conservancy	Deschutes River Basin, Oregon	Internal Revenue Code 501(c)(3) non-profit corporation with 29-member board	Or Rev Stat § 65 (non-profit corporation)	Only Oregon Water Resources Department can hold instream flow water rights: Or Rev Stat § 537.332 (2013)	Donors Partners US Internal Revenue Service Oregon Secretary of State
Freshwater Trust	Oregon	Internal Revenue Code 501(c)(3), non-profit corporation with 24-member board	Or Rev Stat § 65 (non-profit corporation)	Only Oregon Water Resources Department can hold instream flow water rights: Or Rev Stat § 537.332 (2013)	Donors Partners US Internal Revenue Service Oregon Secretary of State

Oregon Water Resources Department	Oregon	State government department	Personhood for purposes of water rights limited to capacity to acquire water rights for instream flows	Can hold instream flow water rights: Or Rev Stat § 537.332 (2013)	Oregon citizens Water Resources Commission Governor of Oregon
Walla Walla Watershed Management Partnership	Walla Walla Basin (Water Resource Inventory Area 32), Washington State	Local public agency governed by nine-member board	Personhood limited by legislation: Wash Rev Code § 90.92.050	Wash Rev Code § 90.42 Pilot Local Water Management Program (2014) Wash Rev Code § 90.92	Funders Local community Washington Department of Ecology Washington state legislature
Washington Council of Trout Unlimited	Washington State	Internal Revenue Code 501(c)(3) non-profit corporation (an affiliate of national Trout Unlimited)	Wash Rev Code § 24.03 (non-profit corporation)	Water Resource Management, Wash Rev Code § 90.42 (2014)	Local chapters and members Donors Trout Unlimited (national) Partners US Internal Revenue Service Washington Secretary of State

continued

Table 5.2 Continued

EWM	*Geographical extent of activities*	*Organisation type*	*Source of legal personhood rights and duties*	*Source of water holding and management capacities*	*Accountability: to whom does this organisation report?*
Washington Water Trust	Washington State	Internal Revenue Code 501(c)(3) non-profit corporation with nine-member board	Wash Rev Code § 24.03 (non-profit corporation)	Water Resource Management, Wash Rev Code § 90.42 (2014)	Donors Partners US Internal Revenue Service Washington Secretary of State Washington Department of Ecology
Washington Department of Ecology	Washington State	State government department	Personhood under Washington Water Resource Management Act limited to establishment of Trust Water Program	Water rights transferred to instream flow via Trust Water Program Wash Rev Code § 90.42 (2014)	Washington citizens Office of Financial Management Governor of Washington
Idaho Water Resource Board	Idaho	State government agency	Limited personhood as set out in Idaho Code Ann § 42.1732-34 (2014)	Right to acquire water rights as set out in Idaho Code Ann § 42.1734 (2014)	Idaho citizens Funders Governor of Idaho

Colorado Water Trust (CWT)	Colorado	Internal Revenue Code 501(c)(3) non-profit corporation with 13-member board	Colo Rev Stat §7.121-137 (non-profit corporation)	As a private person, CWT can acquire water rights via change of water right process: Colo Rev Stat § 37-92-103(5) CWT cannot hold instream flow rights: Colo Rev Stat § 37-92-102(3) (2015)	Donors Partners Colorado Water Conservation Board US Internal Revenue Service Colorado Secretary of State Colorado Department of Revenue
Colorado Water Conservation Board (CWCB)	Colorado	State water resource agency with 15-member board	Limited personhood as a function of state agency: Colo Rev Stat § 37-60 (2015)	Only CWCB can hold instream flow rights: Colo Rev Stat § 37-60-123(7), 37-92-102(3) (2015)	Colorado citizens Funders Department of Natural Resources, Division of Water Resources Governor of Colorado

Table 5.3 Objectives of the environmental water managers of the Columbia Basin and the state of Colorado

EWM	*Objectives*
Clark Fork Coalition	Mission: 'The Clark Fork Coalition is dedicated to protecting and restoring the Clark Fork River basin.' Vision: 'The Clark Fork Coalition envisions a future when the Clark Fork River system flows with clean, cold, and abundant waters that ensure the people, fish, and wildlife of the region flourish for generations to come...' Strategies: 'Protect clean water strongholds, past gains, and ongoing restoration investments; restore resiliency and improve the vital signs of our waterways; engage and inspire people to care for the waters that provide for us all; and sustain the momentum and increase the Coalition's capacity to achieve the vision.' Source: Clark Fork Coalition, *Strategic Plan 2013–2017* (Clark Fork Coalition, 2013) 3, 7.
Trout Unlimited MT Water Project	Mission: 'To conserve, protect, and restore Montana's world-class coldwater fisheries and their watersheds.' Source: Montana Trout Unlimited, 'Projects' (2016) http://montanatu.org/projects/
Montana Fish, Wildlife, and Parks Department (FWP)	Mission: to provide 'for the stewardship of the fish, wildlife, parks, and recreational resources of Montana, while contributing to the quality of life for present and future generations'; to do this, the FWP Fisheries Division 'preserves, maintains, and enhances aquatic species and their ecosystems to meet the public's demand for recreational opportunities and stewardship of aquatic wildlife'. FWP's Instream Flow Protection aims to 'physically and legally protect, restore, and manage the instream flows required to sustain Montana's aquatic species, their habitats, and related ecosystems with focus on the increasing competition for the water resources, limited supplies and changing hydrologic conditions'. Source: Montana Fish, Wildlife, and Parks, *Montana Statewide Fisheries Management Plan 2013–2018* (Montana Fish, Wildlife, and Parks, 2013) 7, 63.
Deschutes River Conservancy	Mission: 'To restore streamflow and improve water quality in the Deschutes Basin.' Source: Deschutes River Conservancy, 'Mission' www.deschutesriver.org/about-us/mission.
Freshwater Trust	The Freshwater Trust 'protects and restores freshwater ecosystems... [u]sing science, technology and incentive-based solutions'. Source: Freshwater Trust, 'About Us' (2015) www.thefreshwatertrust.org/about-us/.

Table 5.3 Contnued

EWM	*Objectives*
Oregon Water Resources Department	Mission: 'To serve the public by practicing and promoting responsible water management through two key goals: to directly address Oregon's water supply needs, and to restore and protect streamflows and watersheds in order to ensure the long-term sustainability of Oregon's ecosystems, economy, and quality of life.' Source: Oregon Water Resources Department, 'About Us' www.oregon.gov/owrd/Pages/about_us.aspx.
Walla Walla Watershed Management Partnership	Vision for the Walla Walla Basin: 'A place where water is managed locally to achieve and sustain a healthy river system where human and natural communities thrive and flourish now and in the future.' Source: Walla Walla Watershed Management Partnership, *Strategic Plan Update 2012–2015* (Walla Walla Watershed Management Partnership, 2012) 2.
Trout Unlimited Washington Water Project	Mission: 'To conserve, protect and restore cold water fisheries, their watersheds, and ecosystems as a means of maintaining our quality of life.' Source: Washington Council of Trout Unlimited, 'Home' (3 February 2016) www.troutunlimitedwashington.org/index.html.
Washington Water Trust	Washington Water Trust is 'a neutral, nonregulatory nonprofit, dedicated to improving and protecting stream flows and water quality throughout Washington state'. Source: Washington Water Trust, 'About Us' (2016) www.washingtonwatertrust.org/about-us.
Washington Department of Ecology	Mission: 'To protect, preserve and enhance Washington's land, air and water for current and future generations.' Source: Department of Ecology, State of Washington, 'About Us' www.ecy.wa.gov/about.html.
	Mission of the water resources programme: 'To manage water resources to meet the current and future needs of the natural environment and Washington's communities.' Source: Department of Ecology, State of Washington, 'Ecology Programs' www.ecy.wa.gov/programs.html.
	The Department of Ecology is 'committed to meeting current water needs and ensuring future water availability for people, fish and the natural environment'. Source: Department of Ecology, State of Washington, 'Water Resources Program' www.ecy.wa.gov/programs/wr/wrhome.html.

continued

Table 5.3 Contnued

EWM	*Objectives*
Idaho Water Resource Board	Objective: 'The conservation, development, management, and optimum use of all unappropriated water resources and waterways of this state in the public interest' (Idaho Code Ann § 42-1734A). Source: Idaho Water Resource Board, *Idaho State Water Plan* (Idaho Water Resource Board, 2012) 6.
Colorado Water Trust	Mission: 'To restore and protect streamflows in Colorado to sustain healthy aquatic ecosystems' by engaging in and supporting voluntary efforts and market-based transactions. Source: Colorado Water Trust, 'About Us' (2016) www.coloradowatertrust.org/about-us.
Colorado Water Conservation Board	Mission: 'To conserve, develop, protect and manage Colorado's water for present and future generations.' Source: Colorado Water Conservation Board, 'About the CWCB' http://cwcb.state.co.us/about-us/about-the-cwcb/Pages/main.aspx. Goal of the Instream Flow Program: 'To preserve and improve the natural environment to a reasonable degree' by appropriating, acquiring, protecting, and monitoring instream flow and lake-level water rights. Source: Colorado Water Conservation Board, 'Instream Flow Program' http://cwcb.state.co.us/environment/instream-flow-program/Pages/main.aspx.

The NGO EWMs are much more active in water rights acquisition and management, even though in many cases they may not continue to hold the formal title to a water right after it has been converted to instream use. The NGO EWMs are often referred to as the *retail arm* of the government EWMs, and when water rights are acquired it is most often a result of an NGO EWM working with the irrigator to identify a win-win solution (e.g. water savings, shorter irrigation seasons, or shifting diversion points downstream).[53] NGO EWMs may also be involved in making sure the instream flows are enforced by the state government. The NGO EWMs are clearly identifiable legal persons, and take the form of not-for-profit corporations with Internal Revenue Code 501(c)(3) status as charitable organisations. This status limits their ability to advocate for instream flows, and although they contribute to legal reform when required, this is not their primary role.

In each state of the Columbia Basin (except Idaho), private and public EWMs work in partnership to protect and restore instream flows (Table 5.2). In Colorado this partnership is especially close. The CWT works hand in hand with the CWCB's Instream Flow Protection Program to recover water for the environment:

> We run a simultaneous process with Linda [head of Instream Flow Program at CWCB] and let her know – where it can be used, how much, the stream miles, what is health of the water right – and make sure she's interested in acquiring the water right ... Our most critical key partner is Linda and her team.[54]

> The Colorado Water Trust is a close partner with us on acquisitions of water. They bring us water to acquire for instream flow use ... The advantage of the Colorado Water Trust is that they have a team; it takes us a lot longer to investigate water rights. The Colorado Water Trust is helpful for us and the water user because [it is] faster.[55]

The EWMs of both the Columbia Basin and Colorado (Table 5.2) use a range of state legal frameworks to establish themselves as identifiable organisations with the required legal powers to hold and manage water rights for instream flows.

Each state in the Columbia Basin, and the state of Colorado, has a combination of government and non-government EWMs (except Idaho). These organisations work very closely together to protect and restore instream flows, and these working relationships have been further enhanced by the NFWF Western Water Program.

It is the operation of the EWMs that really highlights the emerging tension between the multiple constructions of the aquatic environment in water law.

Operation of the EWMs: appropriation and acquisition

The EWMs of the Columbia Basin and the state of Colorado focus on both protection and restoration of instream flows. Government EWMs are responsible for appropriation of new water rights for the environment, which enables them largely to avoid two significant challenges: the financial cost of acquiring water rights, and the controversy of potentially reducing water availability for other users.

NGO EWMs, however, focus on restoration of instream flows by acquiring water rights. They depend on convincing potential funders that they can improve the existing environmental condition, so they target locations where the return of instream flows will generate a significant ecological response. However, they can struggle to complete acquisitions, because the NGO EWMs in the western USA aim for water transactions that result in wins for the environment, the irrigators, *and* the broader community (unlike Australia, where individual water purchase decisions are made based on a price acceptable to only the EWM and the individual irrigator).[56] Requiring each transaction to be acceptable to all three groups necessarily slows down transactions, as the EWMs must work with irrigators to find ways to increase instream flows without shutting down irrigation.

The strong partnership that has evolved between government and NGO EWMs in each state reflects the limitations on who can hold instream flow rights. This partnership has been enhanced by the ability of NGO EWMs to obtain funding and work closely with potential sellers (or leasers) of water rights.

All EWMs are vulnerable to changing community values of instream flows, and depend on the continued desire to maintain and improve instream flows for the aquatic environment. The objectives of the EWMs in the western USA are broader than those of the EWMs in Australia, and seek explicitly to connect the health of the aquatic environment to better outcomes for people (Table 5.3). Many of the NGO EWMs explicitly reject a 'pure' environmental focus, as a staff member from Trout Unlimited Montana explained:

> [The] majority [of members] are strong fly fishermen. So it's basically identified as a fishing organisation that does conservation work, which is a much better vehicle than a self-identified environmental group.[57]

The breadth of objectives in Table 5.3 highlights the difficulty of constructing the aquatic environment in law as an entity that is important for its own sake, and demonstrates the ongoing importance of human value for healthy, functioning aquatic ecosystems.

The multiple objectives of the EWMs of the western USA (Table 5.3) demonstrate the challenge of combining legal personhood, which is a narrow, powerful legal construct of the environment, with the broader and legally weaker constructs of the socio-ecological concept and legal object (Chapter 2). The objectives of many of the EWMs emphasise the socio-ecological aims of the EWM: protecting the aquatic environment to support human activities, such as fishing. Government EWMs also embed their streamflow protection activities as part of a broader programme of balanced water resource management, reflecting the nature of newly appropriated instream flows to act more as a limit on others' activities than as a clear legal right.

However, the way the staff of the EWMs describe their activities presents a much clearer vision of the EWMs: 'Our mission is really to make sure water goes instream'[58] and 'The water acquisition program was started as a tool to provide for protecting the environment.'[59]

The next sections describe how the EWMs undertake the two major activities to provide instream flows: appropriation of new water rights and acquisition of existing water rights.

Appropriation of instream flows: protection

> The primary tool for protecting flow is appropriating new junior water rights.[60]

Government EWMs are responsible for the appropriation of new water rights for instream flows, which forms part of a planning and prioritisation phase. Appropriation of instream flows began in response to the concern that streams were regularly drying out, which was causing significant problems for migratory fish species. Many of these species are now listed under the federal ESA, and in some instances avoiding a federal agency intervention was a significant driver for the establishment of state-based programmes to appropriate new instream flow rights:

> At around 1973 ... environmental consciousness was increasing. There was an issue occurring with big water projects, the federal agencies were starting to impose bypass flows to protect environment, and state water users didn't like that. They wanted more control over water in Colorado, so the instream flow program was created as an alternative to the federally mandated bypass flows. We work with the federal agencies to show that we can meet their goals through the state program, so we can retain state control over stream flows.[61]

This is a challenge that continues to inform state water planning processes today, as a staff member from the Washington Department of Ecology noted: 'We also have ESA responsibilities; 80 per cent of watersheds in the state have listed species.'[62]

State water planning processes include the concept of protecting instream flows as part of broader water resource plans in response to increasing urban demands.[63] Several states have also attempted to close basins to new consumptive appropriations (which has been overruled) or to require any new appropriation for consumptive use to be offset by improving water availability (though water savings or water purchase) elsewhere.

The appropriation programmes of the government EWMs operate in practical terms to construct the environment as a weak legal object, requiring and deserving of protection (Chapter 2). The limits on appropriation programmes are designed to retain this 'weak and deserving' construction of the environment. For example, early instream flow programmes placed legal limits on the appropriation of instream flows to the minimum necessary to preserve the environment, and this remains the case today in Idaho, where despite an instream programme being in place since 1978, only 2 per cent of stream miles in the state are protected under 291 instream flow rights.[64] In Colorado the ability to appropriate instream flows beyond that needed to preserve the environment was only lifted in 2001; and in addition to creating new challenges for the government EWM (the CWCB), this only applies to acquisition rather than appropriation:

> For a new instream flow right, we aim to preserve the natural environment to a reasonable degree; we use quantification techniques to

> establish the base flow. In 2001 the Board was given authority to improve the natural environment, and this has been controversial, we're being asked for more definition on what this actually means, as this requires flows above that basic preservation amount to provide additional useable habitat for fish. This is something more we can do with the acquired water.[65]

The ability to appropriate instream flows lacks the flexibility to respond to changes in water availability under climate change, ecological needs, and social demands for environmental amenity. New appropriations of instream flows, except in almost pristine rivers, are incapable of protecting the full suite of environmental flows required, and often only result in the protection of a minimum flow, which may be sufficient to keep a river running but will not provide the necessary spawning or migration triggers to fish species.[66] This emphasis on protection of existing environmental quality, combined with the lack of flexibility, reduces the legal right created by the appropriation into little more than a legal object that limits the activities of other users. It is easy to focus on the *formal* nature of the newly appropriated water rights as legal rights, and their requirement to be held by a legal person, but in such a stringently use-oriented water law paradigm this construction of the aquatic environment was necessary to give it any place at all.

In the states of the Columbia Basin and Colorado, instream flow appropriations still far outnumber the instream flow rights that have been acquired from existing users.[67] In Colorado the CWCB has appropriated over 1,900 instream flow rights (including 476 lake level protections), and these rights protect over 30 per cent of the state's perennial river miles.[68] These programmes are of long duration and represent a significant commitment to protecting existing environmental condition in many rivers in these states. However, their overall success has been mixed:

> More than 98% of the CWCB's instream flow water right portfolio (by number of water rights) is junior to 1973 ... often making them some of the most junior water rights in the State's prior appropriation system.[69]

As a CWT staff member argued:

> We should be amplifying the ability to move senior water into the instream flow program – this water is climate change durable, voluntary, market based, less regulatory; there is a real desire to see a lot more senior water in the program.[70]

Acquisition of instream flows: restoration

Across the USA, environmental water acquisition is increasing: 'environmental water transactions have gained a prominent role as an important tool in protecting and restoring water-dependent ecosystems'.[71] In the period 1987–2007 over 2,800 transactions delivered over 10 million acre-feet of water to streams, for a price tag of over US$500 million.[72] In the Columbia Basin transactions to improve instream flows grew steadily over the decade from 2003 to 2012.[73] They included permanent purchases, long-term and short-term leases, water conservation projects, and donations (which can be permanent or temporary).

Acquisitions of existing water rights for instream flows solve several key problems: acquisitions give the environment access to senior water rights, enabling flows to be restored as well as protected; acquisitions can be used to increase flexibility, by restoring a particular flow at a particular time; and acquisitions can be undertaken in chronically or periodically dewatered rivers, not just in rivers where water remains for appropriation.

Typically, water markets that enable water transfers between users are only effective when total water use has been capped, so that new demands for water must be met from the existing pool of water rights.[74] However, the water laws of the western USA do not typically set formal caps on water use. In the Columbia Basin and Colorado, the wide range of seniority of rights creates opportunities for EWMs to target the specific rights they need. Senior water right holders have the first call on water in the stream, and during low-flow periods they retain the right to extract their full amount, which can cause the stream to dry out. EWMs therefore focus on these senior water right holders:

> Knowing where you want to work is important and typically, now we do a basin assessment to consider where the rights are, who owns them, who the most senior right holder is, where it [the senior right] is ... We only work with senior water right holders, so we start with the most senior water right holders; if they're at the bottom of the reach and the most senior that's ideal, as the water is there all the way down the reach.[75]

However, although this heterogeneity creates an entry point for targeted environmental water recovery via water transfer, the process remains extraordinarily slow and expensive:

> The transaction cost element is very expensive. It's very different to new appropriations, the process to transfer a water right and the transaction costs are much more significant, there's a lot more work on the front end. And it's not a uniform process, there are messy negotiations...[76]

The acquisition programmes are all relatively recent, as they depend on the legal reforms that recognise the environment as a beneficial use and enable the transfer of existing water rights to instream flows. When EWMs acquire water rights to protect or improve habitat for threatened species (under the federal ESA) or wildlife refuges,[77] these programmes are typically supported by government EWMs. The government agency may partner with an NGO EWM to undertake the actual transaction (even if it ends up as a transfer to a government EWM), by providing funding or other agency support. For example, the Bonneville Power Administration is a federal government agency that provides funding for the Columbia Basin Water Transactions Program, where the water acquisitions are predominantly carried out by NGOs.

There is often a high degree of overlap between the priorities of government and NGO EWMs:

> Used to be 'come one, come all', but now we're overlaying our priorities with conservation initiatives.[78]

> In the Upper Clark Fork, for example, we work with NRDP [the Natural Resource Damage Program] to identify tributaries that are the most important for native fish recovery in the basin. We also work with DFWP [Department of Fish and Wildlife] across the basin to identify high-priority tributaries from a fishery perspective.[79]

> Sometimes motivation for landowners is enforcement driven … that really drives business; water transactions are often ESA driven, as in all the areas we work in there are listed fish.[80]

However, the NGO EWMs retain flexibility to acquire water, and can be more opportunistic when necessary (such as when water is recovered for a wider range of purposes, like angling and duck hunting):

> We don't have a rigid science model, because there are a whole bunch of different factors: for example, maybe you need to get to this dewatered tributary by working on another tributary, because you've got the relationship there first; often there's multiple stages. Often we'll do opportunistic leases, because they help us get where we're trying to go…[81]

In the Columbia Basin and Colorado, only Idaho conducts its instream flow programme without a significant private partner EWM (probably because the instream flow programme in Idaho is almost solely focused on appropriation of new water rights).[82] In all other locations the NGO EWMs work alongside the government EWMs to acquire instream flows.[83] There is widespread recognition that, in the western USA in particular, there is a real benefit to using a private organisation as the face of environmental water transactions:

> I think that a non-profit organization is much better equipped to work with private landowners than the government. In the western United States, there's a lot of baggage ... Negotiating with the government about water is more than farmers can handle, but private non-profit hasn't got that baggage, and can often be comprised of local community members, which can open doors. Government can never do that, that's the main benefit of the non-profit: they can have conversations that government can't have with people about their property.[84]

The legal limits on who can hold instream flow rights, combined with the preference of irrigators in the western USA to avoid doing business directly with government, have positioned the NGO EWMs as the 'retail arm'[85] of the government EWMs. In the absence of a highly functional water market, the NGO EWMs are dependent on negotiating one-on-one with landholders to obtain the voluntary transfers of water rights. Although the NGO EWMs are supported by government agencies as well as private funders, their real power lies in their ability to open the conversation with irrigators and other water users. As a result, the EWMs are vulnerable to changing community perceptions and work very hard to maintain a good relationship with the water user community: 'We're advocating for policies to do the work more effectively, but trying very hard not to alienate other water users.'[86]

Legal personhood through collaboration and partnership

The role of the NGO EWMs in procuring voluntary transfers of water rights for instream flows needs to be understood as part of a wider legal context in the western USA. Following passage of the ESA in 1973, a number of court cases demonstrated the power of the law to construct the environment as an object with the capacity to limit the activities of others significantly, and created an 'us or them' mentality in the western USA. First, there was the long-winded spotted owl litigation, which pitted environmentalists against loggers and local communities.[87] Second, a decision to withhold water from irrigators to protect threatened fish species inflamed the community of the Klamath Basin in southern Oregon and northern California.[88] Attempting to acquire instream flows in the aftermath of these law suits was phenomenally challenging. The Oregon Water Trust discovered this during its first decade of operations, when it found it difficult to find water rights to acquire for the environment, leaving it with funds it could not spend.[89] Even just over a decade ago, at the beginning of the Columbia Water Transaction Program, NGO EWMs were still encountering serious pushback from irrigators: 'the notion back in 2003 that anyone would even consider water instream was enough to get run out of Dodge. It was really considered a traitorous act…'[90]

As a result, the NGO EWMs had to construct the aquatic environment and instream flows as something that could exist alongside agriculture, without being a threat to communities or a way of life. NGO EWMs are very wary of any attempt to present instream flows as an alternative to agriculture:

> We aim to keep the landscapes working, we don't want to 'buy it up and dry it up', we don't want to perpetuate that; obtaining the flow targets in a variety of different ways appeals to the communities.[91]

Constructing the environment in this way required the NGO EWMs to focus on efficiency savings, which take longer but ultimately generate greater community support for instream flows. Almost all water transfers are the result of an investment to increase efficiency of water use, change the time or location of water use, or alter aspects of an irrigator's business so that less water is needed.[92] This shift in approach created the possibility of mutually acceptable outcomes for the EWM, the irrigators, and the community: 'people realized that if you can offer efficiency, you can make their lives a little easier and still have water in stream'.[93]

Both appropriation and acquisition of instream flows are contingent on the legal personality of the EWMs and their ability to hold and acquire water rights. However, in both cases this formal legal construction is limited in important ways. In most states only nominated agencies can hold environmental water. Appropriation is limited to locations where a clear case can be made that both the environment is worthy of protection and the means to protect it without affecting other users' rights exist. Acquisition programmes were designed as a way to work around the zero-sum outcomes of the ESA, but in doing so have constructed the aquatic environment as a legal person that depends on its ability to coexist with other users of the water resource. Although the formal construction of the environment as a legal entity with power to acquire senior water rights increases the ability of the EWMs to improve environmental flows, the inability of the EWMs to access this power without undermining their ongoing legitimacy in their communities is a real weakness.

Conclusion

The prior-appropriation water laws of the western USA construct the aquatic environment along similar lines to the water laws of Australia. First, water law reforms *recognised* the environment as a broad socio-ecological concept by establishing the environment as a beneficial use of water, to protect ecological health and the social values that are dependent on healthy aquatic ecosystems (such as recreational uses like angling and duck hunting).

Second, the ESA has been used to limit the activities of existing water users by *translating* the environment into a legal object, but one which remains of limited legibility to water law, which focuses on *rights* to water. In addition, water laws established legal rights to water for the purposes of instream flows via appropriation, a hybrid construction which blends elements of the legal object and legal subject.

Lastly, the aquatic environment was *personified* as a legal subject by establishing organisations with the legal powers necessary to hold water rights (the EWMs). With the more recent ability to *acquire* existing water rights and retain their seniority, the aquatic environment was constructed as a more powerful legal person, although still affected by limits on who can hold the instream flow rights. Even then, the organisations tasked with responsibility to acquire these water rights, most often the NGO EWMs, constructed the environment as a subtly weaker version of itself: something that must coexist with other uses of water, without requiring a significant reduction in agricultural use of water to support environmental outcomes.

The NGO EWMs depend on the support of irrigation communities for their continued access to water rights, and while they will litigate if necessary to enforce a contract or protect their own water rights, they largely avoid framing the environment in opposition to agriculture. This construction has evolved over time in response to a painful history of environmental litigation in the western USA, as well as a low-functioning water market which means every water transaction needs to be negotiated on a case-by-case basis. This requirement to engage in a time-consuming and expensive conversation slows down instream flow transactions, but also provides an opportunity to address explicitly the tensions between the legally powerful EWM (which can acquire water rights) and the need to convince the broader community that the environment deserves those water rights.

Chapters 4 and 5 show how the aquatic environment is constructed in water law in south-eastern Australia and the western USA. Chapter 6 builds on this detailed analysis to explore what happens when the aquatic environment is constructed as a legal person. In particular, Chapter 6 shows how shifts in the cultural narrative underpinning the different constructions of the aquatic environment can lead to legal reform that limits the ability of the EWMs to protect and improve the health of the aquatic environment.

Notes

1 A Dan Tarlock, 'Prior Appropriation: Rule, Principle or Rhetoric?' (2000) 76 *North Dakota Law Review* 881, 882.
2 *Baker Ditch Co. v. District Ct.*, 824 P 2d 260 (Mont, 1992).
3 Steven Malloch, *Liquid Assets: Protecting and Restoring the West's Rivers and Wetlands through Environmental Water Transactions* (Trout Unlimited, 2005) 4.

4 Lawrence J MacDonnell, 'Return to the River: Environmental Flow Policy in the United States and Canada' (2009) 45(5) *Journal of the American Water Resources Association* 1087, 1089.
5 Janet C Neuman, 'The Good, the Bad and the Ugly: The First Ten Years of the Oregon Water Trust' (2004) 83 *Nebraska Law Review* 432, 438.
6 Sasha Charney, *Decades Down the Road: An Analysis of Instream Flow Programs in Colorado and the Western United States* (Colorado Water Conservation Board, 2005) 11–12.
7 National Fish and Wildlife Foundation, 'Western Water Program' (2016) www.nfwf.org/wwp/Pages/home.aspx#.Vu9b2OJ97IU.
8 National Fish and Wildlife Foundation, 'Walker Basin Restoration Program' (2014) www.nfwf.org/walkerbasin/Pages/home.aspx; National Fish and Wildlife Foundation, 'Desert Terminal Lakes Restoration Program' (2 July 2014) www.nfwf.org/dtl/Pages/home.aspx; National Fish and Wildlife Foundation, 'Rio Grande Water Transactions Program' (archived) www.nfwf.org/archive/Pages/riogrande.aspx.
9 Neil E Ward and David L Ward, 'Resident Fish in the Columbia River Basin: Restoration, Enhancement and Mitigation for Losses Associated with Hydroelectric Development and Operations' (2004) 29 *Fisheries* 10.
10 Columbia Basin Water Transactions Program, *Annual Report 2012: A Decade of Outcomes 2003–2012* (National Fish and Wildlife Foundation, 2012).
11 Dustin Evan Garrick, *Water Allocation in Rivers Under Pressure: Water Trading, Transaction Costs, and Transboundary Governance in the Western USA and Australia* (Edward Elgar, 2015).
12 Bureau of Reclamation, 'Law of the River' (March 2008) Bureau of Reclamation, Lower Colorado Region www.usbr.gov/lc/region/g1000/lawofrvr.html.
13 L W Daesslé et al., 'The 2014 Water Release into the Arid Colorado River Delta and Associated Water Losses by Evaporation' (2016) 542 *Science of the Total Environment* 586.
14 A Dan Tarlock, 'Mexico and the United States Assume a Legal Duty to Provide Colorado River Delta Restoration Flows: An Important International Environmental and Water Law Precedent' (2014) 23(1) *Review of European Community & International Environmental Law* 76.
15 Colorado Water Trust, 'About Us' (2016) www.coloradowatertrust.org/about-us.
16 Charney, above n 6.
17 Columbia Basin Water Transactions Program, *Annual Report Financial Year 2011* (National Fish and Wildlife Foundation, 2011).
18 Committee on Western Water Management, *Water Transfers in the West: Efficiency, Equity and the Environment* (National Academy Press, 1992) 70.
19 Zachary Donohew, 'Property Rights and Western United States Water Markets' (2009) 53 *Australian Journal of Agricultural and Resource Economics* 85, 88.
20 Tarlock, above n 1, 881.
21 Richael K Young and Nicholas Brozović, 'Innovations in Groundwater Management: Smart Markets for Transferable Groundwater Extraction Rights' (2016) 17 *Technology and Innovation* 219.
22 Bruce Aylward, *Water Markets: A Mechanism for Mainstreaming Ecosystem Services into Water Management?* (Briefing Paper, Water and Nature Initiative, IUCN, 2008).
23 Amanda E Cronin and Lara B Fowler, *The Water Report #102: Northwest Water Banking* (Envirotech Publications, 2012).
24 Kelly Mistry, 'Columbia River Flows to Be Protected' Centre for Environmental Law and Policy www.celp.org/tag/celp/.
25 Tarlock, above n 14.

26 Interview CWT.
27 Tarlock, above n 1.
28 Lawrence J MacDonnell, 'Environmental Flows in the Rocky Mountain West: A Progress Report' (2009) 9(2) *Wyoming Law Review* 335, 335.
29 Donohew, above n 19.
30 Committee on Western Water Management, above n 18, 73–76.
31 Patrick A Byorth, 'Conflict to Compact: Federal Reserved Water Rights, Instream Flows and Native Fish Conservation on National Forests in Montana' (2009) 30 *Public Land and Resources Law Review* 35.
32 *United States v. Adair*, 723 F.2d 1394, 1414 (9th Cir. 1984).
33 *Winters v United States* 207 U.S. 564 (1908); *Arizona v. California*, 373 U.S. 546 (1963); *Cappaert v. United States* 426 U.S. 128, 133 (1976).
34 John E Thorson et al., 'Dividing Western Waters: A Century of Adjudicating Rivers and Streams, Part II' (2006) 9(2) *Water Law Review* 299.
35 D Garrick, N Hernandez-Mora, and E O'Donnell, 'Water Markets in Federal Countries: Comparing Coordination Institutions in Australia, Spain and the Western USA' (2018) 18 *Regional Environmental Change* 1593.
36 Donohew, above n 19, 96.
37 Janis M Carey and David L Sunding, 'Emerging Markets in Water: A Comparative Institutional Analysis of the Central Valley and Colorado-Big Thompson Projects' (2001) 41 *Natural Resources Journal* 283, 284.
38 Jedidiah Brewer et al., '2006 Presidential Address. Water Markets in the West: Prices, Trading, and Contractual Forms' (2008) 46(2) *Economic Inquiry* 91, 108.
39 National Water Commission, *Australian Water Markets: Trends and Drivers 2007–08 to 2012–13* (National Water Commission, 2014).
40 Poh-Ling Tan, 'A Property Framework for Water Markets: The Role of Law' in Jeff Bennett (ed.), *The Evolution of Markets for Water: Theory and Practice in Australia* (Edward Elgar, 2005) 56.
41 Carey and Sunding, above n 37.
42 Garrick, Hernandez-Mora, and O'Donnell, above n 35.
43 David M Gillilan and Thomas C Brown, *Instream Flow Protection: Seeking a Balance in Western Water Use* (Island Press, 1997).
44 A Dan Tarlock, *The Law of Water Rights and Resources* (West Publishing, 2008).
45 Jesse A Boyd, 'Hip Deep: A Survey of State Instream Flow Law from the Rocky Mountains to the Pacific Ocean' (2003) 43 *Natural Resources Journal* 1151.
46 Holly Doremus and A Dan Tarlock, 'Fish, Farms and the Clash of Cultures in the Klamath Basin' (2003) 30 *Ecology Law Quarterly* 279.
47 *Riverside Irrigation District v Andrews* 758 F.2d 508 (10th Cir. 1985) (for the Clean Water Act); *O'Neill v U.S.* 50 F.3d 677 (9th Cir. 1995); *Klamath Water Users Protective Association v Patterson* 204 F.3d 1206 (9th Cir. 1999).
48 Holly Doremus and A Dan Tarlock, *Water War in the Klamath Basin: Macho Law, Combat Biology and Dirty Politics* (Island Press, 2008).
49 Janet C Neuman and Cheyenne Chapman, 'Wading into the Water Market: The First Five Years of the Oregon Water Trust' (1999) 14 *Journal of Environmental Law and Litigation* 135; John J Ferguson, Barbara Chilcott Hall, and Brianna Randall, 'Private Water Leasing: Working Within the Prior Appropriation System to Restore Streamflows' (2006) 27 *Public Land and Resources Law Review* 1.
50 Malloch, above n 3, 52.
51 Dustin Garrick and Erin O'Donnell, 'Exploring Private Roles in Environmental Watering in Australia and the US' in Jeff Bennett (ed.), *Protecting the Environment, Privately* (World Scientific Publishing, 2016) 203.

52 Department of Ecology, State of Washington, 'Water Market' (3 February 2012) Water Resources www.ecy.wa.gov/programs/wr/market/market.html.
53 The Freshwater Trust, 'Tools for Stream Flow Restoration' (2011) www.thefreshwatertrust.org/conservation/stream-flow/tools; National Fish and Wildlife Foundation, 'Finding Balance – Typical Tools' (3 February 2012) Columbia Basin Water Transactions Program www.cbwtp.org/balance/TypicalTools.htm.
54 Interview CWT.
55 Interview CWCB.
56 Columbia Basin Water Transactions Program, above n 10.
57 Interview TUM.
58 Interview WWT.
59 Interview WDE 1.
60 Interview CWT.
61 Interview CWCB.
62 Interview WDE 2.
63 Thorson et al., above n 34.
64 Idaho Water Resource Board, *Idaho Minimum Stream Flow Program* (Idaho Department of Water Resources, 2013).
65 Interview CWCB.
66 Byorth, above n 31.
67 Charney, above n 6, 18.
68 Dan Merriman and Anne M Janicki, *Colorado's Instream Flow Program – How It Works and Why It's Good for Colorado* (Colorado Water Control Board, 2005).
69 Zach Smith and Edalin Koziol, *The Water Report* (Colorado Water Trust, 2014).
70 Interview CWT.
71 Malloch, above n 3, 35.
72 Brandon Scarborough, *Environmental Water Markets: Restoring Streams Through Trade* (Property and Environment Research Centre, 2010).
73 Columbia Basin Water Transactions Program, above n 10.
74 Terry L Anderson and Gary D Libecap, *Environmental Markets: A Property Rights Approach* (Cambridge University Presss, 2014).
75 Interview WWT.
76 Interview CWT.
77 Malloch, above n 3, 6.
78 Interview NFWF.
79 Interview CFC.
80 Interview FWT.
81 Interview TUM.
82 Laura Ziemer and Scott Yates, 'Montana, Idaho and Wyoming: Obstacles and Opportunities in State Water Right Change Process – The Good, the Bad and the Ugly' paper presented at Water in the West: Environmental Water Transactions, 15–16 January 2014, Stanford University; Edna T Loehman and Sasha Charney, 'Further Down the Road to Sustainable Environmental Flows: Funding, Management Activities and Governance for Six Western US States' (2011) 36(7) *Water International* 873.
83 Garrick and O'Donnell, above n 51.
84 Interview DRC.
85 Interview WWT.
86 Interview CFC.
87 Barry R Noon and Kevin S McKelvey, 'Management of the Spotted Owl: A Case History in Conservation Biology' (1996) 27 *Annual Review of Ecological Systems* 135; Jeb Boyt, 'Struggling to Protect Ecosystems and Biodiversity under

NEPA and NFMA: The Ancient Forests of the Pacific Northwest and the Northern Spotted Owl' (1993) 10(2) *Pace Environmental Law Review* 1009.

88 Doremus and Tarlock, above n 46.

89 Neuman, above n 5.

90 Interview WWT.

91 Interview FWT.

92 Columbia Basin Water Transactions Program, above n 10.

93 Interview WWT.

6 Competing narratives and the paradox of the environmental water managers

In south-eastern Australia and the western USA the EWMs have the rights and powers of legal persons and operate within water law to construct the aquatic environment as a legal subject. The two case studies show that the EWMs sit alongside other constructions of the aquatic environment in law: the socio-ecological concept and the legal object.

This chapter brings the findings of the case studies together to show how the constructions of the aquatic environment in water law interact and, ultimately, what happens when the aquatic environment is constructed in law as a legal subject. In doing so, this chapter explores the 'critical relationship between concepts of ownership and agency, and the extent to which the environment is seen as an equal partner in human–environmental interactions'.[1]

Chapter 6 uses the conceptual framework developed in Chapter 2 to demonstrate the importance of cultural narratives and the relationship between narrative and regulatory response. The EWM, as an organisation with legal personality, legal rights to water, and (at least some) funding, is a legally powerful construction of the environment that can compete with existing water users. The EWMs then choose which legal powers to use to conduct their activities, and these choices can be understood as deliberate strategies to align their operations with a dominant cultural narrative about the role of the aquatic environment. However, the multiple constructions of the aquatic environment in water law mean that the competing narratives remain present, shaping conflicting responses to the activities of the EWMs. This chapter draws on the perspectives of the EWM staff, through their interviews, to examine the way that the EWMs are defined by both their formal legal powers and the choices made by their staff to use a particular subset of those powers.

In highlighting the potential for both competition and collaboration with other water users, this chapter uncovers the paradox of the EWMs: that more power can lead to fewer protections.[2] Other water users, confronted with the legal power of the EWMs, and most particularly their capacity to compete in the water market, can become afraid of the EWMs. One response to this fear is legal reform that constrains the legal personhood powers of the EWMs in ways that other water users are not constrained. This legal reform strengthens the narrative that the aquatic environment, when constructed as a legal person, does not require and should not receive any 'special' protection. The experience of the EWMs shows that increasing the legal power of the aquatic environment (by constructing it as a legal person) can also weaken the cultural narrative (and the laws) that supports the protection of the environment in the first place.

Legal power and the ability to use it

The EWMs are organisations that have been accorded legal personality, which includes the formal capacity to 'bear a legal right and so to participate in legal relations'.[3] Chapters 4 and 5 demonstrate that the EWMs of Australia and the USA have the power to use these legal rights by acting on their own behalf, but their ability to do so is constrained by both their legal form and the choices they themselves make.

First, the powers and rights of the EWM are often expressly limited under statute. Legal personality is a particular 'constellation of rights'[4] and duties associated with a specific legal subject, and the EWMs, even when created using a generic corporate form, are usually limited in their legal capacities by water laws. Notably, these often specify which EWMs can formally hold water for the purpose of instream flows (see Chapter 5) and limit the capacity of the EWMs to buy and sell water rights (Chapter 4).[5] These limits are specifically imposed on the EWM as the manager of water for environmental purposes, and do not apply to other water users.

Second, there are also specific legal rights and powers that the EWMs are *reluctant* to use because of the social and political contexts in which they operate. The EWMs in both south-eastern Australia and the western USA exhibit this reluctance in various ways. In Australia the EWMs choose to limit their participation in the water market by conducting acquisition through various geographically limited reverse auctions, to reduce their potential effect on the water market and competition with other water users.[6] In the western USA this reluctance is most obviously exhibited in a refusal to acquire water rights that would result in the former water user ceasing to operate.[7]

The staff of individual EWMs exhibited this reluctance in different ways. In Australia staff from the VEWH expressed considerable ambivalence on the capacity of the VEWH to act as it sees fit: 'We ... inform the minister, we don't wait for him to clear it, it's our call; we assert our independence'[8] and 'the VEWH as an organisation is very mindful of its reputation'.[9]

In the USA the EWMs' employees were optimistic about their ability to influence outcomes, but also acknowledged the position and power of the other water users: 'We are a leadership voice in water policy and we have an outsize influence on water policy...'[10] and 'The irrigation districts, the water users themselves, are really at the top of the hierarchy in terms of affecting water management.'[11]

The following sections examine in more detail both the limits imposed in law and those set by the EWMs themselves.

Creation of the EWMs: legal form

The EWMs of south-eastern Australia and the western USA use a variety of legal methods to create legal personhood (see Chapters 4 and 5). The most significant difference in legal form depends on whether the organisation is part of government or an independent private entity.

Non-government EWMs

The simplest method of creating legal personhood is used by the NGOs in each jurisdiction: the corporate form. In the USA the EWMs take the form of non-profit corporations which are incorporated under the relevant state legislation and operate under the US Internal Revenue Code as either a 501(c)(3) or 501(c)(4) entity.[12] The main distinction between these two designations relates to the role of the organisation in influencing political outcomes or legislation: a 501(c)(3) organisation is prohibited from engaging in lobbying or political activities, or it risks losing its not-profit designation; a 501(c)(4) organisation, on the other hand, may engage in political activities as long as it is consistent with the purpose of the organisation and its role in promoting social welfare. Most of the non-government EWMs in the western USA have chosen to incorporate as 501(c)(3) organisations to avoid being seen as overtly 'political' actors. One of the rare 501(c)(4) examples is the NFWF, and the importance of that difference is primarily related to how it receives funding:

> We have a unique designation by Congress, which allows NFWF to partner with federal agencies to leverage their dollars with non-federal dollars. That unique legal form positions us in a way that other funders aren't positioned.[13]

The NFWF is an example of the exception that proves the rule: although the NFWF does have legal personhood, it does not act as an EWM except for some very limited circumstances in Nevada, where it owns both land and water rights as an interim step before converting the land to dryland farming. Interestingly, this is also an exception to the 'buy it up and dry it up' philosophy, and is only undertaken by an organisation that is not generally operating as an EWM.

In general, the formal construction of NGO EWMs in the western USA frames the EWMs as non-threatening charitable organisations, beholden to the community in which they operate:

> ... we're speaking out for the work, but we walk a fine line ... our mission doesn't involve sustainable agriculture, but we have to make it work for the agriculture community too.[14]

In Australia the non-government EWMs use a variety of legal forms, including an incorporated association (an inexpensive way to establish an incorporated entity under state legislation) and a trust, where the trustee is a registered company under the Australian Corporations Act 2001 (Cth). In each case the organisation has focused on finding the form that best suits their specific needs:

> It might be an issue if you had a larger amount of water that was being provided to you, by say the federal government, they might have some further requirements about what sort of company structure you have, organisational structure, but for us it's never mattered.[15]

Government EWMs

The situation is more complicated for government organisations. In both Australia and the USA the government EWMs face the challenge of creating separate legal personhood while retaining the connection to the democratic process. This challenge is not unique to the EWMs, and affects all statutory agencies which operate at arm's length from government.[16] In 2010 Hendry argued that the corporatisation of water service provision was a way to 'regulate the public sector in a similar manner to the private sector and thereby institute comparable efficiencies, whilst still maintaining a public sector ethos'.[17] Government-owned corporations are often termed 'quangos' or 'quagos': quasi-government organisations that operate with a significantly greater degree of independence than government departments, and with very different expectations placed on their staff (although those staff may retain their formal designation as public servants).[18]

In south-eastern Australia corporatisation has been explicitly adopted by the states as a way of introducing commercial operating principles (including cost recovery, transparency, and independence) to the provision and management of water services.[19] For the VEWH, a statutory corporation,[20] being the same formal type of organisation as the other water authorities was considered to be an important factor in the choice of legal form:

> [T]he body corporate provides ... the VEWH a better standing in the industry ... The legislation was changed so that all the water corporations would be the same organisational form; if you have another part of that water industry, why wouldn't you use the same model [the corporate form]? ... I believe it's sending the right signals on what a professional organisation needs to be and that it is a legitimate user of water ...[21]

The staff of the VEWH considered that the legal form was important, and were able to articulate why the corporate form was important to achieving specific outcomes:

> There is a sharper focus because you know that you can sue or be sued, you know that you have that legal personality.[22]

> The organisational form does matter; it ensures that there is a discipline in its objectives and what the VEWH is trying to achieve.[23]

> The corporate form probably has got advantages because it brings awareness of responsibilities and accountabilities, there is no one to hide behind, you have to establish policies and practices that are right for you.[24]

However, the staff of the Commonwealth Environmental Water Office, which supports the activities of CEWH (a statutory legal person but not a separate body corporate),[25] were much more ambivalent about the importance of legal form: 'I don't think it really does matter too much'[26] and 'I don't really know why this form was used ... We've got what we've got, and we're working with that...'[27]

Both Australia and the USA include examples of government departments with limited legal personality to enable them to hold and manage water rights. In Australia government departments can be the environmental water licence holder, which is the case in New South Wales after the RiverBank programme was reabsorbed into the government department: 'the [team] which provides the environmental water governance unit support ... That unit is the water licence holder.'[28] In South Australia, 'The minister's licence acts as a surrogate environmental water holder.'[29]

In the western USA each state has a government department or government agency that holds instream flow rights on behalf of the environment.[30] As in Australia, these government organisations are often responsible for multiple objectives, which can blur their accountability for managing instream flows for environmental outcomes. In Colorado, for example, the instream flows programme is part of the CWCB:

> Our agency has a lot of different functions, and instream flow is just one ... It's a water policy and planning agency, we're all state employees, and the state agency is under the umbrella of the Department of Natural Resources, similar to Colorado Parks and Wildlife and the Division of Water Resources, our sister agencies in the same department.[31]

In Washington the instream flow rights are held in trust by the Washington Department of Ecology:

> We are a state government agency … The trust water right program is operated within the Department of Ecology, in the Water Resources Program … It acts as a bank vault – where water rights are put to prevent relinquishment; it's a structural mechanism.[32]

> We have no board or commission, which can be good for leaving politics behind, but we can also be seen as out of control and making decisions in private; we make every effort to show elected officials that we're trying to engage the public in our processes.[33]

The importance of legal form and independence

Chapters 2 and 3 establish the crucial importance of the legal rights and powers of an entity in establishing legal personality. For EWMs these rights and powers are established by the legal form used to create the EWM, and this makes legal form particularly important. In addition, for government EWMs a distinct legal form enables their decisions and actions to be treated as distinctly environmental, and separate to the broader policies of the government.

However, the ambiguity expressed by some of the EWM staff about the importance of legal form may simply reflect a lack of awareness of the ramifications of specific legal forms. In both case studies the EWM staff were very clear about the importance of *organisational* form for independence and accountability, even where they were less clear about the particular importance of *legal* form. In Australia the staff indicated that the desirability of independence and accountability in the government EWMs was linked to the necessity of being seen as separate to the politics. Staff from the CEWH believed that 'It's implicit in the legislation that it was quite a deliberate thing to separate it from the politics of the government of the day.'[34]

However, although the Office of Commonwealth Environmental Water was created to establish a 'firewall between management and purchase'[35] of environmental water rights, the CEWH is still perceived by others as being too close to the government department: 'I'm well aware of criticisms and public perceptions of the CEWH because it's not a separate organisation.'[36]

This potential for conflation of the CEWH with the Australian federal government creates problems for the identifiability of the EWM, and makes it difficult for individuals to hold the CEWH to account for its environmental water decisions (as distinct to whole-of-government policies). From the perspective of irrigators participating in the water market, the conflation of the CEWH (the decision-maker) with the water purchase programme in the MDB exacerbates their fear of the CEWH: 'This places irrigators with small pockets in the same marketplace as the Commonwealth with large deep pockets.'[37]

In Victoria the staff of the VEWH linked its statutory form to permanence, as well as providing some insulation from changing political mores:

> Statutory is good – it ensures legitimacy; the VEWH is in legislation, [it] can't be written off with a stroke of a pen ... What is important are the specifics of how VEWH is independent is in legislation, [the] limits on [the] minister's direction power.[38]

In Victoria this independence is enshrined in statute, by first creating the VEWH as a statutory body corporate, a legally distinct organisation to the department and the minister,[39] and second preventing the minister from directing the VEWH on how to use its available water in any given year.[40] The minister may set rules for the operation of the VEWH in the longer term, but the decisions of the VEWH are insulated from political interference in the short term.[41] The separation from the relevant government department was also considered as important for the VEWH:

> [Being] separate from DSE [Victorian Department of Sustainability and Environment] is incredibly useful and important, [it's a] separation of policy and service delivery ... [the VEWH] doesn't set policy but is a service delivery agent; this is very much a benefit and emphasises independence of decision-making.[42]

The persistent concerns about the CEWH being too close to government and the ability of the VEWH to differentiate itself from government can be traced to two critical differences between the legal forms of the VEWH and the CEWH. First, the VEWH is explicitly insulated from ministerial interference, a protection that the CEWH does not have.[43] In 2010 this vulnerability was publicised in the federal election, when the then opposition party campaigned on a platform that included a commitment to issue directions to the CEWH on how and where to use its environmental water. Second, the VEWH is a statutory body corporate, which gives it distinct legal personality and formally establishes its separation from the government department. In addition, the CEWH is undertaking the more politically sensitive activity of water recovery, whereas the VEWH is only responsible for managing water that has already been recovered.

In the western USA formal separation of the EWMs from government was seen as crucial, and the acquisition of water rights has been outsourced to private EWMs (although they can receive government funding):

> I think that a non-profit organization is much better equipped to work with private landowners than the government ... the main benefit of the non-profit: they can have conversations that government can't have with people about their property.[44]

Further, the specific creation of the NGO EWMs in the USA as organisations which do not profit from the environmental water transaction was critical:

> In this work, being independent and non-regulatory, with no ties, and also non-profit, that was a much better combination and structure. As a non-profit, people are less scared about somebody making money off their water. Tea Party folks still think you are; but we don't hold any of the water, and we don't function as a land trust (which always will buy at a discount and resell and profit from the sale). The state itself does buy water, but there's so much more suspicion about going to a regulatory agency, you're much less likely to have someone calling you up and saying 'hey, let's do a deal'.[45]

Even though the NGO EWMs in many states in the western USA must legally transfer the acquired water right to the nominated government department to enable this water to be considered as instream flows, it is the NGO EWM which remains the face of the water transaction in the eyes of the community.

While the role of NGO EWMs in Australia is much more limited to date, EWM staff still considered that a non-profit, non-government form of organisation could be critical to the success of environmental water recovery: 'because of the sort of organisation we were, we got agreement and provided the water'.[46]

In summary, all EWMs have the formal legal capacity to acquire and hold water rights, to sue and be sued, and to enter contracts. However, their specific legal forms include a range of specific limitations on their activities, and although the EWMs have been established to facilitate transfer of water rights to the environment as easily as if they were another irrigator, they are limited by the law in ways that other water users, particularly other irrigators, are not. In addition, the EWMs have chosen to emphasise some legal powers over others, so that for each EWM their legal personhood is a combination of their specific legal powers and the choices that they make. These choices reflect and reinforce the narratives that have emerged about the nature and role of the EWMs in each jurisdiction.

Choices: which personhood powers are the EWMs using?

Naffine's constructivist approach to legal personality emphasises the specific combination of legal rights and powers associated with a particular legal entity, so '[l]egal personality is therefore shifting and variable'.[47] Legal personhood is thus an expression of both form and function. The EWMs in Australia and the USA choose to use subsets of their formal legal powers to meet their responsibility to increase the quantity and efficacy of environmental flows (Table 6.1).[48] These choices act as self-imposed restraints on their legal personalities.

The EWMs of the Columbia Basin and Colorado explicitly frame themselves and their work as non-threatening and non-political. This narrative is strengthened by the relationship between the state agencies and the NGOs, which limits both the role of government in negotiating with individuals and the perceived power of the NGO EWMs by requiring them (in most cases) to transfer the instream flow rights to the government agency. In Australia the EWMs also attempt to position themselves as non-political: government EWMs create a strict separation between the decisions of the EWM and broader government policy. Government EWMs in Australia are also beginning to use NGO EWMs as the faces of community engagement, in both water recovery and water management.[49]

In each jurisdiction the EWMs have adapted their legal personalities to meet their specific needs by the *choices* they make about which legal powers to use (Table 6.1). Although there are differences in the specific legal powers that are considered to be 'off limits', there is a common outcome across both case studies: the EWMs operate to construct *themselves* by their reluctance to use their full suite of legal powers.

Further examination of these choices exposes the different dominant narratives about the role of the EWMs in water resource management in each case study. In south-eastern Australia the EWMs have adopted the narrative of being 'just another user' of water, which aligns most strongly with the construction of the aquatic environment as a legal person, capable of looking after itself. In the Columbia Basin and Colorado the EWMs are framing themselves as collaborators with the community of water users, which is much more dependent on an ongoing public interest in protecting the environment (and the construction of the aquatic environment as a legal object).

Understanding the way the choices of the EWMs operate to reinforce particular cultural narratives gives insight into how the EWMs interact with their legal and social contexts.

EWMs of South-Eastern Australia: 'we're another water user'[50]

The impetus for environmental water recovery in south-eastern Australia originated in the severe degradation of the MDB and emphasised the need to *protect* the aquatic environment (see Chapters 3 and 4). However, experience quickly demonstrated the essential importance of a *voice* for the aquatic environment, with the capacity to engage in both the policy debates and the decisions about how and when environmental water was used.[51] A voice for the environment explicitly engages private interest theories of regulation, and the narrative that the environment can and should look after itself.

Table 6.1 Activities undertaken by the environmental water managers in the two case study locations[1]

Environmental water activity	*EWMs of south-eastern Australia*	*EWMs of Columbia Basin and Colorado*	*Details and example*
Negotiate with existing water users on potential acquisitions		X	NGO EWMs, such as Washington Water Trust
Buy water from other water users	X	X	Mainly NGO EWMs in the USA Mainly government agencies on behalf of EWMs in Australia
Hold water rights	X	X	All EWMs
Hold water rights for environmental use	X	X	All EWMs in Australia Designated EWMs in USA
Make decisions on how water rights will be used (including trade, use instream, or use in wetlands)	X	X	Australian government EWMs were formally established to perform this function US EWMs may be limited in their ability to use or trade instream flows
Enforce water rights (in court if necessary)		X	US EWMs rely on this ability, as water rights are often only enforced on a complaints basis Australian EWMs rely on river operators to do this (although recent experience in Australia has shown that this is not perfect)[2]
Attract donations and acquire tax-deductibility status	X	X	NGO EWMs in both Australia and the USA
Participate in water policy debates as a water user	X		Australian EWMs such as the CEWH, as well as some NGOs such as Murray-Darling Wetlands

Notes

1 Based on Erin O'Donnell, 'Competition or Collaboration? Using Legal Persons to Manage Water for the Environment in Australia and the United States' (2017) 34(6) *Environmental and Planning Law Journal* 503. Reproduced with permission of Thomson Reuters (Professional) Australia Limited, legal.thomsonreuters.com.au.

2 Ken Matthews, *Independent Investigation into NSW Water Management and Compliance: Advice on Implementation* (NSW Department of Industry, 2017).

During the final years of the severe Millennium Drought in south-eastern Australia (2007–2010), it became clear that the most secure environmental water rights were those that were legally almost identical to those of other water users. For example, in New South Wales water plans that had protected environmental flows without creating specific environmental water rights were suspended from 2006 to 2010, effectively reallocating this water to consumptive users.[52] In Victoria the Minister for Water may temporarily 'qualify' legal rights to water in the event that there is insufficient water to meet all demands.[53] During the drought, environmental water was reallocated to meet critical human needs around the state, including in the state capital, Melbourne.[54] In Victoria the only environmental water affected by these qualifications had *fewer* legal protections (similar to the water plans in New South Wales) or *more* legal protections (such as the Thomson and Yarra environmental entitlements, which were the highest reliability water in storage[55]) than the water rights of other users. Environmental water rights that were essentially the same as those held by other water users remained available to the environment.[56] Ever since, both water recovery and water management by EWMs in Australia have emphasised the similarity of their rights to other water users, and continue to position the government EWMs as 'just another user'[57] of water: 'We're a water user; we're another water user, we need to be regulated like everyone else.'[58]

This shift in the narrative in Australia was predicted by Paul Humphries back in 2008, in the first year of the CEWH's existence and two years before the VEWH was established. He also identified the potential problems that it would create:

> [T]he environment becomes just another user, or worse, client, and when it needs more water, it – the government, or us, actually – has to pay for it. It would seem logical to give a substance absolutely critical to maintaining the function of a system, upon which other systems are based, the highest priority. Instead, we have put it on level footing with other users, which might be fine if we knew how much water was needed (and when) to maintain that functioning system. But we don't![59]

As a result, the EWMs of south-eastern Australia focus on their legal personhood, which enables them to operate as any other water user (including having the power to acquire, hold, use, and trade water rights) even though they continue to face additional legal constraints that irrigators do not.[60] First, the EWMs have attempted to rely on the existing output-focused paradigm of water use[61] to legitimise their actions in the eyes of the public and other water users. By focusing on outputs, the EWMs align themselves with the prevailing efficiency norm in Australian water resource management, exemplified by the reliance on water markets. Like irrigators,

Australian EWMs emphasise the volumes of water they hold, and where and how that water has been used.[62] Even the phrasing used by a government employee in New South Wales frames the activities of the EWM like those of an irrigator: 'Did we grow a population of [native] fish? Did we not grow carp?'[63]

Behaving as just another user has already caused problems, for the government EWMs in particular. The CEWH has attempted to rely on the legitimacy of market processes in guiding water management activities, which meant it was slow to react to concerns about its market power. A discussion paper on trading activities was not released until 2011 (four years after water purchase began), and this paper only considered trade in existing environmental water rights, not new water purchases.[64] The CEWH was also slow to grasp the potential for conflation of the decisions it made and decisions made by the government department responsible for water recovery: 'For many people, it's just government – someone representing rules and requirements, the level of government (local, state, federal) is not relevant.'[65]

Furthermore, it was not until 2012 that the CEWH formalised a relationship with a community-based NGO EWM to help manage environmental water. The local partner, Water For Nature, makes proposals to the CEWH each year for use of the water, based on both environmental outcomes and the capacity to build 'strong partnerships with the river community, local community organizations, irrigators and corporates'.[66] This partnership demonstrates a growing awareness of the importance of the broader social context of environmental water management. It was the first time the government EWMs of Australia explicitly acknowledged the need to engage local people, including other water users, in making decisions about, and the outcomes of, the watering. Since then, the VEWH has also been building broader community relationships by holding an annual event that brings together a range of stakeholders, including traditional owners (Indigenous Australians), irrigators, recreational fishers, duck hunters, and representatives of local tourism operators. There is growing recognition of the need to build deeper, lasting support for environmental watering in local communities.[67]

Second, the EWMs of south-eastern Australia have positioned themselves as just another user of water so as to claim membership of water services committees. These committees provide a forum for water users (typically irrigators) to provide feedback to water authorities about the delivery and management of their water rights.[68] This is an explicit customer-service model, and the CEWH attends some of these committees to represent the aquatic environment as another water customer:

> I see the CEWH as the representative of the environment in the market at the Commonwealth level ... I think it represents the environment quite strongly. If you look at NSW, we participate on the customer

> service committees for state water in every catchment, we go to those forums to put forward the view of the environment's needs in terms of the system operations; we provide input to water sharing plan amendments in terms of what will lead to the best environmental outcome.[69]

The CEWH frames this activity as a way to seek 'changes to the way the system operates to get better environmental outcomes',[70] but the capacity for the EWMs to influence outcomes via this forum is now contingent on their role as large water customers rather than on a common understanding of the importance of protecting the environment. It is difficult to frame the environment as a *customer* while not being seen as seeking 'special' treatment for environmental protection: '[the] environment is now the largest customer, so the arrangements will have to be different to a normal irrigator, but without bias of course'.[71]

Australian EWMs have used their construction as a legal person to frame themselves as just another user of water. This narrative gives the EWMs the power of being 'the largest irrigator[s]' in the system, which the EWMs use to give themselves a voice in water policy.[72] The Australian EWMs have strengthened the narrative of the environment as 'just another user' by demonstrating their effective and efficient acquisition and use of water. They have largely relied on their watering outputs for 'output legitimacy', which focuses on the outcomes achieved as the driver of mutual acceptance and support.[73] The US EWMs, however, have gone a different way.

EWMs of the Columbia Basin and Colorado: collaborator, not competitor

> In Montana, the story of [instream flow] legislation is the story of Trout Unlimited and collaboration.[74]

The environmental advocacy movement that helped to create the EWMs in the western USA was strongly influenced by the experience of the controversy and long-term litigation to protect the spotted owl under the ESA in the 1980s and 1990s:[75] 'I was very dedicated to the idea that you could take an issue as controversial as the spotted owl, and find a different path and build it differently from the ground up.'[76] The EWMs, particularly the NGOs, very early adopted the explicit approach of building consensus and collaborating with communities to solve the problem of dewatered streams, rather than relying on unpopular and unpredictable litigation.[77] In doing so, the EWMs deliberately established themselves as different from other environmental organisations: 'the other environmental groups were doing other things (legislation, studies, advocacy, policy, wild and scenic designations, litigation), we were the only group focused on collaboration and projects on the ground'.[78]

The EWMs of the Columbia Basin and Colorado position themselves as collaborators with other water users and their local communities. Collaboration is a central element in the stories of success for NGO EWMs:

> It's more effective, you can move much more quickly to put water instream by offering incentives and compensation rather than using the ESA and litigating for five years. You can get there that way, but you alienate everyone. You're not changing behaviour, you're just forcing people into an enclosure, you're not changing behaviour that way. Even though you have to still have the regulation, you have to have the option for them to do something of their own volition.[79]

This narrative relies on maintaining a public interest in protecting the aquatic environment, and aligns with the broader cultural narrative that the environment should be protected because it cannot (or will not) protect itself.

In stark contrast to Australia, where water purchase is undertaken at arm's length through a tender process, the EWMs in the Columbia Basin and Colorado include water transactions as part of the collaborative process. The EWMs of the western USA frame the ability to pay for water rights as a mechanism to enhance the collaborative experience:

> [T]his would all be done in an environment of collaboration ... The basis of the conversation rests on the agreement that we aren't actually trying to take anything away, we're trying to determine the value and the just compensation for that asset. It does put us squarely in the arena of a business negotiation, not a legal coercion or threat of litigation or that kind of thing.[80]

This is a powerful reframing of water transactions. Rather than a market process, where decisions are made based solely based on the price of water, the water transactions are being used by the EWMs to enhance the legitimacy of environmental water recovery in the eyes of both the water users and the broader community. In part this reflects the relative inactivity of western USA water markets, and the associated increase in transaction costs of the one-on-one negotiations makes it a slower, more expensive process to recover water.[81] However, it remains a useful lesson for EWMs: it is not necessary to cede the narrative of the environment as deserving protection to make use of water markets. This ability of the EWMs of the western USA to construct their water transactions as part of a set of social norms based on trust and mutual respect demonstrates the possibility of using market mechanisms without necessarily adopting market norms (see discussion in Chapter 8).

However, this reliance on collaboration and community support is also a significant weakness for the EWMs and environmental water recovery.[82]

For the NGO EWMs of the Columbia Basin and Colorado, environmental water recovery is secondary to building and maintaining the support of the community. This leaves the NGO EWMs vulnerable to changing community attitudes, and makes the process of water recovery slower and more expensive.[83]

In Montana the Clark Fork Coalition acknowledges that water transactions are 'always dependent on a willing landowner',[84] and 'The biggest concern is validation and objections; landowners get peer pressure from neighbours who are disapproving of them selling water to the Clark Fork Coalition.'[85]

The trust and partnership that the NGO EWMs, in particular, rely on to initiate and complete water transactions successfully is dependent on the EWMs not forcing the issue:

> The sophisticated water user community understands who we are, trusts us, they don't feel threatened, we're a resource, we can partner with them, we bring perspectives and creative solutions that will work for them. If we ever figure out something that is not right, we walk quietly away and don't create problems for them. This trust building has been really critical.[86]

Even more explicitly, one staff member emphasised that success itself is about the partnership, not necessarily the actual outcome:

> There's a different character to the instream flow work ... There's a lot of celebration of success, but the partnership is always celebrated first. The partnership is the success, and what we manage to accomplish together is secondary.[87]

Despite having the requisite legal powers to set their own targets and goals, the EWMs remain reluctant to impose these on the community. In the Deschutes River Basin the local EWM considers community agreement on the desired level of environmental health of the rivers as the primary driver of the outcome: 'That's where the community comes in – it will be their decision as to whether the creek is restored or not, the DRC [Deschutes River Conservancy] ought to listen and respond to them.'[88]

The NGO EWMs can also be reluctant to make use of their legal powers to fully protect their instream flow rights:

> For the period of the lease (when water is in stream) we have to go out and take measurements, we have to make the call to more junior water users (to make them release the water). It can be controversial – some people accept it, some people [say] 'over my dead body'. If the water is being taken by someone else, first we file a complaint with the DNRC

> [Montana Department of Natural Resources and Conservation]; then we litigate. We have not yet had to resort to litigation and it is entirely a last resort.[89]

Although this vulnerability is particularly problematic for the NGO EWMs, which depend much more explicitly on community support, it also affects the government EWMs: 'We just got some flows on the Colorado mainstream, and this never would have happened without stakeholder group support…'[90]

In Oregon, Washington, and Colorado the state government agency must hold the transferred water rights in order for the water rights to be legally recognised as instream flows. In many cases the same government agency is responsible for both holding the instream flows and managing water resources more generally. In Australia this dual (and often incompatible) responsibility was a significant driver for the creation of independent government agencies to hold and manage environmental water. In the western USA this tension can result in the unwillingness of a state agency to enforce instream flow rights:

> Another institution – the Oregon Water Resources Department – holds all the instream water rights; because they are the water right holder, they have some discretion to enforce or not enforce their own water rights. This is one of the issues that's becoming more important as we put more water instream and increase competition for water rights. It's a politically unpopular decision to enforce their own water rights, but do they then let someone continue to take water and injure their instream water rights? Because they are the water right holder and the regulator, they are in a difficult position. The DRC and the other NGOs are required to take on a watchdog role to make sure they are stewarding and protecting the water rights that are being put instream and granted to them … When I look at it from the water users' standpoint, I'd be concerned that the state was overenforcing the instream water rights, I'd be concerned that they were looking out for their interests ahead of other interests. It's not how it's supposed to be, it creates a bit of schizophrenia on the state's part, because of conflict avoidance and politics, typically the state errs on the side of underenforcement of instream flows.[91]

The blurring of the line between the EWM and the government department is a significant constraint on legal personhood, and the government EWMs also acknowledge that they are often caught between the conflicting interests of environmental NGOs and water users: 'we're glad the environmental groups are there watching us. It helps us do our jobs better'[92] and 'environmental organizations watch and query whether we're enforcing our instream water rights; other water users, they hold us accountable more, if they think we're unreasonable in protecting our rights'.[93]

In these instances, the ability of the NGO EWMs to challenge the government EWMs is legally limited because the NGO EWMs are no longer the legal owner of the instream flow rights:

> [B]ecause [the NGO EWM] has a delicate and collaborative relationship with the state, we're not requesting enforcement, we're just pointing out that water rights are not being met and maybe they should do something about it, and that's typically enough to get them to act.[94]

Even when the government agency is not the only holder of instream flow rights, the attitude of the state government to instream flows reflects this unwillingness to create even the perception that the environment is receiving favourable treatment:

> [The state agency] is reluctant to show any special dispensation for environmental transactions. They don't see it as a public benefit or state benefit; so these transactions have as much or more scrutiny as other water transaction.[95]

The government EWMs should in theory be less vulnerable than the NGO EWMs to the potential hostility of some members of local communities to particular instream flow rights; but this is undermined by the duality of the government EWMs' role as both a water right holder and a regulator of all water rights. This potential conflict in responsibilities is exacerbated by the narrative of EWMs as collaborators with local communities.

In sum, the EWMs of the Columbia Basin and Colorado are unwilling to use their legal powers to pursue zero-sum approaches to environmental water recovery, either in the initial transaction (they refuse to 'buy it up and dry it up'), or in the protection of their instream flow rights (they are reluctant to litigate). Instead, they are most willing to use legal powers that support their role as a member of their communities. They present themselves as collaborative actors seeking consensus-based, mutually beneficial solutions. In contrast to the Australian EWMs, these EWMs emphasise 'input legitimacy': access, transparency, accountability, consultation and cooperation, independence, and credibility.[96] These choices constrain the legal personality of the EWMs, and leave them dependent on the cultural narrative that the aquatic environment should be protected because it is too weak to protect itself.

Competing narratives and 'off-limits' legal powers

In both south-eastern Australia and the western USA the aquatic environment is simultaneously constructed in water law as the socio-ecological concept underpinning the need for sustainable water resource management; a legal object that requires protection by imposing limits on the water use activities of others (such as a cap on water extraction, or modification of dams to meet ESA requirements); and a legal subject, capable of protecting its own interests. The EWMs in these jurisdictions have to navigate the tension between their own legal form (an entity constructed as a legal subject) and their objectives within water law, which stem from the other, less legally powerful constructs of the aquatic environment. The EWMs in each jurisdiction exhibit a preference for a particular subset of the powers associated with legal personhood as a way to make sense of the tensions between the narratives underpinning the multiple constructions of the aquatic environment. In each jurisdiction the EWMs have emphasised a particular narrative that has supported their specific form and operations to date.

Although the EWMs of south-eastern Australia were created to improve the health of the aquatic environment, in their operations they have framed themselves as just another irrigator, focusing on their capacity to participate in the market as a competitor with other water users to acquire and manage water. Although the largest and most powerful EWMs in Australia are government agencies, the Australian approach is more closely aligned with private interest theories of regulation, and the narrative of the environment as capable of acting to protect itself through the individual EWMs. This narrative emphasises the environment as a *user* of water, operating in (and competing for) the policy space with all the other users of water. This narrative depends on the environment having its own voice, and the power to use it (see Chapter 2). While the narrative supports the construction of the environment as its own advocate, in doing so it undermines the narrative that the environment needs (and deserves) special protections. For example, 'when RiverBank set up, there was a lot of emphasis on a level playing field, if environment was going to participate with [irrigator] licences, then it had to be on same basis as irrigators'.[97]

It is perhaps surprising to observe the dominance of this narrative in the Australian context, where the largest EWMs are government organisations and often perceived as being part of government, but the EWMs have been deliberately created and operated to distance themselves from government agencies.

This narrative is not missing from the western USA, but is much less dominant. Most EWMs emphasised their role as collaborators with other water users, as highlighted above, but it is worth noting that the legal capacity to grant instream flows in the western USA is contingent on recognising the environment as a beneficial use, the same as all other recognised uses of water. Government EWMs like the CWCB have also attempted to frame themselves as the same as other users when using their legal powers:

> To protect our water rights, we participate in other users' water court applications; where necessary, we oppose them and try to prevent injury to our water rights. We operate like another water user in that system.[98]

However, as discussed above, this legal capacity is only reluctantly used by even the state EWMs, especially when it comes into conflict with their broader roles as water use regulators. More typically, the EWMs of the Columbia Basin and Colorado present themselves largely as community actors, focused on collaborative approaches to improving environmental water quantities. The NGO EWMs typically eschew a combative, litigious approach and focus on working with water users to find ways to improve instream flows without reducing agricultural outputs. Even the government agencies, although historically more likely to enforce their legal rights in court and with a perceived background of a more contentious approach to water management, have been unwilling to use law and regulation to force a shift in water use by the imposition of caps or new conditions on existing users.

Although the NGO EWMs often act as the 'retail arm' of water recovery to avoid the cultural baggage of 'big government', the ultimate approach is more closely aligned with the narrative of the environment as worthy of protection but legally weak and ultimately dependent on the actions of humans to protect it. Collaborating with water users on each water transaction ensures that every time water is traded to the environment, it generates a local champion who can speak to the possibility of improving environmental outcomes without sending irrigators out of business. However, this maintenance of the status quo is likely to be a serious limit on the future water recovery activities of the EWMs.

This narrative also relies on a public interest theory of regulation, and constructs the environment as one of several public interests that should be balanced by policymakers to generate well-rounded regulation and governance. This emphasis on balance was expressed by both NGO and government EWMs:

> We try to balance the activities of mankind with reasonable preservation of natural environment; it is constantly a balancing act that the board does.[99]

> I think [the EWM] would like itself to be viewed as the place where reasonable people come together to do difficult business. It's a place where people can understand one another's needs, and try to meet those needs, without letting extreme views about the environment, property rights, or politics get in the way of doing important business. There's an intentional attempt to avoid being seen as too green or too agriculture-friendly – [the EWM] is a pretty pragmatic, business-minded group of people who can get things done for a lot of different interests.[100]

> It's not pitting the environment against anyone else. We're trying to convey that sentiment; that this is why we're trying to make this work happen. It's never with a notion of trying to pit environment against anything; we're really displaying the balance and the possibility of a solution.[101]

The issue of 'balance' is one that can cut both ways. In the western USA the argument for 'balance' is used to position the EWMs as advocates for a collaborative, consensus-based outcome that suits all users, rather than just the aquatic environment. This concept of balance frames the environment as merely one factor among many. In Australia, however, the need for balance was initially a powerful argument for the establishment of the MDB cap and the recovery of additional water, to redress the historical *imbalance* that had emerged as a result of overallocation of water to irrigators and 'provide a permanent rebalancing between consumptive water use and the environment'.[102] However, as discussed above, the Australian EWMs have come to rely on a narrative that frames their power as dependent on the volume of water entitlements they hold, supplanting balance with the framing of the environment as just another user.

Although each jurisdiction has a clearly identifiable dominant narrative, the tension between the competing narratives about the value of the environment and how it should be protected continues to undermine the dominant narrative. In attempting to shape their personhood to work around this tension, the EWMs of each location have ended up constraining their legal personhood by considering some of their legal powers as off limits.

Figure 6.1 draws on the conceptual framework in Chapter 2 to map the interaction between the regulatory response, the construction of the aquatic environment in law, and the different narratives underpinning the operation of the EWMs in the western USA and south-eastern Australia. By aligning themselves with a particular narrative, the EWMs limited their capacity to resolve the problem of insufficient water for the aquatic environment. In the western USA the EWMs can't afford to compromise their worthiness and community support by engaging in direct competition with water users. In south-eastern Australia the EWMs have successfully participated in water markets, but they have struggled to retain community support for the environment as worthy of protection.

The tension between the multiple constructions of the environment can further crystallise in specific legal limitations imposed on the EWMs, particularly in response to the water users' fear of a legally powerful construction of the environment as a legal subject.

	Legal object	Legal subject
EWM narrative	'Collaboration not competition' EWMs work to maintain worthiness	'Just another user' EWMs act as an any other legal person with water rights
Narrative and regulatory response	'Weak but worthy' Aquatic environment worthy of receiving protection by the state	'Strong enough to speak for itself' Aquatic environment receives limited protection by the state

Figure 6.1 Construction of personhood, narrative, and regulatory response for environmental water managers of Australia and the USA.

Fear of a legally powerful organisation representing the aquatic environment

> [W]ithin the water industry itself, it's started to change people's thoughts on how the environment will operate and that is a very powerful thing…[103]

In law, the EWMs are constructed as legal persons with specific rights and powers, and capable of protecting their own interests. However, the ongoing role of government in setting environmental water recovery targets and providing at least some of the funding for the EWMs means that the EWM is still haunted by the other constructions of the aquatic environment in water law. The EWMs simultaneously strengthen the narrative that the aquatic environment can and should look after itself while also relying on the narrative that the aquatic environment should be protected in the public interest.

These two competing narratives confront each other most dramatically when there is an attempt to assert the power of the aquatic environment as a legal person. In both Australia and the western USA there is evidence of the existing water users' growing fear that an EWM will be more powerful than any one individual water user, and that the EWM could use this power to reshape the water market and water management systems to meet its own needs. As Strang argued, 'ownership of water is integral to political power, and any loss of such control is disempowering',[104] and the water users' fear of losing their existing control is driving legal reform.

Western USA: the need for balance and limits on trade

In the western USA this fear is articulated in the reactions to the concept of instream flow rights held by private non-government EWMs. In the Columbia Basin and Colorado only the state of Montana currently allows instream flows to be held by private organisations; in all other states one government agency is specified in law as the 'person' able to hold water rights for the purposes of instream flows. In Colorado a fear of privately held instream flows rights was explicitly acknowledged: 'There have been attempts to get legislation for private instream flows, and that has always been met with fierce opposition from water users, because they're afraid there wouldn't be that balance.'[105]

In Oregon the EWMs were aware of other water users' fear that the environment's water demands were reshaping water resource management. Even staff in NGO EWMs felt constrained by the desire for balance:

> We were reallocating water in stream at such a scale that it started to concern some people that the train was leaving the station without some of the other water users; that the environmental water demand was going to be met by the DRC's effort and it may be at the expense of other less organized, less explicitly stated water needs of other sectors of the economy and the community. It was really the success of the DRC that raised some of these issues in the community, and forced the DRC to step back and take a broader view of what our role should be.[106]

Even where several private and public organisations are funded to recover water for the environment, such as the Columbia Basin Water Transactions Program, the individual organisations are discouraged from acquiring a portfolio of water that they could use to be economically self-sustaining: for example, Bonneville Power Administration's obligations 'do not allow them to fund the acquisition of an asset that is used for economic purposes'.[107] One of the reasons for this limit is that water recovery is designed to offset the impact of Bonneville Power Administration's hydropower production.[108] However, it is a serious impost on the EWMs of the Columbia Basin, and precludes them from making full use of the water markets. This limit is also a real constraint on the legal personhood of the EWMs funded by Bonneville Power Administration, and demonstrates the vulnerability of NGO EWMs to the values of the wider community.

In contrast, this ability to trade water recovered for environmental purposes is used to make the best use of available water in Colorado, where there is a fear that instream flows lead to water being lost to downstream states:[109]

> What we can do, and what the Colorado Water Trust has done, is that we can remarket the instream flow (based on historic consumptive use) to another user downstream, outside of the instream flow reach.[110]

South-eastern Australia: new limits on water purchase

In south-eastern Australia fear of a legally powerful aquatic environmental organisation emerged in response to the national water recovery programme in the MDB. The Murray-Darling Basin Plan committed to recovering 2,750 GL of water for the environment by 2019, and a further 450 GL by 2024 (although recent amendments in 2018 have potentially lowered this total).[111] In 2010 the federal government allocated A$3.1 billion to purchasing water rights from existing water users and A$5.8 billion to increasing water use efficiency, with the water savings to be allocated to the aquatic environment.[112]

In 2010 the National Farmers' Federation argued that 'The market should be the mechanism to adjust between consumptive use and the environment.'[113] This argument was backed by Productivity Commission comparisons of the relative cost of water purchase versus investment in water efficiency savings.[114] However, by 2015 the water recovery programme had purchased over 1,100 GL and there was growing concern about the volume of water changing hands from irrigators to the CEWH.[115] In response, the federal government legislated to cap the volume of water acquired via purchase to 1,500 GL.[116] This additional limit on the ability of the environmental water recovery programme to acquire water through voluntary transactions was welcomed by the National Irrigators' Council[117] and lauded by the conservative press.[118]

From the perspective of neoclassical economics, it is difficult to understand this limit on water purchase: it increases the cost of water recovery, prevents willing sellers from obtaining the best price for their water, and distorts the water market.[119] Even worse, the environmental water purchases were already undertaken separately to the water market itself, so any irrigator selling to the CEWH was voluntarily and explicitly choosing to do so. The new limit on the CEWH's ability to acquire water can be best understood as an example of the other water users' fear of a powerful EWM, with deep pockets, participating in the water market. This legally powerful construction of the aquatic environment can compete with other water users by raising the cost of water in the market, reducing the availability of water for commercial use, and changing the operation of water delivery and accounting to suit the environment rather than irrigators. The irrigators' fear of the EWMs also reflects a largely unacknowledged windfall gain: today's irrigators depend on the historical health and wellbeing of aquatic ecosystems. A legally powerful EWM could potentially seek reimbursement for these ecosystem services.

This fear of a legally powerful organisation representing the aquatic environment is strongly linked to the narrative of the environment as powerful enough to protect itself, and legal reforms in response to this fear have directly focused on imposing specific limits on the EWMs' powers. The aquatic environment in the form of the EWM is left in the difficult position of being constructed as a legal person but with additional legal limits above those imposed on other water users, and limited capacity to act to protect its interests fully. What is also clear from the evidence in Australia and the USA is that the actions taken by the other water users to limit the powers of the EWMs require those water users to reject the narrative of the environment as deserving of protection (most strongly evidenced in south-eastern Australia). This growing awareness that the aquatic environment is represented by an organisation capable of protecting itself is actively undermining the narrative that the environment is worth protecting.

The interaction between the multiple constructions of the aquatic environment results in each individual construct being 'neither fish nor flesh'.[120] As a legal entity the EWMs do not have access to the full powers of a legal person, and yet they are unable to access the full suite of legal protections previously accorded to the environment.

The paradox of legal personhood

What emerges from this analysis is a paradox: the EWMs increase the legal power of the aquatic environment by giving it legal personhood, but their operation may be driving legal reform that lowers environmental protection by weakening the cultural narratives that support protecting the environment. This is an unexpected and unforeseen outcome of the creation and operation of the EWMs, which are intended to improve the health and function of the aquatic environment by recovering additional water and managing this water efficiently and effectively. As the paradox appears to be a consequence of the legal personhood of the EWMs, this is a significant problem for legal rights for rivers.

As legal persons, the EWMs are a step change in the way that the aquatic environment is represented in, and made legible to, law. By constructing the aquatic environment as a legal subject, the EWMs give it the formal capacity to bear legal relations, including rights and duties, and to speak on its own behalf. The EWMs have also achieved real improvements in environmental flows by increasing the volume of water available to the aquatic environment and the efficiency of its management.[121] The EWMs use this legal personhood to position the environment itself as a participant in water markets and a user of water in its own right. Even in the western USA, where the public interest, EWM-as-collaborator narrative is strongest, the EWMs use their legal personality to enable them to negotiate water transactions on an individual basis and will, where absolutely necessary, use their legal powers to protect their water rights.

However, in both Australia and the western USA the EWMs exhibit a reluctance to make use of all the legal powers attendant on legal persons. In both jurisdictions the EWMs have limited themselves so as to appear less threatening to other water users. In Australia this manifests as a portrayal of the EWMs as an irrigator of the environment, operating under the same regulations as all other irrigators. The EWMs are attempting to 'grow' environmental outcomes in the same way that irrigators grow crops, but the metrics of assessing agricultural productivity and environmental protection are very different. The EWMs of south-eastern Australia are 'continually confronted by the differences between the way they present themselves, and what they actually need from water resource managers, and how they account for their use of water to the public'.[122] By framing themselves as just another user of water, the Australian EWMs undercut the 'special' nature of the environment.

In the Columbia Basin and Colorado the EWMs are presented as community-oriented collaborators which work with agricultural users of water to seek a balanced outcome by improving instream flows and maintaining agricultural production. This strategy has been highly effective in creating the necessary legal changes that enable EWMs to operate, and in weakening opposition to environmental water recovery. However, the very success of this approach deepens the outrage of other water users and communities in circumstances in which the EWM would be required to act more selfishly and compete with other water users. For example, the EWMs are extremely reluctant to use litigation to protect their rights at all. In addition, the requirement to find water transactions which are mutually acceptable to the EWM, the irrigators, and the community both increases transaction costs and reduces the water potentially available to the environment. The current operation of the EWMs as collaborators encourages communities to believe that the environment can (and should) only receive protection where this does not require substantial changes to human activity. The activities of the EWMs have strengthened the idea that all solutions to the problems of environmental degradation will be negotiated, collaborative, consensus-based outcomes, which obscures the need sometimes to make tough choices. When the needs of the aquatic environment directly compete with those of human users, the EWMs have no ability to resolve this competition without destroying their community support.

The construction of the EWMs as legal persons simultaneously empowers the aquatic environment in law and weakens the cultural values and social norms that consider the environment as worthy of protection. This paradox has emerged through the detailed examination of the EWMs and their role in water law, but the conceptual framework developed in Chapter 2 indicates that the paradox may not be limited to the EWMs. The next chapter examines the creation of legal rights for rivers in more detail, and considers whether, and how, these findings may affect these new legal persons.

Notes

1 Veronica Strang, *Gardening the World: Agency, Identity and the Ownership of Water* (Berghahn Books, 2009) 23.
2 E O'Donnell, 'Legal Rights for Rivers: More Power, Less Protection?' (International Water Law Project blog, 2018) www.internationalwaterlaw.org/blog/2018/04/23/legal-rights-for-rivers-more-power-less-protection/.
3 Ngaire Naffine, 'Who Are Law's Persons? From Cheshire Cats to Responsible Subjects' (2003) 66(3) *Modern Law Review* 346, 350.
4 Ngaire Naffine, *Law's Meaning of Life: Philosophy, Religion, Darwin and the Legal Person* (Hart Publishing, 2009) 10.
5 Water Act 2007 (Cth) s 106.
6 Australian Government, *Commonwealth Environmental Water: Trading Framework* (Commonwealth Environmental Water Office, 2014).
7 Columbia Basin Water Transactions Program, *Annual Report 2012: A Decade of Outcomes 2003–2012* (National Fish and Wildlife Foundation, 2012).
8 Interview VEWH 1.
9 Interview VEWH 3.
10 Interview TUM.
11 Interview DRC.
12 Internal Revenue Code 26 USC § 501(c).
13 Interview NFWF.
14 Interview CFC.
15 Interview HRA.
16 Marshall E Dimock, 'Government Corporations: A Focus of Policy and Administration, I' (1949) 43(5) *American Political Science Review* 899; Richard Boyer, 'The Statutory Corporation as a Democratic Device' (1957) 16(1) *Australian Journal of Public Administration* 29; A Barker, 'Quangos in Politics' (2001) *International Encyclopedia of the Social & Behavioral Sciences* 12631.
17 Sarah Hendry, 'Ownership Models for Water Services: Implications for Regulation' in Aileen McHarg et al. (eds), *Property and the Law in Natural Resources* (Oxford University Press, 2010) 257, 276.
18 R L Wettenhall, 'Quangos, Quagos and the Problems of Non-Ministerial Organization' (1983) 42(1) *Australian Journal of Public Administration* 5.
19 Department of Sustainability and Environment (Vic), *Victorian Government White Paper: Securing Our Water Future Together* (State of Victoria, 2004) Chapters 6 and 7.
20 Water Act 1989 (Vic) s 33DB.
21 Interview VEWH 3.
22 Interview VEWH 1.
23 Interview VEWH 3.
24 Interview VEWH 1.
25 Water Act 2007 (Cth) ss 105–117.

26 Interview CEWO 1.
27 Interview CEWO 2.
28 Interview OEH.
29 Interview DEWNR.
30 Sasha Charney, *Decades Down the Road: An Analysis of Instream Flow Programs in Colorado and the Western United States* (Colorado Water Conservation Board, 2005); Edna T Loehman and Sasha Charney, 'Further Down the Road to Sustainable Environmental Flows: Funding, Management Activities and Governance for Six Western US States' (2011) 36(7) *Water International* 873.
31 Interview CWCB.
32 Interview WDE 1.
33 Interview WDE 2.
34 Interview CEWO 2.
35 Interview CEWO 2.
36 Interview VEWH 1.
37 National Farmers' Federation, *Submission to Productivity Commission's Draft Research Report: Market Mechanisms for Recovering Water in the Murray-Darling Basin* (National Farmers' Federation, 2010) 14. Although this report cautions against the direct purchase of water rights on the open water market (which the CEWO has avoided by using separate tender programs), it underscores the persistent fear of a well-resourced, legally powerful EWM.
38 Interview VEWH 2.
39 Water Act 1989 (Vic) s 33DB.
40 Water Act 1989 (Vic) s 33DS(2).
41 Erin O'Donnell, 'Institutional Reform in Environmental Water Management: The New Victorian Environmental Water Holder' (2012) 22 *Journal of Water Law* 73.
42 Interview VEWH 2.
43 Liberal Party of Australia, *The Coalition's Plan for Real Action on the Murray-Darling Basin* (Liberal Party of Australia, 2010).
44 Interview DRC.
45 Interview WWT.
46 Interview HRA.
47 Naffine, above n 4, 30.
48 Erin O'Donnell, 'Competition or Collaboration? Using Legal Persons to Manage Water for the Environment in Australia and the United States' (2017) 34(6) *Environmental and Planning Law Journal* 503.
49 Commonwealth Environmental Water Office and Nature Foundation SA, 'Press Release: Commonwealth Works with Nature Foundation South Australia to Deliver Water' (24 October 2012).
50 Interview OEH.
51 Daniel Connell, 'The Role of the Commonwealth Environmental Water Holder' in Daniel Connell and R. Quentin Grafton (eds), *Basin Futures: Water Reform in the Murray-Darling Basin* (ANU E Press, 2011) 982; O'Donnell, above n 41.
52 NSW Department of Primary Industries, 'Drought Management' (2016) www.water.nsw.gov.au/water-management/water-availability/drought-management.
53 Water Act 1989 (Vic) s 33AAA.
54 West Gippsland Catchment Management Authority, *Drought Measures – Thomson EWR* (West Gippsland Catchment Management Authority, 2010); Department of Sustainability and Environment (Vic), *Victorian Water Accounts 2006–2007* (State of Victoria, 2008); Department of Sustainability and Environment (Vic), *Victorian Water Accounts 2007–2008* (State of Victoria, 2010); Department of Sustainability and Environment (Vic), *Victorian Water Accounts 2008–2009* (State of Victoria, 2010).

55 Bulk Entitlement (Thomson River – Environment) Order 2005 (Hansard, Parliament of Victoria, 2005); Yarra Environmental Entitlement 2006 (Hansard, Parliament of Victoria, 2006).
56 O'Donnell, above n 41.
57 Interview CEWO 1.
58 Interview OEH.
59 Paul Humphries, 'The Drought We Had to Have?' (Science Alert, 15 August 2008) www.sciencealert.com/opinions/20081508–17809–4.html?utm_source=feedburner&utm_medium=feed&utm_campaign=Feed%25253A+sciencealert-latestnews+%252528ScienceAlert-Latest+Stories%252529.
60 Water Act 2007 (Cth) s 106; Water Act 1989 (Vic) s 48OB.
61 This output focus extends from the Dublin Principles about the need to account for use of water for commercial purposes, and is entrenched in the water accounting frameworks of south-eastern Australia. Every commercial user of water in south-eastern Australia has its use of water recorded by water meters, which are read by government officials, to ensure compliance at individual and basin-wide levels.
62 Victorian Environmental Water Holder, *Reflections: Environmental Watering in Victoria 2015–16* (State Government of Victoria, 2016).
63 Interview OEH. In the Australian context, carp is an introduced species and classified as a pest.
64 Australian Government, *Commonwealth Environmental Water – Trading Arrangements Discussion Paper* (Commonwealth Environmental Water Office, 2011).
65 Interview OEH.
66 Nature Foundation SA, 'Water For Nature: Our Work' www.naturefoundation.org.au/what-we-do/water-for-nature/our-work.
67 Erin O'Donnell et al., 'Cry Me a River: Going Beyond the Crisis Response: Building Trust and Maintaining Legitimacy in Environmental Flows' (Academy of Social Sciences Australia, 2018) www.assa.edu.au/academy-workshop-report-cry-me-a-river/.
68 Water NSW, 'Customer Services Committees' www.waternsw.com.au/customer-service/feedback/committees.
69 Interview CEWO 1.
70 Interview CEWO 1.
71 Interview VEWH 3.
72 Warwick Long, 'Coalition Split as Commonwealth Environmental Water Holder Stays with Environment Department' (23 September 2015) www.abc.net.au/news/2015–09–23/anger-over-environmental-water-holder-split-from-water-departmen/6797094; Warwick Long, 'Increase the Flow: Irrigators Call on Authorities to Increase Floodwaters in the Murray-Darling Basin' *ABC Rural* (15 September 2016) www.abc.net.au/news/2016–09–15/flood-the-murray-darling-basin/7844736.
73 Karl Hogl et al., 'Legitimacy and Effectiveness of Environmental Governance – Concepts and Perspectives' in Karl Hogl et al. (eds), *Environmental Governance: The Challenge of Legitimacy and Effectiveness* (Edward Elgar, online edn, 2012) 1.
74 Interview TUM.
75 Barry R Noon and Kevin S McKelvey, 'Management of the Spotted Owl: A Case History in Conservation Biology' (1996) 27 *Annual Review of Ecological Systems* 135.
76 Interview TUM.
77 See, for example, Columbia Basin Water Transactions Program, above n 7; D Garrick et al., 'Water Markets and Freshwater Ecosystem Services: Policy

Reform and Implementation in the Columbia and Murray-Darling Basins' (2009) 69 *Ecological Economics* 366; Brandon Scarborough, *Environmental Water Markets: Restoring Streams Through Trade* (Property and Environment Research Centre, 2010); Steven Malloch, *Liquid Assets: Protecting and Restoring the West's Rivers and Wetlands Through Environmental Water Transactions* (Trout Unlimited, 2005).

78 Interview CWT.
79 Interview WWT.
80 Interview DRC.
81 Productivity Commission, *Market Mechanisms for Recovering Water in the Murray-Darling Basin (Final Report, March)* (Productivity Commission, 2010); Dustin Evan Garrick, *Water Allocation in Rivers Under Pressure: Water Trading, Transaction Costs, and Transboundary Governance in the Western USA and Australia* (Edward Elgar, 2015).
82 P L Tan, K H Bowmer, and C Baldwin, 'Continued Challenges in the Policy and Legal Framework for Collaborative Water Planning' (2012) 474 *Journal of Hydrology* 84; Cameron Holley and Darren Sinclair, 'A New Water Policy Option for Australia? Collaborative Water Governance, Compliance and Enforcement and Audited Self-Management' (2014) 17(2) *Australasian Journal of National Resources Law and Policy* 189.
83 Dustin Garrick and Bruce Aylward, 'Transaction Costs and Institutional Performance in Market-Based Environmental Water Allocation' (2012) 88(3) *Land Economics* 536.
84 Interview CFC.
85 Interview CFC.
86 Interview CWT.
87 Interview TUM.
88 Interview DRC.
89 Interview CFC.
90 Interview CWCB.
91 Interview DRC.
92 Interview WDE 1.
93 Interview CWCB.
94 Interview DRC.
95 Interview CFC.
96 Hogl et al., above n 72.
97 Interview OEH.
98 Interview CWCB.
99 Interview CWCB.
100 Interview DRC.
101 Interview WWT.
102 Commonweath of Australia, *Water for the Future: Restoring the Balance in the Murray-Darling Basin* (Australian Government Department of the Environment, Water, Heritage and the Arts, 2010), 1.
103 Interview VEWH 3.
104 Strang, above n 1, 22.
105 Interview CWCB.
106 Interview DRC.
107 Interview NFWF.
108 N J Leonard et al., 'The Challenge of Managing the Columbia River Basin for Energy and Fish' (2015) 22 *Fisheries Management and Ecology* 88.
109 David M Gillilan and Thomas C Brown, *Instream Flow Protection: Seeking a Balance in Western Water Use* (Island Press, 1997) 167.
110 Interview CWCB.

111 Murray-Darling Basin Authority, *Murray-Darling Basin Plan* (Commonwealth of Australia, 2012) ss 04, 7.09.
112 Commonwealth of Australia, *Securing Our Water Future* (Australian Government Department of the Environment, Water, Heritage and the Arts, 2010).
113 National Farmers' Federation, above n 37, 10.
114 Productivity Commission, above n 80.
115 Greg Hunt and Bob Baldwin, 'Joint Media Release: Coalition Delivers Election Commitment with 1500GL Water Buyback Cap' (Commonwealth of Australia, 14 September 2015).
116 Water Amendment Act 2015 (Cth) Schedule 1.
117 Tom Chesson, '1500 GL Cap on Water Buybacks Legislated' (National Irrigators' Council, 14 September 2015) www.irrigators.org.au/assets/uploads/news/sep-2015–2.pdf.
118 Dairy News Australia, '1500 GL Cap Delivers Certainty to Farmers' (15 September 2015) www.dairynewsaustralia.com.au/general-news/1500-gl-cap-delivers-certainty-to-farmers.html; Sid Maher, 'Senate Passes 1500GL Cap on Murray Darling Water Buybacks' *The Australian* (15 September 2015) www.theaustralian.com.au/national-affairs/climate/senate-passes-1500gl-cap-on-murraydarling-water-buybacks/news-story/f59442bd44b3f98e33ba4b27542dc779.
119 Productivity Commission, above n 80.
120 John Heywood, *A dialogue conteinyng the nomber in effect of all the prouerbes in the englishe tongue compacte in a matter concernyng two maner of mariages* (Imprinted at London in Fletestrete by Thomas Berthelet prynter to the kynges hyghnesse, 1546), Early English Books Online, *Text Creation Partnership* http://quod.lib.umich.edu/e/eebo/A03168.0001.001?view=toc.
121 Scarborough, above n 76; Brandon Scarborough and Hertha L Lund, *Saving Our Streams: Harnessing Water Markets: A Practical Guide* (Property and Environment Research Centre, 2007); Murray-Darling Basin Authority, *Towards a Healthy, Working Murray-Darling Basin: Basin Plan Annual Report 2014–15* (Murray-Darling Basin Authority, 2015).
122 O'Donnell, above n 48, 520.

7 Rivers as legal persons

Competition and collaboration

In 2017 rivers in Aotearoa New Zealand, India, and Colombia were recognised as being the subject of legal rights and given the status of legal persons. The novelty of constructing rivers as people fired the imagination of people around the world, and as each new river was given legal rights, it was generally seen as a cause for celebration and a step forward for environmental protection.[1] Legal rights for rivers certainly sounds like a good idea: it means giving rivers the legal tools to protect themselves,[2] and expands legal systems to include consideration of the needs and rights of nature as well as of humans.[3] However, the conceptual framework developed in Chapter 2 highlights three significant problems that emerge when nature is personified in law.

First, just what is 'nature'? The expression of nature in law as a *socio-ecological concept* (Chapter 2) is extremely vulnerable to shifting definitions and changes in the social value of 'nature'. In particular, Western legal frameworks tend to perpetuate the dichotomy between the 'natural' and the 'human', which operates to disconnect people from nature.[4] When nature has legal rights of its own, this disconnection can be exacerbated by the potential for the relationship between humanity and the environment to become adversarial (Chapter 6).

Second, constructing nature as a separate legal person can fracture the powerful bonds between Indigenous and First Nations peoples and Country (Indigenous peoples of Australia have a close and personal relationship with the land, which they refer to as Country).[5] Legal rights for rivers in Aotearoa New Zealand have emerged specifically in response to the Māori worldview of the river as an ancestor, so the challenges that this paradigm may create for other Indigenous peoples are important to understand.

Third, why *should* nature need to protect itself in law? Modern environmental law is essentially public law created to protect collective values and interests in a clean and healthy environment (Chapter 2). It is part of a broader set of public interest laws intended to ensure that the law acts on behalf of those too institutionally weak to speak up for themselves in an adversarial context.[6] Giving rivers legal rights replaces this emphasis on the collective good with individual rights, most particularly the right to sue and be sued (legal standing), so that rivers can go to court and advocate for their own interests. In 1972 Christopher Stone made a compelling argument as to why legal standing is so important: without it, harm to the river can only be recognised if it is also harm to human beings.[7] But standing law has evolved significantly since 1972, and many environmental organisations can now speak on behalf of the environment.[8] So is this ability to go to court still so necessary? In fact, the experience of the EWMs in Australia highlights that rather than the ability to go to court, it is the ability to participate in policy debates that is much more important. Australian EWMs use their legal personality to give a 'voice' to the environment, enabling the EWMs to compete for regulatory outcomes (Chapters 4 and 6).

Finally, legal rights are only of value to the extent that they can be enforced. If nature has a 'voice' and is expected to compete for its own regulatory outcomes, it must have the real world power (particularly funding and organisational capacity) to make its voice heard.[9] Without this power, legal rights for nature can create a false perception of a level playing field between human interests and nature's interests.[10]

Bringing together the conceptual framework (Chapter 2) with the evidence of the EWMs (Chapters 3–6) shows that constructing the aquatic environment as a legal person (even via the operation of organisations like the EWMs that do not directly create legal rights for rivers) can create a paradox where increasing legal power can actually lead to less legal protection. This chapter examines the creation of legal rights for rivers around the world to see how these new legal rights are interacting with water law and governance, and to identify any evidence, even at this early stage, of the paradox of the EWMs.

Legal rights for rivers: an idea whose time has come

Constructing rivers as people with legal rights of their own is a transformative idea. The combination of a profound shift in the environmental law paradigm and the apparent novelty of the concept has resonated with communities around the world. The successful application of the idea in Aotearoa New Zealand, India, and Colombia has inspired other jurisdictions to explore the possibilities. In Nigeria there is a campaign to extend legal rights to the River Ethiope, which has important cultural as well as ecological values.[11] In Western Australia the Traditional Owners of the Mardoowarra (Fitzroy River) are exploring legal personhood as a way to recognise the river as a living entity, and local communities in south-west Western Australia have begun a grassroots campaign for legal rights for the Margaret River, a major tourist destination famed for its natural beauty.[12] In the USA an environmental NGO filed suit in the Federal District Court in Colorado, seeking to recognise the legal rights of the

Colorado River.[13] In Oregon another environmental NGO filed an action on behalf of the Siletz River ecosystem, attempting to prevent the aerial spraying of pesticides within the river catchment.[14] Although neither of these attempts was successful, they raised the profile of legal rights for rivers throughout the USA.[15]

However, despite this perceived novelty, legal rights for nature, and specifically for rivers, is not an especially new idea. In Western legal scholarship the concept of giving non-human entities legal rights goes back over 100 years.[16] Although the idea was still considered 'unthinkable' when Stone published his seminal article in 1972, less than 40 years later rights for nature had been embedded at the constitutional level in Ecuador.[17] In 2011 these new Ecuadorian constitutional rights for nature were tested in a case involving protection of the Río Vilcabamba.[18]

Río Vilcabamba: new legal rights, but no new outcomes

The Vilcabamba River is located in Loja province in southern Ecuador. During the construction of a new road, rocks and other detritus were deposited on the bed and banks of the Río Vilcabamba, which damaged the river banks and the riparian forest, and polluted the water when the river flooded. The Ecuador constitution gives any citizen the right to enforce nature's rights, so local affected citizens brought the case to Ecuador's provincial court (Sala de la Corte Provincial) on behalf of the river. The court held that 'the rights of nature had been violated – more specifically nature's right "to exist, to be maintained and to the regeneration of its vital cycles, structures and functions"'.[19] However, the court stopped short of preventing the construction of the road, instead choosing to impose environmental protection guidelines on future work and requirements to make good the existing damage. In her analysis of the case, Daly argues that 'additional time, resources and continued persistence on the part of the plaintiffs is needed to ensure compliance with the court's order', and in the end neither the construction company nor the provincial government took the required action to enforce the order.[20]

The Vilcabamba case demonstrates the difficulty in enforcing legal rights for nature, especially when those rights lack any additional institutional support.[21] In Ecuador nature does not have any formally identified guardians, which means that enforcement of the rights relies on individual citizens and NGOs. Further, in the Vilcabamba case the court acknowledged the potential for conflict between the constitutional rights of nature and the human right to economic development, and the final outcome indicates that the court attempted to find a balance between the competing rights of nature and humans. As a result, in the case of the Río Vilcabamba the new legal rights for nature did not create any new solutions to the existing problems facing environmental protection in law.

The legal rights for rivers created in 2017 are much more specific, and for the most part are attached to named rivers. In each case the grant of legal rights was accompanied by the nomination of specific guardians to act on behalf of the rivers. Each of the three main examples of legal rights for rivers (Aotearoa New Zealand, India, and Colombia) is examined in detail.

Whanganui River, Aotearoa New Zealand

The Whanganui River is located on the south-west of Aotearoa New Zealand's North Island (Figure 7.1), and runs for 290 kilometres from its source to the Tasman Sea. The river begins on the slopes of Mount Tongariro, and up to 80 per cent of the river flow is diverted for use in the Tongariro hydropower scheme. The upper reaches of the Whanganui River are located within a national park, but much of the catchment has been cleared for farming. Water quality in the river is affected by erosion, sewage discharge, and nutrient and manure pollution from farms. The river is central to the culture and livelihoods of local Māori, and is a popular tourist destination for kayaking, hiking, and heritage tours.

On 15 March 2017 the government of Aotearoa New Zealand set an international precedent by granting legal personhood to the Whanganui River. The passage of the legislation created headlines around the world, but it is important to remember that the legislation was the result of eight years of negotiation by the Whanganui Iwi (local Māori) and the Crown over ownership and control of the river, and part of an ongoing dispute since 1873.

The new legislation stems from the findings of the Waitangi Tribunal and the Treaty of Waitangi settlement process for the Atihaunui-ā-Pāpārangi iwi (referred to in this book as the 'Whanganui Iwi') regarding their claims to the Whanganui River.[22] The Whanganui Iwi had lived along the river for nearly a thousand years before the Crown attempted to take ownership in 1903. The Whanganui is classed as a 'navigable' river, and it was on this basis that the Crown claimed ownership of the river and its bed.

In 2011 the Record of Understanding between the government of Aotearoa New Zealand and the Whanganui Iwi (Māori) indicated that the Whanganui River would be granted the status of a legal person. This development was of great interest for environmental and Indigenous legal scholars, but until the legislation was passed in 2017 there was significant uncertainty as to what the new legal rights would entail.[23] Even now, as implementation of the new legal arrangements proceeds, there are still significant unresolved issues for water and catchment management.

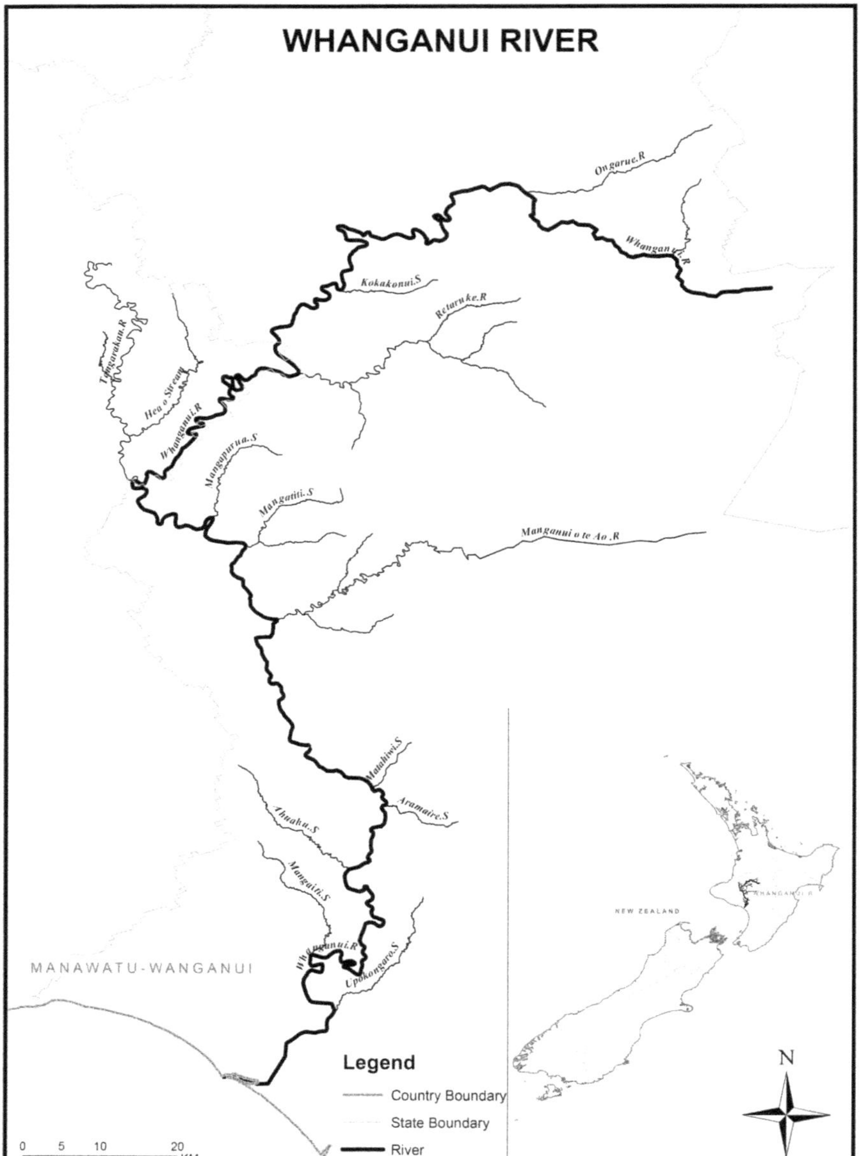

Figure 7.1 Whanganui River, Aotearoa New Zealand.

Water resource management in Aotearoa New Zealand

Aotearoa New Zealand experiences high annual rainfall, and water scarcity is not traditionally a problem. However, water quality and irregular water flow are significant problems, and are the focus of new national water reform.[24] Aotearoa New Zealand does not have an active water market and there is only a very low incidence of informal water trading.[25]

Water resource management is regulated under the Resource Management Act 1991 (RMA), which takes an ecosystem approach underpinned by the concept of sustainable management.[26] Warnock and Baker-Galloway describe the RMA as providing a highly integrated legal framework for natural resource management.[27] Water is vested in the Crown, and temporary rights to take and use water (a 'resource consent' lasting up to 35 years) under the RMA are granted by consent authorities, typically local councils.[28] Under Part 9 of the RMA, any person may apply to the Minister for the Environment for a 'water conservation order' to protect environmental or cultural water values.

Protecting cultural and ecological values

At present the RMA requires consent authorities to recognise and provide for the 'relationship of Maori and their culture and traditions with their ancestral lands, water, sites, waahi tapu [sacred sites], and other taonga [treasures]'.[29] The RMA supports the use of collaborative co-management arrangements with the Māori for the governance of natural resources, including rivers. Following settlement of Māori claims under the Treaty of Waitangi, these co-management arrangements include new local authorities with representatives from both the Māori and the national government (such as the Waikato River Authority).

However, the national government in Aotearoa New Zealand is currently pursuing major freshwater management reform. In 2010 a survey of regional councils across Aotearoa New Zealand found that although all have objectives or policies regarding water quantity and quality, only six of the 17 councils have given these policies regulatory force. A proposed national environmental standard has been developed that would set interim ecological flows and provide guidance on how to undertake environmental flows assessments consistently, but this document has been shelved pending the outcomes of the current reform process.[30] The consultation document prepared by the Ministry for Environment emphasises the importance of managing water quality, respecting Iwi values, and honouring the Treaty of Waitangi, and it seems likely that co-management arrangements will continue to be part of Aotearoa New Zealand's water law and governance framework.

Legal personhood for the Whanganui River

The outcomes of the treaty settlement negotiations for the Whanganui River are very similar to previous treaty settlements, and in many ways the new legal arrangements for the Whanganui are simply an adaptation of the co-management arrangements that characterise river governance in Aotearoa New Zealand.[31] However, reaching agreement on the Whanganui required resolving the problem of who would legally own the riverbed. The Whanganui Iwi were opposed to the Crown retaining ownership of the riverbed, and the Aotearoa New Zealand government sought to avoid the political complexity of handing over the riverbed to Iwi.[32] The proposal to grant legal personality to the river itself became a circuit-breaker in these negotiations, enabling agreement to be reached.

Accordingly, the Te Awa Tupua (Whanganui River Claims Settlement) Act 2017 (NZ) granted the Whanganui River 'from the mountains to the sea, incorporating all its physical and metaphysical elements' the same duties, rights, powers, and liabilities as a legal person.[33] Under the new legislation, ownership of the riverbed has been transferred from the Crown to the new legal entity, Te Awa Tupua, which effectively enables the river to own itself.[34] This means that although the Whanganui River is the first river to receive legal rights of its own, this happened as part of a process that did not explicitly intend to create legal rights for nature, nor necessarily to establish a new international legal precedent.

However, although legal rights for nature were not a primary driver of the new legislation, the Māori worldview of the river as an ancestor was central to the final outcome. Recognising the river and its catchment as an interconnected, living whole, protected by an appointed guardian, places the Whanganui Iwi's relationship with the river at the heart of the new legislation. The Māori principle of *kaitiakitanga* (guardianship) broadens the focus of the Te Awa Tupua Act from resource management, and establishes a profoundly different relationship for all people with the river. Further, the legislation specifies 'intrinsic values' that 'represent the essence of Te Awa Tupua', including the relationship of Iwi to the river: *Ko au te Awa, ko te Awa ko au* (I am the River and the River is me).[35] In this way, although the legal person of Te Awa Tupua (the Whanganui River) is distinct from the Whanganui Iwi, it avoids the traditional Western dichotomy of nature and human.

Institutional and governance arrangements

Te Awa Tupua, the legal person that is the river and its catchment, is represented by a guardian, Te Pou Tupua. The guardian comprises two people, one appointed by the national government (the Crown) and the other by the Whanganui Iwi.[36] The guardian is the human face of the river, responsible for promoting and protecting the health and wellbeing of Te

Awa Tupua.[37] Te Pou Tupua will administer a NZ$30 million contestable fund to support the operations of the new governance arrangements.

Te Pou Tupua will be supported by a new advisory group, Te Karewao, established under the legislation. The future management of Te Awa Tupua will be guided by a new strategy document, Te Heke Ngahuru, which will be developed and monitored by a strategy group, Te Kopuka na Te Awa Tupua. This group provides an opportunity for all stakeholders in Te Awa Tupua to be engaged in the process of developing and implementing future strategy, and will consist of up to 17 representatives: six from Iwi with interests in the Whanganui River, and the remaining 11 from local and central government, tourism, conservation, recreation and wild game interests, and Genesis Energy, the operator of the Tongariro power scheme (located near the source of the Whanganui River).[38]

However, despite the long negotiations and careful development of these complex new collaborative management arrangements, there is a major gap when it comes to water governance. The legislation creating legal rights for the Whanganui River expressly states that nothing in the Act 'creates, limits, transfers, extinguishes, or otherwise affects any rights to, or interests in, water' (s 16). This means that the river, although it includes the entire catchment from the mountains to the sea, does not own the rights to its own water.

Ganga and Yamuna Rivers, India

Uttarakhand is a state of India located on the northern border of India and Nepal. The state contains the headwaters of the Ganga and Yamuna Rivers (including their source glaciers), and parts of the Himalayas. The Ganga and Yamuna Rivers flow across India, and in the case of the Ganga all the way into Bangladesh, before entering the Bay of Bengal (Figure 7.2). Both rivers are considered sacred by Hindus, and the confluence of the rivers at Allahabad is considered a holy site.

In 2017, days after the news broke that the Whanganui River had received legal rights, the High Court of Uttarakhand released an extraordinary ruling. On 20 March 2017 the court held that:

> the Rivers Ganga and Yamuna, all their tributaries, streams, every natural water flowing with flow continuously or intermittently of these rivers, are declared as juristic/legal persons/living entities having the status of a legal person with all corresponding rights, duties and liabilities of a living person.[39]

Ten days later the same court ruled that all of nature in the state of Uttarakhand had legal rights:

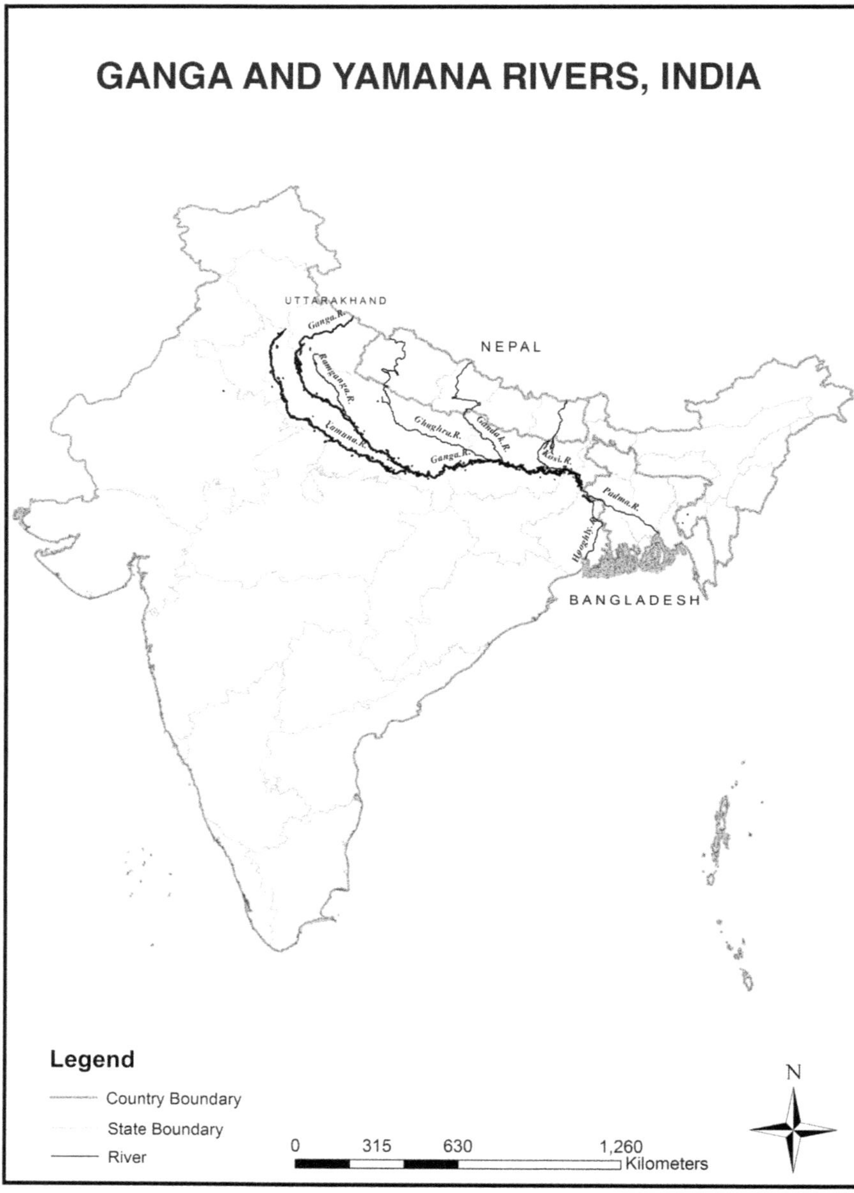

Figure 7.2 Ganga and Yamuna Rivers, India.

> the Glaciers including Gangotri and Yamunotri, rivers, streams, rivulets, lakes, air, meadows, dales, jungles, forests wetlands, grasslands, springs and waterfalls, legal entity/legal person/juristic person/juridical person/ moral person/artificial person having the status of a legal person.[40]

The first case (referred to here as the *Ganga and Yamuna* case) has been appealed to the Supreme Court of India, which stayed the effect of the original ruling when it agreed to hear the appeal.[41] No such appeal has been filed for the second case (referred to as the *Glaciers* case). The legal status of the Ganga and Yamuna Rivers remains in limbo.

Water resource management in the Ganges Basin, India

The Ganga and Yamuna Rivers are located within the Ganges–Brahmaputra–Meghna watershed, which extends across India, Bangladesh, Pakistan, Nepal, and China. In this region water security is closely linked to issues of national security.[42] Hanasz describes the Ganges–Brahmaputra 'problemshed' as a place of both 'plenty and scarcity'.[43] The headwaters of the Ganga are located in some of the most water-rich regions of the world, but the combination of extreme weather events and a lack of water storage infrastructure 'creat[es] a situation of too much water in the wet season and too little water in the dry season'.[44]

Across the Ganges–Brahmaputra Basin agricultural use accounts for approximately half of all water use, although rapid urbanisation is also increasing water demands.[45] In the upper Ganga there are several large dams located on the main river channel, as well as on some of the tributaries. Water stored in these dams is used to irrigate 2.7 million hectares via three canal systems (the Upper, Madhya, and Lower Ganga canals).[46]

Across India more generally, over 62 per cent of water used for irrigation is sourced from groundwater and canal irrigation is declining.[47] Water markets in India are predominantly operating in groundwater (sourced via tubewells with pumps run on electricity or diesel), and these markets are informal, seasonal, and dependent on local negotiations between water sellers and buyers.[48] Water resources are locally managed, with varying levels of local control of water prices and access.[49]

Protecting cultural and ecological values

The Ganga and Yamuna Rivers are sacred under Hindu mythology. The Ganga represents a goddess reincarnated on Earth, and is believed to have the power to wash away sin and ensure salvation for those who bathe in the river's waters.[50] However, the health of both the Ganga and Yamuna Rivers continues to suffer from the impacts of hydropower generation, irrigation, flooding, sedimentation, cultural uses, and pollution from urban and rural sources.[51]

Although the Ganga is revered by hundreds of millions of people as a holy or sacred river, this does not necessarily translate into protection of the river and its flows, which are primarily managed to provide water for irrigation and hydropower generation. Work by Lokgariwar and others in 2014 showed that although believers valued the physical attributes of the river, they also felt that the power of the river as a sacred entity did not necessarily depend on the health of the river.[52]

Both the Ganga and the Yamuna remain highly polluted. The government of India has developed action plans for both rivers and a national project, Namami Gange, to provide an integrated water and development regulatory framework for the Ganga River. However, these plans are criticised for being far too slow, with the Namami Gange expected to take more than 20 years to generate any improvements to the health of the Ganga.[53]

In 2013 the cultural and ecological values of the river came together in the triannual celebration of Kumbh at Allahabad, an event which brings millions of visitors to the banks of the Ganga River.[54] This celebration depends on sufficient flow in the river to support 'cultural rituals including bathing ... and taking a few millilitres of Ganga River water into the mouth'.[55] During the festival, by agreement between the state government water resource manager (Uttar Pradesh Irrigation and Water Resources Department) and the Tehri Hydro Electric Corporation, water was released to meet environmental flows requirements during the Kumbh event, and this was seen as a successful culmination of social, cultural, and ecological outcomes.

The primary rationale for the state court decisions to grant legal rights to rivers and other natural objects in Uttarakhand was that the extraordinary threats posed by pollution and climate change demanded an extraordinary solution: 'The very existence of the rivers, forests, lakes, water bodies, air and glaciers is at stake due to global warming, climate change and pollution.'[56] In the *Ganga and Yamuna* case the existential threat to the ecological health of the rivers was compounded, in the eyes of the court, by the status of the rivers as 'sacred and revered ... central to the existence of half the Indian population'.[57]

Rivers as children: a legal/living person hybrid

In both the *Glaciers* and *Ganga and Yamuna* cases the court ruled that the rivers (and other natural objects in Uttarakhand, including the two named glaciers) had the 'status of a *legal* person' as well as all the 'rights, duties and liabilities of a *living* person' (emphasis added).[58] This conflation of legal person and living person was reinforced by the court in the *Glaciers* case, when it stated that the rights of the new legal persons 'shall be equivalent to the rights of human beings, and the injury/harm caused to these bodies shall be treated as harm/injury caused to the human beings'.[59]

Finally, the court nominated specific guardians for the rivers, and stated that these guardians were to act in *loco parentis* for the rivers and other natural objects. The phrasing here is particularly interesting, as it infers that the rivers are legal minors – in effect, children.[60] The combination of these two elements (the conflation of legal and living person, and the guardians in *loco parentis*) creates a new hybrid form of legal person, and it is unclear what effects this will have on the legal rights and liabilities of the rivers.

Institutional and governance arrangements

In the case of the Ganga and Yamuna Rivers the court declared that:

> The Director NAMAMI Gange, the Chief Secretary of the State of Uttarakhand and the Advocate General of the State of Uttarakhand are ... the human face to protect, conserve and preserve Rivers Ganga and Yamuna and their tributaries. These Officers are bound to uphold the status of Rivers Ganges and Yamuna and also to promote the health and well being of these rivers.[61]

On behalf of the glaciers, rivers, forests, mountains, and other natural objects in the state of Uttarakhand, similar duties were extended to:

> ...the Chief Secretary, State of Uttarakhand, Director NAMAMI Gange Project, Mr. Praveen Kumar, Director (NMCG [National Mission for Clean Ganga]), Mr. Ishwar Singh, Legal Advisor, NAMAMI Gange Project, Advocate General, State of Uttarakhand, Dr. Balram K. Gupta, Director (Academics), Chandigarh Judicial Academy and Mr. M.C. Mehta, Senior Advocate, Hon. Supreme Court...[62]

However, the court had no power to provide funding for these new arrangements, so the guardians were left to take on these responsibilities in addition to their existing roles. As Lokgariwar argued:

> The persons the court has nominated as the guardians of the Ganga and the Yamuna are themselves responsible for the sad state of these rivers today, and they have failed to really achieve any improvement in the condition of these rivers. What hope is there for these rivers if these same persons are now declared as parents of these rivers now? Moreover, the Uttarakhand officials will have no powers beyond the borders of Uttarakhand.[63]

Indeed, the state government of Uttarakhand has demonstrated considerable reluctance to assume guardianship responsibilities for the Ganga and

Yamuna. Shortly after the decision of the High Court, the state government appealed this decision to the Indian Supreme Court, which stayed the effect of the original ruling (effectively removing the legal rights of the Ganga and Yamuna once more), but has not yet reached a final decision on the status of the rivers.[64]

Río Atrato, Colombia

The Atrato River (el Río Atrato) is the longest river in Colombia, and is located in the state of Chocó on the Pacific coast (Figure 7.3). The river basin covers over 40,000 square kilometres and is considered to be one of the most biologically diverse places on the planet.[65] Over 90 per cent of Chocó is protected forest area, but current and historical impacts of gold and silver mining and logging threaten these natural values. Governments in Colombia have been characterised by 'fragility of the rule of law',[66] exacerbated by weak territorial control by the central government. In the state of Chocó almost half the population live in poverty, and the combination of a historically weak central government and challenging geography has left the state largely isolated from the rest of the country.[67]

In May 2017 the Constitutional Court of Colombia released to the public a groundbreaking decision made in 2016. In this decision (referred to as the *Tierra Digna* case), the court recognised the Río Atrato (including the river, its tributaries, and the basin) as an *entidad sujeto de derechos* (legal person).[68] This decision was based on Colombia's Constitución Ecológica (Ecological Constitution), which enshrines the protection of the environment at the constitutional level.[69] In particular, articles 79 and 80 provide for the human right to a healthy environment, and establish corresponding responsibilities of the state to protect the environment, including preventing environmental deterioration.

Water resource management in Colombia

National policy on water resource management is developed and promulgated by the Ministry of Environment and Sustainable Development.[70] However, each region is managed by an autonomous regional corporation (CAR), which has primary responsibility for implementing national policies, and these bodies have a high degree of financial and administrative autonomy. The CARs are responsible for water allocation, pollution control, and ecosystem protection (particularly ecosystems related to the hydrological cycle).[71]

CARs develop 'watershed ordering plans', which guide water resource management within each catchment (or 'watershed'). The local CAR is responsible for issuing water concessions (or permits), which are issued based on an assessment of water availability on a 'first come, first served'

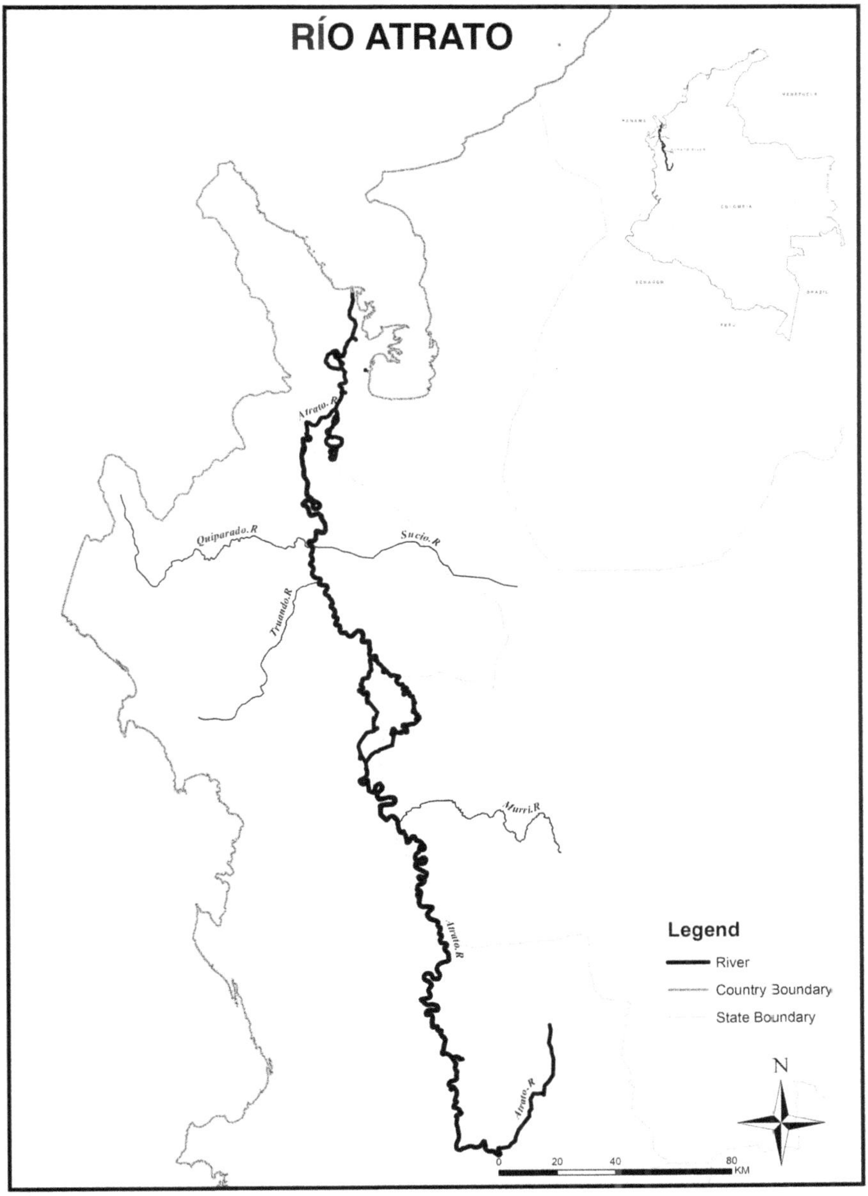

Figure 7.3 Río Atrato, Colombia.

basis. Trading of water rights is possible but not widespread.[72] The CAR sets the water use charge (based on volume), although the minimum water tariff is set by the national ministry. The CAR is responsible for collecting these fees, which must be used on watershed management within the same basin as the water extraction. CARs are also responsible for issuing licences to discharge into water bodies.[73] However, the historical isolation of the region means that government has played a relatively small role in the management of water resources in the state of Chocó.

Cultural and ecological values in Chocó, Colombia

Local communities along the Río Atrato are almost entirely composed of Indigenous people and Afro-Colombians (descendants of the Spanish slave trade). These communities occupy 'ancestral territories, called *resguardos* (in the case of Indigenous people) and *consejos mayores* (in the case of Afro-Colombian communities)', and maintain traditional livelihoods based on small-scale 'artisan' gold and silver mining, hunting, fishing, and traditional agriculture.[74]

People of both the *resguardos* and the *consejos mayores* receive particular legal protections under International Labour Organization Convention 169,[75] and the Constitutional Court in Colombia has previously recognised the status of the Afro-Colombian communities as being equal to that of any other ethnic community in Colombia. Like the Whanganui Iwi, for these communities 'the river is everything. It is their way of measuring time, the place where children play and learn how to swim, and the only highway to other parts of the region.'[76]

However, the river is under threat. Although small-scale artisan mining of gold and silver has been part of traditional livelihoods for centuries, illegal modern extraction mining is now occurring in many locations along the river. Combined with illegal logging, the river is afflicted with increasing loads of silt, as well as heavy metal contamination which has entered the food supplies of local communities. In the *Tierra Digna* case the court described this as 'a humanitarian, social and environmental crisis without precedent'.[77]

Biocultural rights for the river

In 2015 the people of the Río Atrato Basin sought the help of Tierra Digna, an NGO, to bring a case to the Constitutional Court of Colombia on the grounds that the illegal mining operations had violated the constitutional rights of the local people. Under article 86 of the constitution, any Colombian citizen may apply for an order of protection of their fundamental rights to life and a healthy environment when those rights are threatened by either an act or, importantly, an omission by a public or private authority. In this case, although the activities that were threatening the local people were illegal, it was the omission by the public authorities which had allowed those acts to continue.

The Constitutional Court upheld the claims of the local communities, and held that the failure of the government to prevent illegal mining was a breach of their fundamental rights. However, the court did not stop there. In a judgment that explicitly acknowledged the example of the Whanganui River (and the national park, Te Urewera), the court recognised the river itself as a legal person, with its own rights to protection, conservation, and where necessary restoration. The court expressed these rights as reflecting the 'profound unity between nature and the human species', based on the 'collective rights of the ethnic communities in relationship to their cultural and natural surroundings, which are called, "biocultural rights" '.[78]

The close relationship between the Indigenous and Afro-Colombian communities and the river played a key role in this decision. However, like the Uttarakhand High Court, the Colombian Constitutional Court explicitly followed a more ecocentric line of argument, stating:

> Its importance is obviously due to the human beings who inhabit it and the need to have a healthy environment to lead a dignified life in conditions of well-being, but is also for the other living organisms with which the planet is shared, understood as entities worthy of protection in [and] of themselves. This means being conscious of the interdependence that connects all living things on the Earth; that is, to recognise that we are integral parts of the global ecosystem and biosphere, before applying normative categories of domination, simple exploitation or utility.[79]

Although groundbreaking, the decision of the Constitutional Court has already been followed in a recent decision by the Colombian Supreme Court (Corte Suprema de Justicia, Sala de Casación Civil) to grant legal rights to the Amazon rainforest in Colombia. This case was brought by a coalition of young people and the NGO Dejusticia, who argued that failure to halt deforestation was contributing to climate change, which breached the right to a healthy environment in the future.[80]

Institutional and governance arrangements

The Colombian court ordered that a guardian be appointed to protect the rights of the river, and proposed a similar model to that of Te Pou Tupua: one guardian would be appointed by the government and one from the river communities. However, as the government and the communities negotiated the process of implementation, it was decided to include representatives from the seven main *resguardos* and *consejos mayores*, which each appointed one male and one female guardian for the river. Along with the government representative of the Ministry for Environment and Sustainable Development, there are now 15 guardians of the river.[81]

Although the court lacks the power to allocate funding, it did make a number of procedural orders to support the implementation of its ruling. In addition to the nominated guardians, management of the river will be supported by a 'commission of guardians of the Atrato river', which includes the river guardians and an advisory group of experts from NGOs. Implementation of the court orders will be overseen by a new interdisciplinary body, the *panel de expertos*, which brings together experts from ethnic communities, NGOs, and academic organisations and is headed by the Procuraduría General de la Nación. The specific challenges of illegal mining and heavy metal contamination were also addressed by the court, which required the creation of a plan to decontaminate the river and stipulated that government agencies must work to bring a halt to all illegal mining in the Chocó.[82]

Legal rights for rivers: implications for water governance

Each of the three jurisdictions used different legal methods and different justifications to create the legal rights, and the new legal entities have received varying levels of institutional support (Table 7.1). Both India and Colombia explicitly intended to create legal rights for nature (as opposed to Aotearoa New Zealand, where the legal rights for the river were a by-product of the negotiations). Although implementation is still under way in two cases (and indefinitely paused in India), narratives of both collaboration and competition in river management and water governance are already becoming apparent.

Collaboration

Both Aotearoa New Zealand and Colombia have embraced a collaborative co-management approach when it comes to implementing the legal rights of rivers. In each jurisdiction the legal rights for the river have emerged from the need to give effect to legal rights of people, particularly Indigenous communities, and the new legal rights for the rivers reflect the value of the rivers to their local communities.

In Aotearoa New Zealand there is a history of co-management of natural resources between Māori and Pākehā (New Zealanders of European descent), in cases both with legal rights (such as the national park, Te Urewera) and without (such as the Waikato River Authority). These arrangements reflect the pluralism of views on natural resources, and help give effect to the Māori worldview on how these natural objects should be protected. However, this is the first time that the co-management has included both legal rights for the river *and* competing uses of the river (particularly when it comes to hydropower). The experience of the EWMs shows that embedding legal rights within a collaborative approach can result in a reluctance to make full use of those legal rights. Will Te Pou

Table 7.1 Legal rights for rivers in Aotearoa New Zealand, India, and Colombia

Legal and institutional settings	*River and country*		
	Whanganui River, Aotearoa New Zealand	*Ganga and Yamuna Rivers, India*	*Río Atrato, Colombia*
Legal form	Legal person	Legal and living person with the status of a legal minor	Legal person
Legal rights (legal standing, right to enter contracts, right to own property)	Yes	Yes	Legal standing but not property
Human rights for the river	No	Yes (but unclear precisely what rights)	No (but strongly related to human right to a healthy environment)
Explicit intent to create legal rights for nature	No	Yes	Yes
Method of creation	Legislation	State court decision (currently stayed pending Supreme Court appeal)	Constitutional Court decision
Guardians	Te Pou Tupua (appointed by New Zealand government and Whanganui Iwi)	Court-nominated guardians, including members of state government and director of Namami Gange	Guardian of 15 people, including one man and one woman from each of the seven villages, and a representative of the Ministry of Environment
New funding	NZ$30 million contestable fund allocated to support the new arrangements	No (the court cannot allocate funds)	No (the court cannot allocate funds), but the national government has embraced the decision

Tupua be similarly reluctant to take action to protect the rights of the river in future? Will it be possible for Te Pou Tupua to take these actions without compromising the commitment to collaborative co-management?

In Colombia the local communities have developed a sustainable relationship with the river, relying on it for various ecosystem services but not compromising its ecological integrity by their actions. The collaborative approach is less likely to be undermined by competing uses of the river, as the main detriments to the health of the river come from illegal operations. Strengthening the role of government in the Chocó will require significant investment to overcome geographic isolation and historical institutional weakness. It is even possible that, like the government EWMs in the western USA (see Chapter 5), the Colombian government may end up welcoming further actions from the guardians to enforce the rights of the river, to help create impetus for government investment in regulation and enforcement.

However, the historical weakness of the rule of law in Colombia means there is always the potential for corruption. Enforcing environmental protection laws in Central and South America is a dangerous occupation, with several campaigners having been killed in recent years. Finally, ongoing collaboration will depend on maintaining an alignment of interests between the river, the local communities, and the Colombian government. Like Ecuador and Bolivia, Colombia is heavily reliant on exploiting its natural resources, and future development opportunities could create future competition between the rights of the river and the rights of people.

Competition

The narrative of competition emerges most strongly in the Indian example, where the rivers (and other natural objects in the state of Uttarakhand) were given legal rights explicitly to help protect them against future competing uses of the river. In the *Glaciers* case the court imposed an extremely broad definition of harm: 'plucking of one leaf, grass blade also damages the environment universally'.[83] The court then imposed a strict liability approach, strengthening the rights of the rivers even further (emphasis added):

> Any person causing any injury and harm, *intentionally or unintentionally* to the Himalayas, Glaciers, rivers, streams, rivulets, lakes, air, meadows, dales, jungles and forests is liable to be proceeded against under the common law, penal laws, environmental laws and other statutory enactments governing the field.[84]

The construction of the rivers (and other natural objects) as legal minors has stoked the fires of competition between humans and the river. In the weeks after the *Ganga and Yamuna* decision was handed down, an environmental advocate filed a police report asking the Agra police to investigate 'an attempt to murder the Yamuna by poisoning'.[85] This is an extreme interpretation of an already extreme ruling, but it highlights the willingness of environmental advocates in the region to use all legal powers at their disposal to protect the rivers.

The corollary of this outcome is that it creates an adversarial environment in which the new legal rights for the rivers will be interpreted. The new guardians for the rivers, most of whom are bureaucrats within the state government (or, in the case of the director of Namami Gange, the head of a national agency), were given the task of representing and advocating for the rights of rivers used by people for a wide range of social, agricultural, energy, and religious uses. The nominated guardians of the Ganga and Yamuna Rivers face the particular challenge of being responsible for rivers that extend across the country (well beyond the state of Uttarakhand) and into neighbouring Bangladesh (Figure 7.2), and the report of attempted murder shows the willingness of environmental advocates to test these new legal rights in court.

In a move that echoed the responses of some of the EWMs in the western USA, the new guardians were reluctant to use these legal powers – so much so that they rejected the entire premise. The state government of Uttarakhand almost immediately appealed the decision of the High Court of Uttarakhand to the Supreme Court of India, and this appeal was made for two reasons. First, as state bureaucrats, they requested clarification on the extent of their responsibilities and sought a ruling on the ability of the High Court of Uttarakhand to impose responsibilities on the state government outside the state borders. Second, the state government was afraid that recognising the Ganga and Yamuna Rivers as legal minors, both living and legal entities, could result in them being held accountable for the 'actions' of the river when it next flooded. As the guardians, acting in *loco parentis* for the rivers, they were afraid that they could be sued for flood damages.[86] The Supreme Court has upheld the right to appeal, but has not yet ruled on the appeal. However, in the interim it has stayed the effect of the original decision, stripping the Ganga and Yamuna Rivers of their legal person status.

In the Indian example, the strength of the narrative that the rivers can (and therefore should) look after themselves has eroded the narrative of the rivers as deserving of protection with remarkable speed. The experience of the Ganga and Yamuna Rivers shows how quickly the paradox of legal personhood can operate: increased legal powers for the rivers led to a fear of being sued, which then resulted in the loss of those legal powers. The irony is that the implementation of the original court decision in the *Ganga and Yamuna* case would only have been possible if the guardians had been willing to coordinate with all other departments and agencies across the river basins, but the narrative of competition has precluded the potential for collaboration.

The potential for competition is by no means absent in Colombia and Aotearoa New Zealand. In Colombia, although the Constitutional Court recognised a wide range of legal rights for the river and explicitly acknowledged that it was a legal person, the court did not explicitly include a right for the river to own itself.[87] If the river is confronted with the need to manage competing interests into the future, the absence of these property rights weakens the Río Atrato from the outset.

In Aotearoa New Zealand the Whanganui River owns its riverbed but has no rights to the water within it, nor does the new legislation alter the existing hydropower arrangements, which divert up to 80 per cent of the river flows to the Tongariro hydropower scheme. This represents a major competing use of the waters of the river, and failing to address this issue in the current co-management arrangements leaves open the possibility for future legal action. If Te Pou Tupua is reluctant to take action itself, it is possible that the guardian could be sued by environmental groups for failing to fulfil its responsibilities.

Lessons from the EWMs for the rivers

Extending legal rights to rivers is emerging as a transnational legal concept and being applied in a wide range of contexts to improve river protection. It is a concept embedded in environmental law, but also reflects the growing pluralist legal frameworks in many countries, as it can give effect to diverse cultural and religious views on the value of rivers. However, giving rivers legal rights also has significant implications for water governance. Water resource management has typically focused on the *use* of rivers for human benefit, and recognising the rivers as legal persons introduces a new set of competing interests in the management of rivers.

The conceptual framework developed in Chapter 2 shows that the multiple constructions of the river in law can strengthen conflicting narratives about the social value of the river. The evidence of the EWMs has shown that construction of the river as a potential competitor, and the associated legal response (which can lead to legal reforms that weaken legal rights), will be more likely in circumstances where the guardians of the river are required to flex their legal muscles and take action to protect the health of the river in ways that compete with human uses of rivers and catchments.

Applying the lessons from the conceptual framework and the EWMs to the emerging jurisprudence on legal rights for rivers shows that the rapid shift from protection to competition to legal reform in India may be repeated. As legal rights for rivers (and nature more broadly) remains an area of growing legal interest, it is increasingly urgent that we understand why and how this happens, and how to mitigate it.

Notes

1 Ashish Kothari, Mari Margil, and Shrishtee Bajpai, 'Now Rivers Have the Same Legal Status as People, We Must Uphold Their Rights' *Guardian* (21 April 2017) www.theguardian.com/global-development-professionals-network/2017/apr/21/rivers-legal-human-rights-ganges-whanganui.

2 Lida Cano Pecharroman, 'Rights of Nature: Rivers That Can Stand in Court' (2018) 7(1) *Resources* 10.3390/resources7010013.

3 David R Boyd, *The Rights of Nature: A Legal Revolution That Could Save the World* (ECW Press, 2017).

4 Lee Godden, 'Preserving Natural Heritage: Nature as Other' (1998) 22(3) *Melbourne University Law Review* 719.
5 Virginia Marshall, 'Overturning Aqua Nullius – An Aboriginal Perspective on Personhood' International Water Law Project blog (9 April 2018) www.internationalwaterlaw.org/blog/2018/04/09/overturning-aqua-nullius-an-aboriginal-perspective-on-personhood/; Carwill Bjork James, 'Bolivia's New Mother Earth Law to Sideline Indigenous Rights' *Climate Connections* (2012) http://climate-connections.org/2012/08/29/20968/.
6 Cass R Sunstein, *After the Rights Revolution: Reconceiving the Regulatory State* (Harvard University Press, 1990).
7 Christopher D Stone, 'Should Trees Have Standing? Towards Legal Rights for Natural Objects' (1972) 45 *Southern California Law Review* 450.
8 Blake R Bertagna, '"Standing Up" for the Environment: The Ability of Plaintiffs to Establish Legal Standing to Redress Injuries Caused by Global Warming' (2006) 2006 *Brigham Young University Law Review* 415; Brian Preston, 'The Role of Public Interest Environmental Litigation' (2006) 23 *Environmental and Planning Law Journal* 337.
9 Erin O'Donnell and Julia Talbot-Jones, 'Legal Rights for Rivers: What Does This Actually Mean?' (2017) 32(6) *Australian Environment Review* 159.
10 Stephen P Croley, 'Theories of Regulation: Incorporating the Administrative Process' (1998) 98(1) *Columbia Law Review* 1.
11 Earth Law Centre, 'Rights for the River Ethiope, Nigeria' (28 February 2018) www.earthlawcenter.org/blog-entries/2018/2/rights-for-the-river-ethiope-nigeria.
12 Jane Gleeson-White, 'It's Only Natural: The Push to Give Rivers, Mountains and Forests Legal Rights', *Guardian (Aus)* (1 April 2018) www.theguardian.com/australia-news/2018/apr/01/its-only-natural-the-push-to-give-rivers-mountains-and-forests-legal-rights.
13 Julie Turkewitz, 'Corporations Have Rights. Why Shouldn't Rivers?', *New York Times* (26 September 2017) www.nytimes.com/2017/09/26/us/does-the-colorado-river-have-rights-a-lawsuit-seeks-to-declare-it-a-person.html?mcubz=0.
14 Dahr Jamail, 'Oregon Ecosystem Files Lawsuit to Defend Its Rights' (26 July 2017) www.truth-out.org/news/item/41391-oregon-s-siletz-river-ecosystem-files-lawsuit-to-defend-its-rights.
15 Reed D Benson, 'Does a River Have a Right to Life?' *High Country News* (13 December 2017) www.hcn.org/articles/opinion-we-should-recognize-the-legal-rights-of-rivers.
16 Roderick Frazier Nash, *The Rights of Nature: A History of Environmental Ethics* (University of Wisconsin Press, 1989).
17 Constitution of the Republic of Ecuador 2008, articles 71–74.
18 *Wheeler c. Director de la Procuraduria General Del Estado de Loja*, Juicio No. 11121–2011–0010 (Vilcabamba case) http://blogs.law.widener.edu/envirolaw blog/2011/07/12/ecuadorian-courtrecognizes-constitutional-right-to-nature/.
19 Cano Pecharroman, above n 2, 7.
20 Erin Daly, 'The Ecuadorian Exemplar: The First Ever Vindication of Constitutional Rights of Nature' (2012) 21(1) *Review of European Community and International Environmental Law* 63, 64.
21 Mary Elizabeth Whittemore, 'The Problem of Enforcing Nature's Rights Under Ecuador's Constitution: Why the 2008 Environmental Amendments Have No Bite' (2011) 20(3) *Pacific Rim Law and Policy Journal* 659.
22 Waitangi Tribunal, *Whanganui River Report (Wai 167)* (Waitangi Tribunal, 1999).

23 L Hardcastle, 'Turbulent Times: Speculations About the Whanganui River's Position as a Legal Entity' *Maori Law Review* (February 2014) http://maorilawreview.co.nz/2014/02/sir-edward-taihakurei-durie-student-essay-competition-2013-turbulent-times-speculations-about-the-whanganui-rivers-position-as-a-legal-entity/.

24 Ministry for the Environment (New Zealand), 'Next Steps for Fresh Water: Consultation Document' (2016).

25 OECD, *OECD Environmental Performance Reviews: New Zealand* (OECD Publishing, 2017).

26 Resource Management Act 1991 (NZ) s 5.

27 C Warnock and M Baker-Galloway, *Focus on Resource Management Law* (CCH Australia, 2014).

28 Resource Management Act 1991 (NZ) s 14.

29 Resource Management Act 1991 (NZ) s 6.

30 Ministry for the Environment (New Zealand), 'Proposed National Environmental Standard on Ecological Flows and Water Levels: Discussion Document' (2008).

31 Elizabeth Macpherson and Erin O'Donnell, '¿Necesitan derechos los ríos? Comparando estructuras legales para la regulación de los ríos en Nueva Zelanda, Australia y Chile [Do Rivers Need Rights? Comparing Legal Structures for River Regulation in New Zealand, Australia and Chile]' (2018) 25 *Revista de Derecho Administrativo Economico* 95.

32 Julia Talbot-Jones, 'The Institutional Economics of Granting a River Legal Standing' (PhD thesis, Australian National University, 2017).

33 Te Awa Tupua (Whanganui River Claims Settlement) Act 2017 (NZ), ss 12, 14.

34 O'Donnell and Talbot-Jones, above n 9.

35 Te Awa Tupua (Whanganui River Claims Settlement) Act 2017 (NZ), s 13.

36 Zaryd Wilson, 'Whanganui River Representatives Appointed' *New Zealand Herald* (5 September 2017) www.nzherald.co.nz/nz/news/article.cfm?c_id=1&objectid=11916893.

37 Te Awa Tupua (Whanganui River Claims Settlement) Act 2017 (NZ), s 19.

38 Erin O'Donnell and Julia Talbot-Jones, 'Creating Legal Rights for Rivers: Lessons from Australia, New Zealand, and India' (2018) 23(1) *Ecology and Society* 7.

39 *Mohd Salim v State of Uttarakhand & others*, WPPIL 126/2014 (High Court of Uttarakhand) 2017 [19] (Ganga and Yamuna case) http://lobis.nic.in/ddir/uhc/RS/orders/22–03–2017/RS20032017WPPIL1262014.pdf.

40 *Lalit Miglani v State of Uttarakhand & others*, WPPIL 140/2015 (High Court of Uttarakhand) 2017 64 (Glaciers case) http://lobis.nic.in/ddir/uhc/RS/judgement/31–03–2017/RS30032017WPPIL1402015.pdf.

41 *State of Uttarakhand & others v Mohd Salim & others*, Petition for Special Leave to Appeal 016879/2017 (Supreme Court of India) 7 July 2017.

42 V Asthana and A C Shukla, *Water Security in India: Hope, Despair, and the Challenges of Human Development* (Bloomsbury Academic, 2014).

43 Paula Hanasz, *Transboundary Water Governance and International Actors in South Asia: the Ganges–Brahmaputra–Meghna Basin* (Routledge, 2017) 158.

44 R A Vaidya and E Sharma (eds), *Research Insights on Climate and Water in the Hindu Kush Himalayas* (International Centre for Integrated Mountain Development, 2014) 3.

45 A Dinar et al., *Bridges Over Water: Understanding Transboundary Water Conflict, Negotiation and Cooperation* (World Scientific Publishing, 2007).

46 Chicu Lokgariwar et al., 'Including Cultural Water Requirements in Environmental Flow Assessment: An Example from the Upper Ganga River, India' (2014) 39(1) *Water International* 81.

47 T Shah, 'Past, Present and Future of Canal Irrigation in India' in P Tiwari and A Pandey (eds), *India Infrastructure Report* (Oxford University Press, 2011).
48 T Shah et al., 'Is Irrigation Water Free? A Reality Check in the Indo–Gangetic Basin' (2008) 37(2) *World Development* 422.
49 Aditi Mukherji, 'Implications of Alternative Institutional Arrangements in Groundwater Sharing: Evidence from West Bengal' (2007) 30 June *Economic and Political Weekly* 2543.
50 D Eck, 'The Goddess Ganges in Hindu Sacred Geography' in A Bavishkar (ed.), *Waterlines* (Penguin Books, 2003) 28.
51 Paula Hanasz, 'Muddy Waters: International Actors and Transboundary Water Cooperation in the Ganges–Brahmaputra Problemshed' (2017) 10(2) *Water Alternatives* 459.
52 Lokgariwar et al., above n 46.
53 P K Agarwal, 'A Review of Ganga River Pollution: Reasons and Remedies' (2015) 35(3) *Journal of Indian Water Resources Society* 46.
54 S K Singh and Anshika Bisht, 'Environmental Management in Mass Gatherings: A Case Study of Maha Kumbh Mela 2013 at Prayag, India' (2014) 1(7) *International Journal for Innovative Research in Science & Technology* 107.
55 Andrew Harwood et al., *Listen to the River: Lessons from a Global Review of Environmental Flow Success Stories* (WWF-UK, 2017) 88.
56 *Glaciers* case, above n 40, 42.
57 *Ganga and Yamuna* case, above n 39, [11], [17].
58 Ibid., [19]; *Glaciers* case, above n 40, 64 (emphasis added).
59 *Glaciers* case, above n 40, 65.
60 Chicu Lokgariwar, 'The Sad State of These Persons Called Ganga & Yamuna – Can State Protect Them?' South Asia Network on Dams, Rivers and People (11 April 2017) https://sandrp.in/2017/04/11/the-sad-state-of-these-persons-called-ganga-yamuna-can-state-protect-them/.
61 *Ganga and Yamuna* case, above n 39, [19].
62 *Glaciers* case, above n 40, 64–65.
63 Lokgariwar, above n 60.
64 Erin O'Donnell, 'At the Intersection of the Sacred and the Legal: Rights for Nature in Uttarakhand, India' (2018) 30(1) *Journal of Environmental Law* 135.
65 Juan Carlos Bello, *Atlas de La Biodiversidad de Colombia* (Instituto Alexander von Humboldt, 2000).
66 C C LeGrand, 'Legal Narratives of Citizenship, the Social Question, and Public Order in Colombia, 1915–1930 and After' (2013) 17 *Citizenship Studies* 530, 543.
67 Jaime Bonet, *¿Por qué es pobre el chocó? Documentos de Trabajo Sobre Economía Regional* (Banco de la República, Centro de Estudios Económicos Regionales, 2007).
68 Centro de Estudios para la Justicia Social, *'Tierra Digna' and Others v President of the Republic and Others No T-622 of 2016*, Corte Constitucional [Constitutional Court], Sala Sexta de Revision [Sixth Chamber] (Colombia) (10 November 2016) 137 (*Tierra Digna* case); English translation by Elizabeth Macpherson and Felipe Clavijo Ospina, 'The Pluralism of River Rights in Aotearoa New Zealand and Colombia' (2018) 25 *Journal of Water Law* 283.
69 Oscar Darío Amaya Navas, *La Constitución Ecológica de Colombia: Análisis Comparativo Con El Sistema Constitucional Latinoamericano* (Universidad Externado de Colombia, 2002).
70 OECD, *Water Resources Allocation: Sharing Risks and Opportunities* (OECD Publishing, 2015).

71 James Blanco, 'Integrated Water Resource Management in Colombia: Paralysis by Analysis?' (2008) 24(1) *International Journal of Water Resources Development* 91.
72 OECD, above n 70.
73 Blanco, above n 71.
74 Macpherson and Ospina, above n 68.
75 Convention Concerning Indigenous and Tribal Peoples in Independent Countries (No 169) (1989) 28 ILM 1382 (entered into force 5 September 1991) (Convention 169).
76 Macpherson and Ospina, above n 68.
77 *Tierra Digna* case, above n 68, 109.
78 Ibid., 42.
79 Ibid.
80 *Barragán and Others v President of the Republic and Others, No STC4360 of 2018*, Corte Suprema de Justicia [Supreme Court], Sala de Casación Civil (5 April 2018).
81 E MacPherson, E O'Donnell, and F Clavijo Ospina, 'Meet the River People: Who Speaks for the Rivers?' Lines on the Water Blog (19 March 2018) http://linesonthewater.blogspot.com/2018/03/meet-river-people-who-speaks-for-rivers.html.
82 *Tierra Digna* case, above n 68, 159.
83 *Glaciers* case, above n 40, 62.
84 Ibid., 63.
85 Lokgariwar, above n 60.
86 O'Donnell, above n 64.
87 Macpherson and Ospina, above n 68.

8 Legal rights for rivers

A cause for celebration or concern?

Rivers around the world are under threat. As urban populations increase the water footprint of cities grows larger, and water-stressed cities are already eyeing environmental flows as a potential future source of water.[1] When the health of rivers is pitted against the human right to water, the rivers themselves will need a powerful and effective voice in these water policy debates.

However, integrated water resource management requires a coordinated, collaborative approach to water use, enabling competing users to work together. The human right to water fundamentally depends on maintaining healthy, functional aquatic ecosystems to provide safe freshwater supplies. The recent declaration of water reserves in 300 basins across Mexico reflects this approach, by linking human water rights with environmental flows in new water reserves to protect both against future commercial water demands.[2] But would this collaborative approach be possible when rivers are perceived as competitors, and when they have legal rights of their own?

The transnational movement to recognise the legal rights of rivers is also centred on the relationship between people and place. In Australia, the Yarra River of Melbourne has been given a new legal status that identifies the river as 'one living and integrated natural entity'.[3] Although this legislation falls short of giving the river legal rights, it is Australia's first piece of bilingual legislation, and centres the values of Indigenous Australians, and their relationship to the river, in a manner comparable to the Whanganui River Claims Settlement (Te Awa Tupua) Act 2017 in Aotearoa New Zealand.[4] Giving rivers legal rights can increase competition between humans and rivers, but it can also be a powerful way to respect and embed the values of non-Western cultures within a Western legal framework.[5]

So are legal rights for rivers a cause for celebration or concern? As more rivers around the world gain legal rights and are recognised as legal persons, one question is becoming increasingly important: *what happens to water law and governance when the aquatic environment is constructed as a legal subject?* The answer is an unexpected and significant paradox:

constructing the environment as a legal subject, although it brings a suite of new legal powers and is often necessary to support significant improvement in environmental outcomes in the context of water rights and water markets, can undermine the cultural narrative that considers the environment worthy of protection at all. This final chapter brings together the evidence presented throughout the book to identify some key lessons, and possible ways to resolve this apparent paradox.

How this book helps to answer the question: should rivers have rights?

In this book, a new conceptual framework is developed that articulates the relationship between the environment, its multiple constructions in law, the processes that create them, and the role of the cultural narratives that underpin them (Chapter 2). In particular, this framework identifies the *contested space* in which competing narratives underpinning the multiple constructions of the environment can interact, and shows how these competing narratives can affect the broader socio-legal concept of the environment in law. The framework also creates a dialogue between two very different ideologies on the role of the environment in law: the legal rights for nature movement (which has its origins in Earth jurisprudence), and market environmentalism. Although the concept of a backlash to effective environmental laws is well established, the paradox of legal rights identified in Chapters 6 and 7 highlights two particular issues of concern: first, constructing the environment as a legal subject (and thus as a potential competitor) can undermine cultural narratives of the environment as worthy of protection; and second, other constructions of the environment can be affected by this narrative shift.

The new framework has been applied to the groundbreaking but still relatively new examples of legal rights for rivers (Chapter 7), but to understand the potential outcomes fully this book has focused on a much older, if indirect, form of legal personhood for rivers: the EWMs. The EWMs have the attributes of legal personality, including the particular powers to hold and deal with water rights, to enter and enforce contracts, and to sue and be sued (legal standing). They operate within (and are often created by) water law, which is typically rather isolated from the development of environmental law more broadly. This isolation has two consequences: the legal requirements to protect the environment are usually explicitly stated, making them easy to identify; and the broader context of environmental law may have been overlooked in the attempt to create new legal mechanisms. Water laws in water-scarce regions also create legal rights to use water, and water resource managers have rapidly adopted water markets as a mechanism for managing water use efficiently,[6] making water law a good example of a shared resource market in which the environment can participate (see Chapters 2 and 3).

A new way of understanding the environment in water law and governance

Using the law to solve environmental problems requires the law to 'see' and comprehend the environment, and this is not straightforward. The history of modern environmental law can be viewed as a quest to make the environment *legible* to law, by altering the way in which law *constructs* the environment. The conceptual framework developed in Chapter 2 identifies the multiple ways in which the environment is constructed *in* law and which enhance legibility *to* law (Figure 2.1). This conceptual framework also makes the connection between these constructions and the underpinning cultural narratives about the nature and value of the environment in human society. In doing so, the framework exposes the relationship between the construction of the environment in law, the cultural narratives, and the regulatory response to environmental problems.

Constructing the environment in law

The first step towards legibility was the *recognition*, and articulation, of the environment in law as a *socio-ecological concept* which is more than the mere physical background to other legally legible activities. Once the law was capable of 'seeing' the environment, the second step was the *translation* of the broad socio-ecological concept into a legal object, and protecting it by placing limits on the actions of others. Even though the translation of the environment into a legal object enabled significant environmental protection (such as limits on pollution emission, and protection of native vegetation from being cleared), this construct was at best only obliquely visible to the law via the actions of legal subjects. As Christopher Stone argued in 1972:

> What does not weigh in the balance is the damage to the stream, its fish and turtles and 'lower' life. So long as the natural environment itself is rightless, these are not matters for judicial cognizance ... The stream itself is lost sight of.[7]

In response, the legal rights for nature movement crystallised around the next step: empowerment of the environment by constructing it as a legal subject, with rights, powers, and duties of its own. However, it was several decades before this movement began to achieve legal reform, culminating most recently in the personification of rivers (and other natural objects) as legal subjects in 2017 and 2018 (Chapter 7). This third construct of the environment is significantly more powerful in law, and the most transformative:

> Through its concept of the person, law helps to define who matters ... legal personification [is a barometer] of social and moral thought and the means of practically enforcing those ideas: of giving them the force of law.[8]

Over the same period, market environmentalism was increasingly applied to manage environmental problems, including the development of water markets.[9] Competition policy and market reforms of the 1980s in both Australia and the USA increased the use of market mechanisms by governments to improve efficiency of resource use and service delivery. Most early environmental markets were either regulatory markets (which capped total pollution emissions and issued transferable pollution permits that could be traded between polluters) or ecosystem service markets (which used market mechanisms to set a price on ecosystem services and paid private individuals to provide them).[10] In each case, environmental organisations could be buyers or sellers, but not both. The emergence of water markets in the late 1980s and 1990s created the 'shared resource' of water rights, with value to both human users and the environment, and enabled environmental organisations to buy and sell water and participate in the market.[11] These shared water resource markets achieved two important outcomes: they enabled competition between the river and human uses to be managed via the market, and they embedded competition as the defining feature of the relationship between humans and rivers.

As Chapter 3 describes, the EWMs emerged as legal subjects in response to the twin challenges of needing to be able to 'see' environmental harm explicitly (rather than through the lens of harm to humans) and needing to establish an entity capable of holding property rights and participating in environmental markets. This was followed by the recognition of rivers as legal persons in Aotearoa New Zealand, Colombia, and India. By constructing the environment as a legal person, the environment (or parts thereof) is directly visible to the law and able to hold and manage property rights.

Narratives shape regulatory response

The constructions of the environment in law are underpinned by cultural narratives about the value of the environment (Table 8.1): 'stories matter to environmental law'.[12] These narratives have the power to shape the regulatory response to environmental problems by aligning particular constructions more closely with public or private interest theories of regulation.[13]

All three constructs of the environment exist simultaneously, and the example of the EWMs shows that the construction of the aquatic environment as a legal person both affects and can be affected by other constructions. The conceptual framework, by making the link between the construction and the cultural narratives, shows that the mechanism of this influence is via the interaction of the underpinning narratives: 'legal stories mediate our engagement in the world and with others; they provide the possibilities and parameters of our own self-definition and understanding'.[14]

Table 8.1 Constructions of the environment in law: processes and narratives

Construct of the environment in law	*Process of construction*	*Underpinning cultural narrative*
Environment as a socio-ecological concept	Recognition	The environment is a concept that is more than the sum of its parts, but simultaneously a contingent, nuanced concept reflecting a dynamic relationship between the physical reality (ecosystems) and social value
Environment as a legal object	Translation	The environment is legally weak, but worthy of protection. This narrative supports public interest theories of regulation: that regulators act to protect vulnerable areas in the interests of broader social good
Environment as legal subject	Personification	The environment has the same legal powers as any other person, so it can, and should, look after itself. This narrative relies on the private interest origins of regulation: that regulation emerges as a result of competing individual interests

Lessons from the conceptual framework

This conceptual framework has three important implications for the way in which the environment is protected in water law. First, what is meant by 'environment' must be constantly and explicitly articulated in the law, and it is often highly variable between different legal contexts. The socio-ecological concept within the law is broad, flexible, and easily adaptable to meet the needs of specific legislation, but the corollary of this flexibility is uncertainty: 'environmental law is not susceptible to simple definition or pigeonholing ... largely because of the nebulous nature of the concept of "environment"'.[15] The need to articulate it constantly makes the socio-ecological concept highly vulnerable to changing cultural narratives about the value of the environment.

Second, there are tensions between the constructions of the environment as a legal object and a legal subject. The construction of the environment as a legal object hinges on the cultural narrative that the environment is worthy of protection but unable to protect itself. Legal limits are imposed on the actions of others precisely because the environment itself cannot defend its own rights; and indeed, as a legal object, has no rights to defend. On the other hand, the construction of the environment as a legal subject confers both legal rights and legal status.[16] As a legal person, the organisation representing the environment has legal rights and is no longer dependent on human protection. The environmental organisation can (at least in theory) stand up for itself.

Third, the conceptual framework highlights the importance of defining the 'environment' to be represented by the legal subject, by explicitly connecting competence and capacity. The EWMs have attempted to resolve the issue of specificity by using an organisational form that acts on behalf of particular parts of the aquatic environment (where water rights are available), with capacity to hold legal rights and the competence to use those rights.[17]

This combination of both capacity and competence is what distinguishes both the EWMs and the new 'river persons', which are specific organisations with clear responsibilities to speak and act on behalf of particular rivers, from earlier attempts to personify the environment in law, such as the broad legal rights created in Ecuador, which depend on other citizens to enforce them, and Bolivia, where the rights of nature were intended to be supported by the creation of the Defensoría de la Madre Tierra, which would operate as an ombudsman for nature's rights. This office has yet to be created, and its absence has weakened Bolivia's legal rights for nature. The clarity of purpose, organisational identity, and clear lines of accountability make it more likely that the legal rights for rivers created in 2017 will have real force and effect in water resource management.[18]

The conceptual framework also helps to make sense of the paradox of legal rights, as a result of the interaction between the competing narratives that underpin the construction of the environment as a legal object and a legal subject. In doing so, the framework places the emergence of this paradox within the broader context of the quest to enhance the legibility of the environment to law.

The paradox of legal rights

Granting rivers legal rights, either directly or indirectly (such as through the EWMs), generates a paradox. Constructing the river as a legal person increases the legal powers available to help protect the river from future impacts. However, in doing so, it strengthens the narrative that the river should protect itself and weakens the narrative that the river is worthy of protection by human action. Shifting narratives can drive legal reform that can weaken (or in the most extreme case entirely remove) the new legal rights (Figure 8.1).

The conceptual framework creates a dialogue between market environmentalism and legal rights for nature, which can highlight opportunities as well as future challenges. In addition, the experience of both the EWMs and the new river persons provides opportunities to examine how they are seeking to understand and redress the paradox, which directly affects their ability to operate effectively.

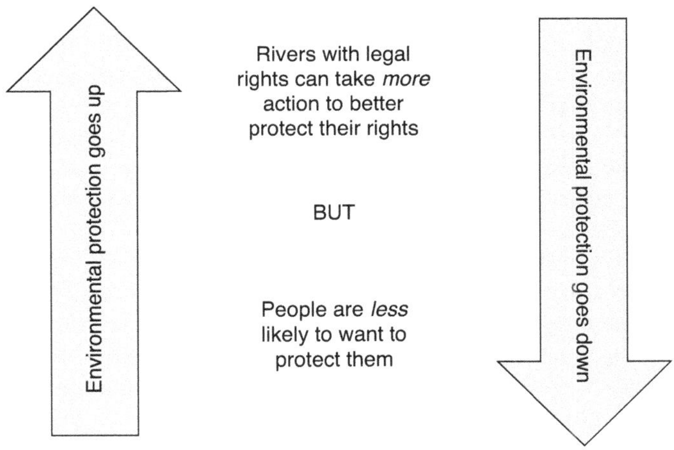

Figure 8.1 The paradox of legal rights.

Understanding the paradox: a new dialogue in a contested space

Legal rights for rivers create a new dialogue between two often ideologically opposed paradigms: legal rights for nature, and market environmentalism (particularly when given effect through water markets). What this book demonstrates for the first time is that *both* paradigms construct the environment as a legal subject, and both rely on the idea that the environment is worthy of protection in order to do so.

The legal rights for nature movement is deeply ecocentric, and seeks to create legal rights for the environment to shift existing legal systems so that they can better protect the environment, and to empower the environment itself to do this: 'we must stop thinking of nature as our slave'.[19] However, Earth law advocates often consider property rights as the antithesis of protecting the environment. Aldo Leopold, one of the early and preeminent voices in environmental protection, argued that 'We abuse land because we regard it as a commodity belonging to us.'[20] Eric Freyfogle specifically drew on the legal object/subject dichotomy when he argued:

> People … are subjects, and the land is merely an object, possessing no moral or legal worth and counting for nothing. There is at work here a distinct dichotomy of subject and object, legally worthy and legally worthless. People are the ones who own and dominate, and the land is the thing that is owned and dominated.[21]

Market environmentalism, however, is 'a mode of resource regulation which promises both economic and environmental ends via market means'.[22] Anderson and Libecap argue that by creating and regulating 'missing markets' it is possible to address the problems of both market failure and government failure, by creating the capacity for innovative and efficient provision of environmental goods.[23] For market environmentalists, markets and property rights, 'rather than being seen as contributing to environmental degradation, are regarded as a large part of the solution'.[24] Water markets, in particular, enable the environment to participate within the market (through the actions of its representative organisation), and depend on a construction of the environment with the necessary legal powers and rights to do so.

Both market environmentalism and the legal rights for nature movement thus focus on a construction of the environment as a legal subject. Acknowledging the intersection between these very different ways of thinking about the environment offers a powerful insight for the legal rights for nature movement. Market environmentalism may offer a pragmatic way towards creating legal rights for nature that may otherwise be difficult to achieve. The growing use of markets to manage resources and minimise environmental problems around the world can thus be seen as an opportunity:

> to accord nature a fraternal rather than an exploited role – even when the resulting institutions resolve in particular cases not to forgo certain human opportunities 'for nature's sake' – [and] might well make us different persons from the manipulators and subjugators we are in danger of becoming.[25]

However, as Anderson and Libecap acknowledge, 'Environmental policy is especially vulnerable to norm invasion.'[26] Environmentalists typically regard neoliberalism and market environmentalism as 'specific, potentially pernicious ideologies' that maintain the 'hegemony of highly individualistic and exclusive property rights over nature'.[27] In a less pointed manner, Dovers argued that:

> market-oriented policy approaches ... are not simply 'another option in the toolbox', but are transformative policy options that carry with them institutional change ... property rights instruments ... shift the policy logic from distributional equity plus some ecological consideration to economic efficiency plus sustainability concerns.[28]

The example of the EWMs highlights the power of applying a market-based solution to an environmental problem, but also demonstrates the capacity of an altered narrative to weaken environmental outcomes. This book is a reminder that although there is a capacity for market environmentalism and legal rights for nature paradigms to engage in meaningful dialogue, there are also real risks in doing so.

Resolving the paradox: lessons from the EWMs and rivers with legal rights

Lessons from the EWMs

> The environment is now the largest customer [for water].[29]

The EWMs are a compelling example of what happens when the aquatic environment enters 'a whole new field [as] an active participant in a water market',[30] and becomes a legal person. The EWMs are environmental organisations with legal rights, and they exist within a legal context defined by modern water rights, water markets, and the extension of modern water rights to include environmental uses.[31] The EWMs have been relatively successful in achieving their objectives: they have recovered significant volumes of water for the environment, and they are using water markets both to acquire and to manage this water.[32] For each of the EWMs, their 'superstructure' (the legal form, their objectives, powers, and capacities, and the mechanisms they use to achieve their goals) has been clearly articulated.[33] However, as Godden pointed out in 1998, environmental law typically treats 'the focus of that regulation as something of an unproblematic "given" ',[34] and this continues to be true of the EWMs. Although they have a clear set of organisational attributes, EWMs do not consistently or clearly articulate the nature of the environment that they aim to manage and protect. This lack of clarity means that the EWMs, while they construct part of the aquatic environment in water law as a legal subject, are vulnerable to shifting cultural narratives about the value of the environment.

Viewing water law, and the EWMs, through the lens of the conceptual framework enables the multiple constructions of the aquatic environment to be identified (Chapters 4 and 5). In water law, each construction of the aquatic environment has emerged in response to a specific need to endow the environment with a particular set of legal characteristics. The EWMs operate alongside other, older constructions of the aquatic environment in water law, and they can affect each other in unexpected or unintended ways through the interaction of the underpinning cultural narratives.

Competition and collaboration

> [I]f you treat the environment like you would irrigation, it might come off second best.[35]

> [If the] environment was going to participate with licences, then it had to be on same basis as irrigators.[36]

The EWMs demonstrate the power of cultural narratives to shape the regulatory response to environmental problems. In the western USA the narrative is one of *collaboration*, and the NGO EWMs in particular work hard at maintaining public support for the idea that the environment is worthy of protection. In south-eastern Australia the narrative is that the aquatic environment is *just another water user*, and can and should look after itself (via the actions of the EWMs). There have been distinct costs imposed on the EWMs as a result of the tension between these narratives (Chapter 6).

The EWMs in both Australia and the USA appear to be aware of the need to bring the narratives underpinning the environment as legal object (deserving of protection) and legal subject (capable of protecting itself) together in water governance, and to strengthen both collaboration and the independence provided by strong legal rights. Each jurisdiction has approached this task differently, but none has fully resolved the problems caused by an organisation with legal personality acting on behalf of the environment.

In Australia there is an increasing awareness of the need to engage with local communities on the value of environmental water, and give an opportunity for input on how that water is used, to shore up the narrative that the aquatic environment is worthy of protection. There is a belief that NGO EWMs provide a way to do this:

> There needs to be a benefit to their local community … What I see is that NGOs can be involved in delivering … 20 per cent of the water but doing it in a way that is highly engaged with communities and at sites of greatest importance to them.[37]

In 2012 the CEWH entered an agreement with a local South Australian NGO to manage environmental water in conjunction with local communities, including irrigators.[38] The CEWH has since entered into more agreements for local management of environmental water, including with the Renmark Irrigation Trust and the Ngarrindjeri Regional Authority (an organisation representing Indigenous Australians).[39] The VEWH has also been building relationships with the broader community: every 18 months it holds an 'Environmental Water Matters' forum with 30 'farming, Aboriginal, environment and recreation community and industry groups'.[40] The VEWH describes these forums as 'a fantastic opportunity to hear from others who are interested in environmental water and for us to get feedback about how environmental watering is managed'.[41] These conversations help to broaden community support for environmental flows, and may eventually help to create more local champions who see the work of the EWMs as part of sustainable water resource management in the community.

In the USA the EWMs have been focused on building collaboration and consensus, and now need to enhance their legal power. One of the ways this could occur is through increasingly efficient water markets, which would enable the EWMs to participate as any other competitor in the market. Although the western USA has significant path-dependent barriers to efficient water markets, there is evidence of ongoing interest in improving the efficacy and efficiency of these markets.[42]

One of the more fundamental problems for the western USA is the legal limit on the organisations which can hold instream flow rights. In every state except Montana, only a nominated government agency can hold water rights for the purposes of instream flows: 'There have been attempts to get legislation for private instream flows, and that has always been met with fierce opposition from water users, because they're afraid there wouldn't be [a] balance.'[43]

Although the government agencies are identifiable as EWMs, they are often part of the same umbrella organisation with responsibility for enforcing access to water rights.[44] As a western US EWM staff member noted:

> It's not how it's supposed to be, it creates a bit of schizophrenia on the state's part, because of conflict avoidance and politics, typically the state errs on the side of underenforcement of instream flows.[45]

As more instream flows are recovered by the EWMs, there will be more pressure on the state organisations to separate these functions formally. In doing this, they will strengthen the narrative that the environment (as represented by the EWM) can, and should, look after itself (through the actions of the EWMs).

Fundamentally, the EWMs must be able to meet two goals: 'to provide more water for the environment, [while also] recognising that the environment is different'.[46] This will require them to engage actively with the way the environment is constructed in law, and the power of the law to construct and shape cultural narratives. Examining how the EWMs navigate the tension between these goals provides further insight into the nature of the paradox and the capacity to resolve it.

Lessons from the rivers

Some of the best evidence of using the legal person to build a collaborative approach to river health comes from Aotearoa New Zealand and Colombia, where the rivers received legal rights as part of a broader recognition of cultural values and the connection between people and the river. In Aotearoa New Zealand the Whanganui River was recognised as a legal person to give effect to the Māori worldview that the river is an ancestor and must be cared for. In Colombia the Río Atrato received legal rights as part of a package of measures identified by the Constitutional Court to protect the communities who live in the river catchment. Linking the rights of the river to human values has deeply embedded the new legal rights into the fabric of social, cultural, and economic values. Instead of establishing rivers as potential competitors with humans, the fate of the river has been intertwined with human values.

India provides a powerful counterpoint: the very basis of the legal rights themselves remains highly controversial, as it drew on the Hindu religion and entirely ignored 'the many diverse peoples who live along the Ganga and are dependent on its healthy flows for their lives and livelihoods'.[47] Although not specifically referenced in the decision of the state government to appeal the state High Court judgment, the controversy generated by the ruling certainly undermined the potential for broad community support.[48]

However, the experience of the rivers also highlights the need to ensure that the new legal rights can be given force and effect.[49] Building a collaborative approach can help, but when it counts, the rivers also need to be able to use their legal rights to protect themselves. This means that the new legal persons need guardians that are clearly identifiable (and thus can be held accountable), with appropriate levels of funding to operate, including going to court if necessary. Both Aotearoa New Zealand and Colombia have appointed guardians that operate at arm's length from government (although government retains a role), and Aotearoa New Zealand has provided funding to establish the new arrangements.

Moreover, the new legal persons need to be effectively embedded within the water governance framework. Aotearoa New Zealand has achieved this most successfully so far, with the new legislation that creates the legal person also creating new institutional arrangements for the management of the Whanganui River, in which the guardian will have a substantial role. It remains to be seen how the guardians of the Río Atrato will be able to affect water governance in Colombia, as the relationship between the Chocó CAR and the guardians is still a work in progress.

The combined experience of both the EWMs and the new river persons highlights a crucial question for water governance: what role do we expect rivers with legal rights to play in integrated water resource management? Rivers have traditionally been protected in water law to varying extents as legal objects, but when they have a voice of their own they acquire the capacity to compete for policy outcome with other water users. This fundamentally changes their roles and responsibilities in water governance frameworks.

Conclusion

Granting rivers legal rights constructs the rivers in water law as a legal subject, and the experience of the EWMs exposes the tension between simultaneous constructions of the aquatic environment as both a legal object and a legal subject. As a legal object, the aquatic environment depends on the narrative that it is worthy of protection but legally weak, and must therefore rely on human action to protect it. Alternatively, as a legal subject, rivers have both legal rights and legal status. As a legal subject, the rivers are no longer so dependent on human protection, and can (at least in theory) take legal action to protect their own legal rights. However, as Goodie argues, 'The environment, as a legal subject, is not simply a physical space; it is a contingent and instrumental concept, determined by human activity, social values and legal and non-legal calculation.'[50]

This makes the aquatic environment especially vulnerable to these shifts in cultural narratives. The cases explored in detail in Chapters 4–7 help to demonstrate the dynamism of the relationship between the aquatic environment and human water users, which changes in response to variability in water availability, ecological change, and shifts in the social value placed on a healthy aquatic ecosystem.

There are no easy answers to the problems of river protection and environmental water recovery. It is unlikely to be possible to maintain all the industries and communities that depend on water use in its current form while also maintaining a healthy and functioning aquatic environment. In Australia the EWMs have attempted to use the market to avoid political decisions on where and how water should be used. In the USA the EWMs have attempted to use community support and collaboration to avoid difficult conversations about long-term sustainability. In Aotearoa New Zealand and Colombia both government and the courts have attempted to avoid issues of competition between the rivers and people by limiting direct effects on property rights (to water and land). These strategies of avoidance simply shift the potential conflict into the future.

This book shows the importance of the broader legal and historical context to understand the implications of granting legal rights to rivers. Where these rights have been embedded within strong cultural frameworks, they appear more likely to create a collaborative approach to river management and water governance.

The new river persons, and the two decades of experience of the EWMs, shift the debate beyond *whether* the aquatic environment can be constructed in law as a legal subject with rights and powers to the question of how this can be *implemented*. In particular, the paradox of legal rights suggests that more attention ought to be paid to exactly *how* 'nature' is given form and power within the law.

Granting legal rights to rivers brings the challenge of good water governance to front and centre. Without appropriate measures to connect people and place, and strengthen cultural values, new legal rights for rivers can easily backfire, leading to legal reform that weakens river protections once again. Ultimately, policymakers need to be clear on the role that the new legal persons will play in water governance. Rivers only really *need* a voice if we expect them to compete for their own outcomes. In that case, giving rivers a 'voice' is arguably an abdication of our responsibilities for protecting our environment, because we are relying on the rivers to look after themselves.

Notes

1 Yoshihide Wada and Marc F P Bierkens, 'Sustainability of Global Water Use: Past Reconstruction and Future Projections' (2014) 9 *Environmental Research Letters* 104003; Julie C Padowski and Steven M Gorelick, 'Global Analysis of Urban Surface Water Supply Vulnerability' (2014) 9 *Environmental Research Letters* 104004.
2 WWF, 'Historic Presidential Decrees Create Hundreds of Water Reserves in Mexico' World Wide Fund for Nature (5 June 2018) http://wwf.panda.org/our_work/water/intro/wetland_conservation/?328874/Historic-presidential-decrees-creates-hundreds-of-water-reserves-in-Mexico.
3 Yarra River Protection (Wilip-gin Birrarung Murron) Act 2017 (Vic) s 1.
4 Katie O'Bryan, 'Giving a Voice to the River and the Role of Indigenous People: The Whanganui River Settlement and River Management in Victoria' (2017) 20 *Australian Indigenous Law Review* (advance).
5 Elizabeth Macpherson and Felipe Clavijo Ospina, 'The Pluralism of River Rights in Aotearoa New Zealand and Colombia' (2018) 5 *Journal of Water Law* 283.
6 R Quentin Grafton et al., 'An Integrated Assessment of Water Markets: A Cross-Country Comparison' (2011) 5(2) *Review of Environmental Economics and Policy* 219.
7 Christopher D Stone, 'Should Trees Have Standing? Towards Legal Rights for Natural Objects' (1972) 45 *Southern California Law Review* 450, 461.
8 Ngaire Naffine, *Law's Meaning of Life: Philosophy, Religion, Darwin and the Legal Person* (Hart Publishing, 2009) 11.
9 Terry L Anderson and Gary D Libecap, *Environmental Markets: A Property Rights Approach* (Cambridge University Press, 2014).
10 Barton H Thompson Jr, 'Markets for Nature' (2000) 25 *William and Mary Environmental Law and Policy Review* 261.
11 Steven Malloch, *Liquid Assets: Protecting and Restoring the West's Rivers and Wetlands Through Environmental Water Transactions* (Trout Unlimited, 2005).
12 Michael Burger, 'Environmental Law/Environmental Literature' (2013) 40 *Ecology Law Quarterly* 1, 56–57.
13 Bronwen Morgan and Karen Yeung, *An Introduction to Law and Regulation: Text and Materials* (Cambridge University Press, 2007).
14 Allan C Hutchinson, *Dwelling on the Threshold: Critical Essays on Modern Legal Thought* (Carswell, 1988) 14.
15 David Grinlinton, 'The "Environmental Era" and the Emergence of "Environmental Law" in Australia – A Survey of Environmental Legislation and Litigation 1967–1987' (1990) 7 *Environmental and Planning Law Journal* 74, 82.
16 Gail Morgan, 'The Dominion of Nature: Can Law Embody a New Attitude?' (1993) 60 *Bulletin of the Australian Society of Legal Philosophy* 43, 46.
17 Ngaire Naffine, 'Who are Law's Persons? From Cheshire Cats to Responsible Subjects' (2003) 66(3) *Modern Law Review* 346.
18 Erin O'Donnell and Julia Talbot-Jones, 'Creating Legal Rights for Rivers: Lessons from Australia, New Zealand, and India' (2018) 23(1) *Ecology and Society* 7.
19 Eric T Freyfogle, 'Ownership and Ecology' (1993) 43(4) *Case Western Reserve Law Review* 1269, 1281.
20 Aldo Leopold, *A Sand County Almanac and Sketches Here and There* (Oxford University Press, 1949), viii–ix.
21 Freyfogle, above n 19, 1274.

22 Karen Bakker, 'Neoliberalizing Nature? Market Environmentalism in Water Supply in England and Wales' in Nik Heynen et al. (eds), *Neoliberal Environments: False Promises and Unnatural Consequences* (Routledge, 2007) 101, 102.
23 Anderson and Libecap, above n 9, xiv, 4, 13.
24 Lee Godden, 'Property in Urban Water: Private Rights and Public Governance' in Patrick Troy (ed.), *Troubled Waters: Confronting the Water Crisis in Australia's Cities* (ANU E Press, 2008) 157, 160.
25 Laurence H Tribe, 'Ways Not to Think About Plastic Trees: New Foundations for Environmental Law' (1974) 83 *Yale Law Journal* 1315, 1346.
26 Anderson and Libecap, above n 9, 5.
27 Nik Heynen et al., 'Introduction: False Promises' in Nik Heynen et al. (eds), *Neoliberal Environments: False Promises and Unnatural Consequences* (Routledge, 2007) 1, 12.
28 Steve Dovers, 'Urban Water: Policy, Institutions and Government' in Patrick Troy (ed.), *Troubled Waters: Confronting the Water Crisis in Australia's Cities* (ANU E Press, 2008) 81, 90.
29 Interview CEWO 2.
30 Interview OEH.
31 Erin O'Donnell, 'Common Legal and Policy Factors in the Emergence of Environmental Water Managers' in C A Brebbia (ed.), *Water and Society II* (WIT Press, 2013) 321.
32 Dustin Garrick and Erin O'Donnell, 'Exploring Private Roles in Environmental Watering in Australia and the US' in Jeff Bennett (ed.), *Protecting the Environment, Privately* (World Scientific Publishing, 2016) 203.
33 Erin O'Donnell, 'Competition or Collaboration? Using Legal Persons to Manage Water for the Environment in Australia and the United States' (2017) 34(6) *Environmental and Planning Law Journal* 503.
34 Lee Godden, 'Preserving Natural Heritage: Nature as Other' (1998) 22(3) *Melbourne University Law Review* 719, 722.
35 Interview DEWNR.
36 Interview OEH.
37 Interview HRA. This interviewee acknowledged that the bulk of environmental water (the 80 per cent) would still need to be managed from a top-down, basin-wide perspective.
38 Commonwealth Environmental Water Office and Nature Foundation SA, 'Press Release: Commonwealth Works with Nature Foundation South Australia to Deliver Water' (24 October).
39 Australian Government Department of Environment and Energy, 'Agreements on the Use of Commonwealth Environmental Water' www.environment.gov.au/water/cewo/publications/agreements-use-commonwealth-environmental-water.
40 Victorian Environmental Water Holder, 'Community Benefits' (2016) www.vewh.vic.gov.au/environmental-water/shared-community-benefits.
41 Ibid.
42 D Garrick, N Hernandez-Mora, and E O'Donnell, 'Water Markets in Federal Countries: Comparing Coordination Institutions in Australia, Spain and the Western USA' (2018) *Regional Environmental Change*, https://doi.org/10.1007/s10113–018–1320-z.
43 Interview CWCB.
44 Garrick and O'Donnell, above n 32.
45 Interview DRC.
46 Interview DEWNR.
47 Chicu Lokgariwar, 'The Sad State of These Persons Called Ganga & Yamuna – Can State Protect Them?' South Asia Network on Dams, Rivers and People

(11 April 2017) https://sandrp.in/2017/04/11/the-sad-state-of-these-persons-called-ganga-yamuna-can-state-protect-them/.

48 Ashish Kothari, Mari Margil, and Shrishtee Bajpai, 'Now Rivers Have the Same Legal Status as People, We Must Uphold Their Rights' *Guardian* (21 April 2017) www.theguardian.com/global-development-professionals-network/2017/apr/21/rivers-legal-human-rights-ganges-whanganui.

49 O'Donnell and Talbot-Jones, above n 18.

50 Jo-Ann Goodie, 'The Invention of the Environment as a Legal Subject' (PhD thesis, Murdoch University, 2006) vi.

Index

Page numbers in **bold** denote tables, those in *italics* denote figures.

www.ingramcontent.com/pod-product-compliance
Ingram Content Group UK Ltd.
Pitfield, Milton Keynes, MK11 3LW, UK
UKHW011011180926
475701UK00004B/674
9780367584160